Let Us Java

Third Revised & Updated Edition

Yashavant Kanetkar

BPB PUBLICATIONS

THIRD REVISED AND UPDATED EDITION 2018

Second Edition 2016

ISBN :978-93-8655-178-8

LIMITS OF LIABILITY AND DISCLAIMER OF WARRANTY

The Author and Publisher of this book have tried their best to ensure that the programmes, procedures and functions described in the book are correct. However, the author and the publishers make no warranty of any kind, expressed or implied, with regard to these programmes or the documentation contained in the book. The author and publisher shall not be liable in any event of any damages, incidental or consequential, in connection with, or arising out of the furnishing, performance or use of these programmes, procedures and functions. Product name mentioned are used for identification purposes only and may be trademarks of their respective companies / owners and are duly acknowledged.

Distributors:

BPB PUBLICATIONS
20, Ansari Road, Darya Ganj
New Delhi-110002
Ph: 23254990/23254991

BPB BOOK CENTRE
376 Old Lajpat Rai Market,
Delhi-110006
Ph: 23861747

COMPUTER BOOK CENTRE
12, Shrungar Shopping Centre,
M.G.Road, BENGALURU–560001
Ph: 25587923/25584641

DECCAN AGENCIES
4-3-329, Bank Street,
Hyderabad-500195
Ph: 24756967/24756400

MICRO MEDIA
Shop No. 5, Mahendra Chambers, 150
DN Rd. Next to Capital Cinema, V.T.
(C.S.T.) Station, MUMBAI-400 001 Ph:
22078296/22078297

Published by Manish Jain for BPB Publications, 20, Ansari Road, Darya Ganj, New Delhi-110002 and Printed him at Akash Press, New Delhi

Dedicated to

Nalinee and Prabhakar Kanetkar

- Yashavant Kanetkar

About The Author

Through his books and Quest Video Courseware DVDs on C, Java, C++, Data Structures, VC++, .NET, Embedded Systems, etc. Yashavant Kanetkar has created, moulded and groomed lacs of IT careers in the last two decades. Yashavant's books and Quest DVDs have made a significant contribution in creating top-notch IT manpower in India and abroad.

Yashavant's books are globally recognized and millions of students / professionals have benefitted from them. Yashavant's books have been translated into Hindi, Gujarati, Japanese, Korean and Chinese languages. Many of his books are published in India, USA, Japan, Singapore, Korea and China.

Yashavant is a much sought after speaker in the IT field and has conducted seminars/workshops at TedEx, IITs, RECs and global software companies.

Yashavant has recently been honored with the prestigious "Distinguished Alumnus Award" by IIT Kanpur for his entrepreneurial, professional and academic excellence. This award was given to top 50 alumni of IIT Kanpur who have made significant contribution towards their profession and betterment of society in the last 50 years.

In recognition of his immense contribution to IT education in India, he has been awarded the "Best .NET Technical Contributor" and "Most Valuable Professional" awards by Microsoft for 5 successive years.

Yashavant holds a BE from VJTI Mumbai and M.Tech. from IIT Kanpur.

Acknowledgments

Let Us Java is not an outcome of my work alone. A book on such a dynamic language required inputs, help and suggestions from several people. Topmost amongst them were our students at Nagpur training centre and the participants in various seminars and workshops. Their inputs have gone a long way in getting this book in the shape and form in which you are holding it.

Over the years, I have used Java to build many applications. All these practical experiences and usage scenarios are factored into Let Us Java.

I am indebted to Manish Jain of BPB Publications who had a faith in this book idea, believed in my writing ability, whispered the words of encouragement and made helpful suggestions from time to time. I hope every author gets a publisher who is as cooperative, knowledgeable and supportive as Manish.

I thank my family for enduring the late nights, the clicking keyboard and mostly for putting up with yet another marathon book effort.

Contents

An Overview of Java

1

You remain well-grounded when you know your roots. Same is true about Java. So a look at how it came into existence and where it stands amongst other programming languages...

Let Us JAVA
3rd Edition

Chapter Contents

- The Evolution
- The Birth of Java
- What is Java?
- Traditional Programming Model
- How is Java Different?
- How Java addresses Security?
- Java or C++?
- The Java Environment
- Tools of the Trade
- Exercise
- KanNotes

Before we can begin to write programs in Java, it would be interesting to find out what really is Java, how it came into existence and how does it compare with other computer languages. Also, it is important to know what tools we are going to use for executing programs in this book, from where to get them and how to install them. In this chapter, we would briefly outline these issues.

The Evolution

Approaches to programing keep evolving all the time. These approaches are more or less driven by the computing needs of those times. When these needs cannot be addressed by languages of that era, a need is felt for a new language. These needs have become more and more complex over the years.

In the early days of computing when the need was that a machine should somehow be able to execute instructions, programming was done by manually keying in the binary machine instructions. So long as the programming task was small, programmers were ready to take the pains of keying in instructions in binary.

As the tasks became more complex and the program lengths increased, need was felt for a new language that makes it easier to write programs. That's when Assembly language was invented. In Assembly, instead of binary, small abbreviations were used to write instructions. These abbreviations were nothing but representations of binary instructions. This made life much easier for the programmer. The assembly language programs were very efficient.

As the demands of computing increased it was felt that learning and using Assembly language is not very easy. To address this need, many languages were invented. These included FORTRAN, BASIC and COBOL. But these turned out to be suitable for specific domains. For example, FORTRAN found widespread acceptance in scientific and engineering applications, whereas, COBOL was typically used for building business applications like payrolls, inventory management, etc.

These languages suffered from three important limitations. They are as follows:

(a) They could not be used across the domains that they were supposed to serve. So a change in domain necessitated a programmer to learn a new language.

(b) They could not be used to write system-level code that could interact with hardware easily.

(c) All these languages were not designed around structured programming principles. Hence, in programs of sizeable length it became difficult to follow the flow of control.

As a result, a feeling started growing—can there not be a universal programming language that can address all these three concerns? The answer came in the form of C language. It was invented by Dennis Ritchie at AT&T's Bell Laboratories. Since it was designed by a programmer, and not driven by a committee, it addressed the programmer's needs very well. These included speed, efficiency and brevity. Programmer's loved it, and it soon became a dominant programming language. This dominance continued for almost two decades.

As new hardware evolved, and computers gained widespread acceptance, demands from the program grew multi-fold. The complexity of programs hit the roof, and this is where C language started showing signs of strain. It simply didn't contain elements that could handle the complexity of the problem being solved. There was a need for a fresh approach to handle the complexity. This gave birth to a new way of organizing a program, called Object Oriented Programming (OOP). C++ was based on these principles and was invented by Bjarne Stroustrup at AT&T's Bell Labs. 1990 was the decade of C++. Since C++ was built on foundation of C, it became easier for programmers to migrate to this new language quite quickly. It was largely accepted that C++ is a prefect language and there would be possibly no need for a new language. But this belief got dented as you would see in the next section.

The Birth of Java

C and C++ were being used for building most applications till late 1990s. The computing world was more or less divided into three camps—Intel, Macintosh and Solaris. Compliers were available that targeted these microprocessors and created machine language instructions that could get executed on these microprocessors. This was alright for the PC world. However, the microprocessor diversity was too much in consumer electronics world. The microprocessors used in washing machines, microwave ovens, and other such devices were so many that creating a full-fledged compiler for each microprocessor was impractical. So a thought started taking shape to create new language that could be used to create software that could run on different microprocessors embedded in various consumer electronic devices. This was the initial motivation that led to the birth of Java.

Thus creation of an architecturally neutral and portable language for consumer electronics devices was the primary factor for Java to come into existence. However, it gained impetus for a very different reason. World Wide Web and the Internet were growing like wildfire, and its programming needs were similar to those that Java was trying to address. There were all types of machines that were getting connected to the Internet. A language was needed that could be used to create programs that could run on machines connected to the Internet and had different microprocessors and operating systems. Java fitted this bill perfectly, because it was designed from ground up with this motive in mind, namely, platform-independence (portability).

So it may not be an exaggeration to state, had Internet and World Wide Web not caught the fancy of the world at the same time that Java was growing, Java would have possibly remained a language to be used in the consumer electronics world.

With that historic perspective under our belt, I think we are well poised to begin learning Java.

What is Java?

Java is a programming language developed at Sun Microsystems in 1995. It was designed by James Gosling. The language derives much of its syntax from C++ (and its predecessor, C), but is simpler to use than C++. Java's reputation has spread wide and far and has captured the imagination of most software professionals. Literally thousands of applications are being built today in Java for different platforms including desktop, web and mobile.

Possibly why Java seems so popular is because it is reliable, portable and easy to use. It has modern constructs that are required to represent today's problems programmatically. Java, like C++ makes use of a principle called Object-Oriented Programming (OOP) to organize the program. This organizing principle has lots of advantages to offer. We would be discussing this in detail in Chapter 8.

Let us now try to understand how Java achieves portability and reliability.

Traditional Programming Model

When we execute a program on any computing device like PC, Laptop, Tablet or Smartphone, the instructions in it are executed by the microprocessor present in that device. However, the microprocessor cannot understand the instructions written in languages like C, C++ or Java. Hence these instructions have to be first converted into instructions that can be understood by the microprocessor. These converted instructions are in machine language. This conversion process is known as compilation.

The machine language instructions understood by a microprocessor are often called its Instruction Set. Problem is that instruction sets of different microprocessors are different. Thus instructions of an Intel microprocessor are different than an ARM microprocessor. Therefore, any program being executed on a specific microprocessor needs to be converted into machine language instructions that that microprocessor understands. Thus, for the same program, corresponding machine language instructions would be different for different microprocessors. Hence if a program is compiled for one microprocessor it may not work on another microprocessor. To make it work on another microprocessor it would have to be compiled for that microprocessor again. This is shown in Figure 1.1.

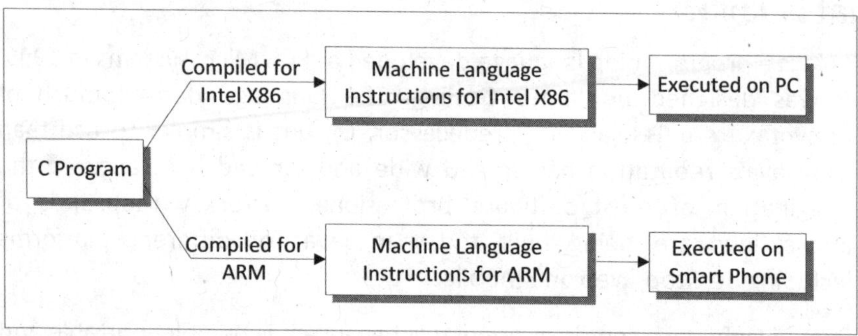

Figure 1.1

Any running program needs to make use of services of an Operating System (OS) during its execution. These include services like performing input/output, allocating memory, etc. You must be aware of the fact that on the same microprocessor, different OS can be used. For example, suppose there are two laptops having same Intel Pentium microprocessor. On one laptop one can run Windows, whereas on the other one can run Linux. But since the way these OSs offer different services is different, during conversion to machine language these changes have to be accommodated. So for the same program, machine language instructions for Intel + Windows combination would be different than those for Intel + Linux combination. This is shown in Figure 1.2.

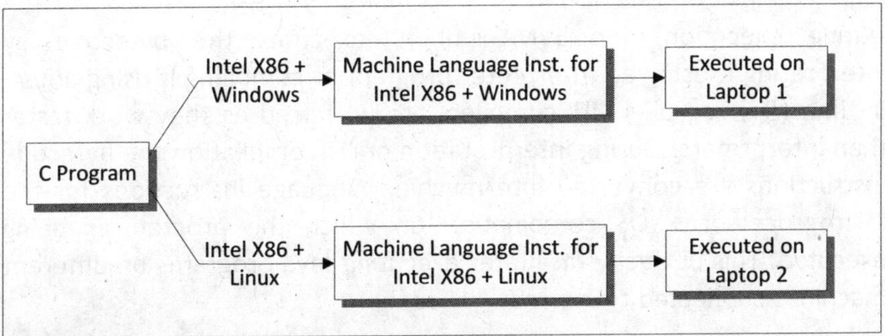

Figure 1.2

Figure 1.1 and Figure 1.2 depict a scenario called "write once, compile anywhere". It means to make the same program work on a different microprocessor + OS combination we are not required to rewrite the program, but are required to recompile the program for that microprocessor + OS combination. This is the approach taken by popular traditional languages like C and C++.

How is Java Different?

Java, takes a different approach than the traditional approach taken by languages like C and C++. It lets application developers follow a "compile once, run anywhere" scenario. This means that once a Java program is compiled, it can get executed on different microprocessors + OS combinations without the need to recompile the program. This makes Java programs immensely portable across different microprocessors + OS combinations. The microprocessor + OS combination is often called "Platform". Hence Java is often called a platform-independent language or architecturally neutral language. Java programs are considered portable since they can be used on different microprocessor + OS combination without making any changes in them.

Java achieves this "compile once, run anywhere" and platform independence magic through a program called Java Virtual Machine (JVM). When we compile Java programs they are not converted into machine language instructions for a specific microprocessor + OS combination. Instead, our Java program is converted into bytecode instructions. These bytecode instructions are similar to machine code, but are intended to be interpreted by JVM. A JVM provides an environment in which Java bytecode can be executed. Different JVMs are written specifically for different host hardware and operating systems. For example, different JVMs are written for Intel + Windows combination, ARM + Linux combination, etc.

During execution, the JVM runtime executes the bytecode by interpreting it using an Interpreter program or compiling it using a just-in-time (JIT) compiler. JIT compilers are preferred as they work faster than interpreters. During interpretation or JIT compilation the bytecode instructions are converted into machine language instructions for the microprocessor + OS combination on which the program is being executed. This perfectly facilitates executing Java programs on different machines connected to Internet.

A Java program is typically stored in a .java file, and the bytecode is usually stored in a .class file. A complex program may consist of many .class files. For easier distribution, these multiple class files may be packaged together in a .jar file (short for Java archive). The working of a Java program discussed above is shown in Figure 1.3.

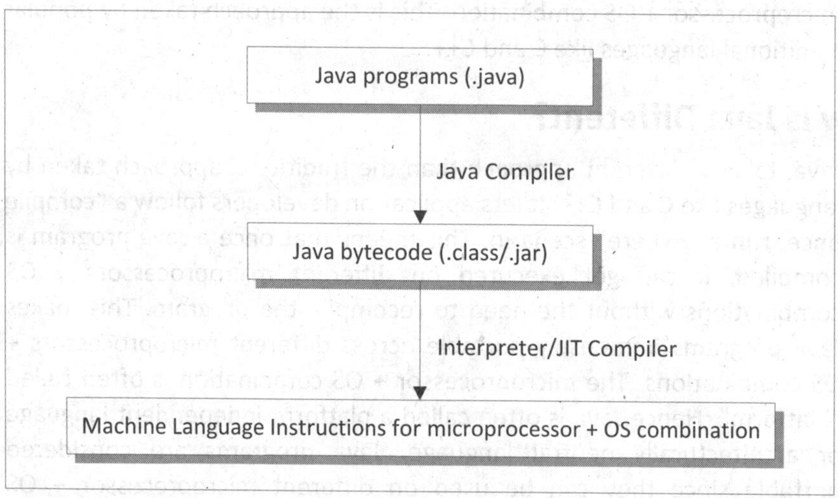

Figure 1.3

How Java addresses Security?

Let us first understand what typically happens when we use some web application on the Internet. Through browser on our PC/Laptop/Tablet/Smartphone we use a URL to reach the application present on some web server on the Internet. The web application sends HTML that gets rendered in our browser. However, except for the simplest of web applications, along with the HTML some executable Java program is also sent to our browser. This program is often small and is called Applet. The purpose of the applet is to make the web application more responsive. For example, if we enter a password, it should be possible to check whether it follows rules for password creation or not right there within the browser using the downloaded applet, rather than sending the password to server and get it verified. This certainly improves user experience. This is because the check is being performed on your machine rather than on the server machine. This saves a roundtrip to the server.

But when we download an applet there is always a possibility that the applet contains malicious code like a Virus or Trojan horse that would cause harm to our machine. JVM prevents this from happening by restricting the applet code from accessing other resources of your machine, other than what it is supposed to. This makes applets secure. Thus JVM solves two dicey issues in one shot—portability as well as security.

Java or C++?

After learning C, it is often a question whether one should migrate to Java or C++. Answer is both; and that too in any sequence that you want. Though both are Object Oriented programming languages, neither is an advanced version of the other. Learning one before the other would naturally help to learn the second.

It is important to note that both address different sets of problems. C++ primarily addresses complexity, whereas Java addresses portability and security. In my opinion both languages would continue to rule the hearts of programmers for many years to come.

As you start learning Java, you would find that there are many features in it that are similar to C and C++. This is not by accident, but by intent. Java designer knew that he has to provide a smooth transition path to learners of Java language. That is why Java uses a syntax which is similar in many ways to that of C and it follows many of the object oriented features of C++, though in a refined fashion.

The Java Environment

As we know JVM contains an Interpreter / JIT that converts bytecode into microprocessor + OS specific machine language instructions. Since instruction sets vary from microprocessor to microprocessor, there exist different JVMs for different platforms. Thus though any JVM can run any Java program, JVMs themselves are not portable.

JVM is distributed along with a set of standard class libraries that implement the Java Application Programming Interface (API). The Java APIs and JVM together form the Java Runtime Environment (JRE). If your need is only to execute Java programs on your machine, all that you need is JRE. For example, if you wish to play a Java-based game on your machine, you need to install only JRE on your machine for the game to run.

However, if you wish to also develop programs on your machine, you need Java Developer Kit (JDK). JDK contains tools needed to develop the Java programs, as well as JRE to run the programs. The tools include compiler (javac.exe), Java application launcher (java.exe), Appletviewer, etc. Compiler converts Java code into bytecode. Java application launcher opens a JRE, loads the class, and calls its **main( )** method. Figure 1.4 shows all these pieces of Java environment.

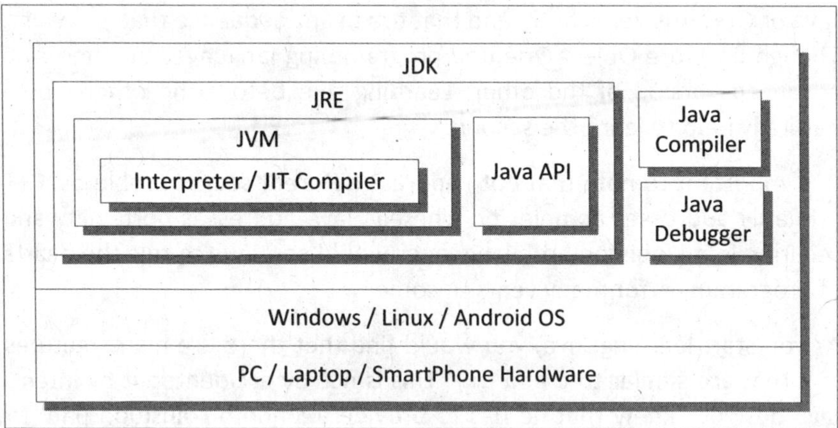

Figure 1.4

Tools of the Trade

To create and run Java programs you need to install two software on your PC. These are

(a) Java Development Kit (JDK)

(b) NetBeans

Remember that JDK must be installed before installing NetBeans. There are multiple versions of JDK and NetBeans available for download from several websites. The latest versions are JDK 8 and NetBeans 8.2. They can be downloaded together from

http://www.oracle.com/technetwork/java/javase/downloads/index.html

On this download page select the appropriate Java SE and NetBeans Cobundle based on the OS (Windows/Mac/Linux) and the Microprocessor (x86 or X64).

JDK is often also called Standard Edition Development Kit or Java SE 8 JDK. Basically JDK contains JVM, JRE, and Java compiler and debugger. A compiler is needed to convert the Java program into its equivalent bytecode. A debugger is needed to detect, analyze and eliminate bugs in the program.

When you are developing a Java program you need an editor to type the program. Small Java programs can be typed in one file. But more sophisticated programs may be split across multiple files. To let you type the program, manage multiple files of your program, compile it and debug it, you need a tool that can let you carry out these tasks in a visual and user-friendly manner. This tool is often called an Integrated Development Environment (IDE). One such IDE that is very popularly used for building programs in Java, is NetBeans. All programs in this book have been created using NetBeans IDE.

Once you download the JDK and NetBeans bundle you need to install it. This is a fairly simple job and I am sure you would be able to do this easily. You simply have to double click the downloaded installer file **jdk-8u141-nb-8_2-windows-i586.exe** (assuming Windows and 64-bit machine configuration), and the installer would guide you through the installation process.

We are now on surer grounds. We now have the historical perspective of what led to creation of Java, what problems it primarily attempts to solve, and what tools we need to install to begin Java program development. It would be a good idea to attempt the exercise on the next page to help you fix these ideas, before we formally begin learning Java language from next chapter onwards.

Exercise

[A] Match the following:

(a) Creator of Java	(1) Provides security and portability
(b) JRE	(2) Platform dependent
(c) Java Program	(3) Bjarne Stroustrup
(d) JVM	(4) Contains compiler and debugger
(e) NetBeans	(5) Needed for executing Java programs
(f) Creator of C++	(6) IDE
(g) JDK	(7) Platform independent
(h) JVM	(8) James Gosling

[B] State which of the following statements are True or False:

(a) Different microprocessors use different Instruction sets.

(b) Same JVM is used for all microprocessor + OS combination.

(c) We can get by just installing JRE on a machine on which we intend to only execute Java programs.

(d) NetBeans is just an IDE and doesn't have a Java compiler built in it.

(e) The Java compiler converts instructions in Java into machine language instructions.

(f) JRE and JDK both are part of JVM.

(g) The way I/O and memory management is done is same across different OSs.

(h) Traditional programming languages like C and C++ follow "write once, compile anywhere" dictum.

(i) Java follows "compile once, run anywhere" dictum.

(j) Java programs cannot run without JVM.

(k) To run a Java program you need to install JDK.

[C] Which of the following is highlighting feature of C, C++ and Java?

(a) Structured
(b) Object Oriented
(c) Portable

(d) Secure
(e) Suitable for Internet programming
(f) Simple syntax
(g) Architecturally neutral
(h) Management of complexity

KanNotes

- 2 categories of software :
    - System software - OS, Compilers, Device Drivers
    - Application software - software for desktop/laptop, Web, Mobile
- Technologies used in Java world for different platforms :
    - Desktop - J2SE, Mobile - J2ME, Web - J2EE
- Reasons of popularity of Java :
    - Same language for varied applications
    - Rapid Application Development (RAD) possible
    - Easy development cycle
    - Easy to manage large projects
- Acronymns:
    - API = Application Programming Interface JVM = Java Virtual Machine
    - JRE = Java Runtime Environment JDK = Java Development Kit
- API = Library of classes in form of packages
- JVM = Memory Manager + Interpreter / Just In Time (JIT) compiler
- JRE = JVM + API
- JDK = JRE + Development tools like javac, java, debugger
- NetBeans, Eclipse are popular development environments
- Nebeans and Eclipse internally use javac, java, debugger
- Different JREs and JDKs have to be downloaded for different Hardware + OS combination
- For execution of Java programs only JRE is needed
- To create and execute Java programs JDK + NetBeans are needed

- In C / C++ our program on building is converted into machine language instructions.
- In Java on building our program is converted into ByteCode instructions.
- During execution of Java programs the ByteCode instruction are converted into machine language instructions and these insrtuctions are executed.
- Byte code instructions for a .java file are stored in corresponding .class file.
- For multiple .java files a .jar (Java Archive) file is created.
- To achieve portability C/C++ use Write once, Compile often principle
- To further improve portability Java uses Compile once, Run often principle

Getting Started

2

Wet your feet, before you take a dip. See how to create a small program in Java...

Chapter Contents

Four important aspects of any language are the way it stores data, the way it operates upon this data, how it accomplishes input and output, and how it lets you control the sequence of execution of instructions in a program. We would discuss the first three of these building blocks in this chapter.

Java Data Types

Before we write even our first Java program, it is important to understand how data is represented in Java. This is done using a data type. A data type specifies two things:

(a) What value can the data type take?
(b) What operations can be performed on the data type?

For example, an **integer** data type can take values in the range -2147483648 to +2147483647, and operations like addition, subtraction, multiplication, division, etc., can be performed on it. Similarly, a **boolean** data type can take a value true or false, and permits comparison operations on it.

Based on where a data type can be created in memory, it is called a **primitive type** (often also known as a **value type**) or a **reference type**.

Java forces primitive data types to get created only in stack and reference types only on heap. For example, an integer (like say, 2341) always gets created in stack, whereas a string (like say "Quest") always gets created in heap. The guiding principle on the basis of which Java does this decision making is—all data types that are small in size are created in stack, and all those that occupy bigger memory chunks are created in heap.

A primitive type as well as a reference type can be further categorized into pre-defined and user-defined categories. Here pre-defined means the data types that Java provides ready-made, whereas, user-defined means the one that a common user like us can create. For example, integer is a pre-defined primitive data type, whereas an Enumeration is a user-defined value type. Figure 2.1 shows the different categories of data types available in Java. Note that the pre-defined value types are often also called Primitives.

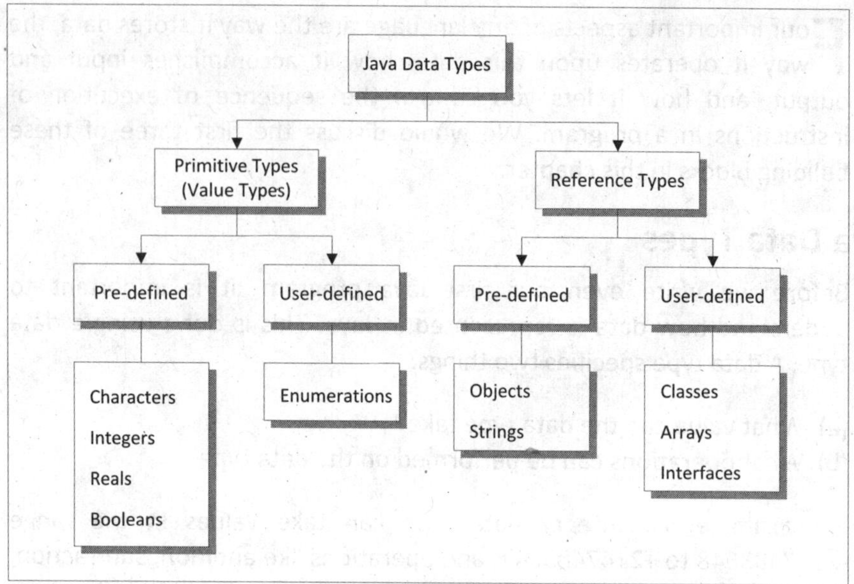

Figure 2.1

Amongst all the data types shown in Figure 2.1, to begin with, we would concentrate on the pre-defined value data types. To use the data types in a Java program we have to create constants and variables. A constant is nothing but a specific value from the range of values offered by a data type, whereas a variable is a container which can hold a constant value. The container is typically a memory location and the variable is the name given to the location in memory. For example, if we use an expression **x = 5**, then the constant value 5 would be stored in a memory location and a name **x** would be given to that location. Whenever, we wish to retrieve and use **5**, we just have to use the variable name **x**. This is shown in Figure 2.2.

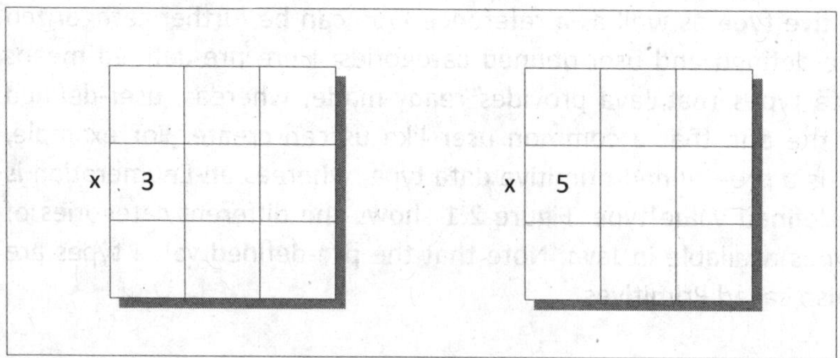

Figure 2.2

As the name suggests, a constant's value cannot change (fixed), whereas, a variable's value can change (vary). A constant is often called a **literal**, whereas, a variable is also known as an **identifier**. Figure 2.3 gives list of commonly used pre-defined primitive data types along with the range of values that they can take and the numbers of bytes they occupy in memory.

Data Type	Range	Size in bytes
char	0 to 65535	2
int	-2147483648 to +2147483647	4
float	-3.4e38 to +3.4e38	4

Figure 2.3

There are certain rules that one needs to observe while creating constants and variables. These are discussed below.

Rules for Constructing Constants

(a) If no sign precedes a numeric constant, it is assumed to be positive.

(b) No commas or blanks are allowed within a constant.

(c) The bytes occupied by each constant are fixed and do not change from one compiler to another.

(d) Only a float constant can contain a decimal point.

(e) A float constant must be followed by a suffix **f**.

(f) A float constant can be expressed in fractional from (example 314.56f) or exponential form (example 3.1456e2).

(g) A character constant is a single alphabet, a single digit or a single special symbol enclosed within single inverted commas. Both the inverted commas should point to the left. For example, 'A' is a valid character constant, whereas 'A' is not.

Given below are examples of some valid constants.

```
426      +78.23    -8000    -7605
true     'A'       '+'      '3'
```

Rules for Constructing Variable Names

(a) A variable name is any combination of alphabets, digits, underscored (_) and dollars ($).

(b) The first character in the variable name must be an alphabet, underscore or dollar.

(c) No commas or blanks are allowed within a variable name.

(d) Variable names are case-sensitive. So, abc, ABC, Abc, aBc, AbC are treated as different variables.

While creating variable names conventions given below are commonly followed.

(a) A variable name usually begins with an alphabet. Ex. speed, average

(b) A variable representing money usually begins with $. Ex. $interest, $salary.

(c) If a variable name containing multiple words the words are either connected using underscore or follow a camel-case notation. Ex. current_speed, currentSpeed, avg_salary, avgSalary.

While following these rules and conventions one must avoid the temptation of creating long variable names, as it unnecessarily adds to the typing effort.

The rules remain same for constructing variables of any type. Naturally, the question follows—how is Java able to differentiate between these variables? This is a rather simple matter. Java compiler makes it compulsory for us to declare the type of any variable name that we wish to use in a program. Here are a few examples showing how this is done.

Ex.:
```
int  si, m_hra ;
float  bassal ;
char  code ;
```

Since, there is no limit on maximum allowable length of a variable name, an enormous number of variable names can be constructed using the above-mentioned rules. It is a good practice to exploit this enormous choice in naming variables by using meaningful variable names.

Thus, if we want to calculate simple interest, it is always advisable to construct meaningful variable names like **prin**, **roi**, **noy** to represent Principal, Rate of interest and Number of years rather than using the variables **a**, **b**, **c**.

Java Keywords

Keywords are the words whose meaning has already been explained to the Java compiler. When we make the declaration

int age ;

age is a variable, whereas **int** is a keyword. When this declaration is made, we are telling the compiler that the variable **age** be treated as a variable of type integer. But we don't have to be so elaborate, just **int age** conveys the same meaning. This is because, the meaning of the keyword **int** has already been explained to the Java compiler.

The keywords cannot be used as variable names because if we do so, we are trying to assign a new meaning to the keyword, which is not allowed. There are only 48 keywords available in Java. Figure 2.4 gives a list of these keywords for your ready reference. A detailed discussion of each of these keywords would be taken up in later chapters wherever their use is relevant.

abstract	class	final	int	return	throw
assert	continue	finally	interface	new	switch
boolean	default	float	long	synchronized	throws
break	do	for	native	short	transient
byte	double	if	package	static	try
case	else	implements	private	strictfp	void
catch	enum	import	protected	super	volatile
char	extends	instanceof	public	this	while

Figure 2.4

The First Java Program

Armed with the knowledge of variables, constants and keywords, the next logical step is to combine them to form instructions. However, instead of this, we would write our first Java program now. Once we have done that we would see in detail the instructions that it made use of.

Before we begin with our first Java program do remember the following rules that are applicable to all Java programs:

(a) Each instruction in a Java program is written as a separate statement. Therefore, a complete Java program would comprise a series of statements.

(b) Blank spaces may be inserted between two words to improve the readability of the statement. However, no blank spaces are allowed within a variable, constant or keyword.

(c) All statements are in small case letters.

(d) Every Java statement must end with a semicolon (;).

Let us now write our first Java program. It would simply calculate simple interest for a set of values representing principal, number of years and rate of interest.

```
// Calculation of simple interest
package calofsi ;
public class CalOfSi
{
    public static void main ( String[ ] args )
    {
        float  p, r, si ;
        int  n ;
        p = 1000.50f ;
        n = 3 ;
        r = 15.5f ;
        si = p * n * r / 100 ;
        System.out.println ( si ) ;
    }
}
```

Now a few useful tips about the program...

- Comment about the program should either be enclosed within /* */ or be preceded by //. For example, the first statement in our program is comment.
- Though comments are not necessary, it is a good practice to begin a program with a comment indicating the purpose of the program, its author and the date on which the program was written.
- Sometimes it is not very obvious as to what a particular statement in a program accomplishes. At such times it is worthwhile mentioning the purpose of the statement (or a set of statements) using a comment. For example

```
/* formula for simple interest */
si = p * n * r / 100 ;
```

- A comment can be split over more than one line, as in,

```
/* This is
   a multi-line
   comment */
```

  Such a comment is often called a multi-line comment.
- A Java program is a collection of one or more packages. Each package can contain multiple classes. Each class may contain multiple functions. Each function can contain multiple instructions. This typical organization of a Java program is shown in Figure 2.5.
- Every instruction used in a Java program should belong to a function. Every function must belong to a class and every class must belong to a package. In our program there is a package called **calofsi**, a class called **CalOfSi** and a function called **main( )**. **package** and **class** both are keywords.

  Right now we do not want to go into the details of package and a class. We would learn about packages and classes in later chapters. But it would be a good time to get introduced to the concept of a function.

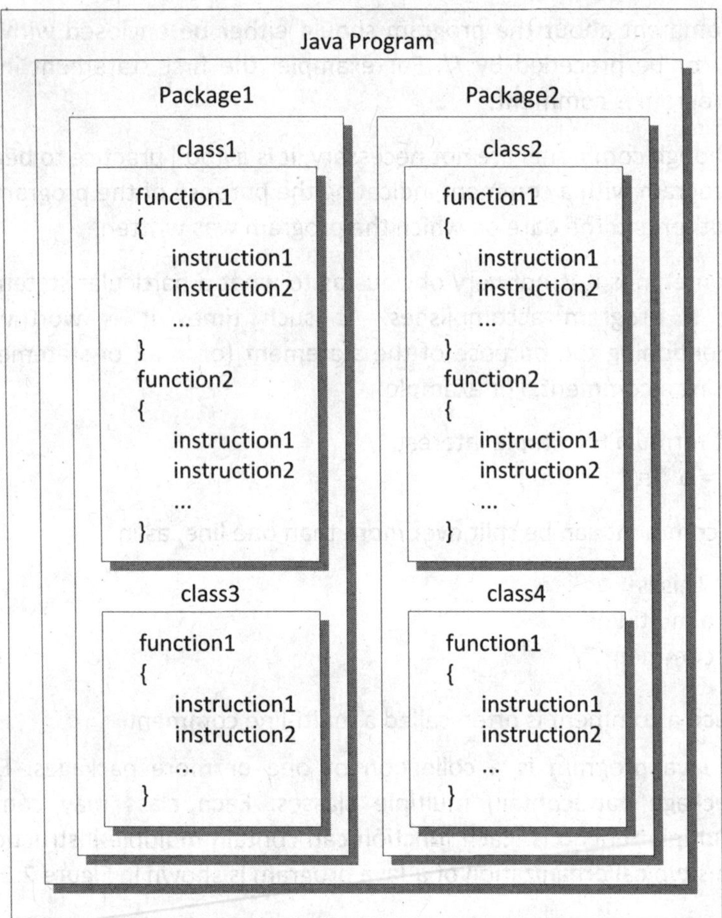

Figure 2.5

- **main( )** is a function. A function contains a set of statements. Though a Java program can contain multiple functions, to begin with, we would concentrate on only those programs which have only one function. All statements that belong to **main( )** are enclosed within a pair of braces { } as shown below.

```
public static void main ( String[ ] args )
{
    statement 1 ;
    statement 2 ;
    statement 3 ;
}
```

– The way functions in a calculator return a value, similarly, functions in Java also return a value. Since we do not wish to return any value from **main( )** function we have to specify this using the keyword **void** before **main( )**. **main( )** is always preceded by the keyword **static**. The purpose of this keyword and detailed working of functions would be discussed in Chapters 9 and 7 respectively.

– Any variable used in the program must be declared before using it. For example,

```
int p, n ;      /* declaration */
float r, si ;   /* declaration */
si = p * n * r / 100 ;  /* usage */
```

– Any Java statement always ends with a semicolon (;). For example,

```
float r, si ;
r = 15.5f ;
```

– In the statement,

```
si = p * n * r / 100 ;
```

***** and **/** are the arithmetic operators. The arithmetic operators available in Java are **+**, **-**, ***** and **/**. Java is very rich in operators. There are totally 41 operators available in Java.

– Once the value of **si** is calculated it needs to be displayed on the screen. Unlike other languages, Java does not contain any instruction to display output on the screen. All output to screen is achieved using ready-made library functions. One such function is **println( )**. We have used it to display the value contained in **si** on the screen.

– Actually speaking **println( )** is a function of **PrintStream** class, and **out** is a **static** object defined in a **System** class. We would learn classes, objects and static members in Chapter 8. As of now, let us just use the syntax **System.out.println( )** whenever we wish to display output on the screen.

– If we wish we can print multiple values using **println( )** function. This is shown below.

```
System.out.println ( si + " " + p + " " + n + " " + r ) ;
System.out.println ( "Simple interest = Rs. " + si ) ;
System.out.println ( "Principal = " + p + " Rate = " + r ) ;
```

The output of these statements would look like this...

465.2325 1000.5 3 15.5
Simple interest = Rs. 465.2325
Principal = 1000.5 Rate = 15.5

Compilation and Execution

We need to carry out the following steps to create, compile and execute our first Java program. It is assumed that you have installed JDK and NetBeans as per the instructions in Chapter 1.

(a) Start NetBeans from Start | All Programs.

(b) Select File | New Project from the File menu. Select 'Java' from 'Categories' list box and 'Java Application' from 'Projects' box. Click on 'Next' button.

(c) Give a proper name for the project in 'Project Name' text box (say **CalOfSi**). Choose suitable location for the project folder, then click on Finish.

(d) NetBeans would provide a skeleton program that would contain a **package** statement, a public class **CalOfSi** and a function **main( )**, all defined in a file called **CalOfSi.java**. Note that the name of the file and the name of the public class are same in all Java programs.

(e) Type the statements of our simple interest program in **main( )**.

(f) Save the program using **Ctrl+S**.

(g) Compile and execute the program using **F6**.

One More Program

We now know how to write an elementary Java program, type it, compile it and execute it. These are the steps that you will have to carry out for every program. So to help you fix your ideas, here is one more program. It calculates and prints average value of 3 numbers.

```
/* Calculation of average */
package calofavg ;
public class CalOfAvg
```

```
{
    public static void main ( String[ ] args )
    {
        int  x, y, z, avg ;
        x = 73 ;
        y = 70 ;
        z = 65 ;
        avg = ( x + y + z ) / 3 ;
        System.out.println ( avg ) ;
    }
}
```

Exercise

[A] Which of the following is invalid variable name and why?

BASICSALARY	_basic	basic-hra
#MEAN	group.	422
population in 2006	over time	mindovermatter
SINGLE	hELLO	queue.
team'svictory	Plot # 3	2015_DDay

[B] Point out the errors, if any, in the following Java statements:

(a) int = 314.562f * 150 ;

(b) name = 'Ajay' ;

(c) varchar = '3' ;

(d) 3.14f * r * r * h = vol_of_cyl ;

(e) k = (a * b) (c + (2.5fa + b) (d + e) ;

(f) m_inst = rate of interest * amount in rs ;

(g) si = principal * rateofinterest * numberofyears / 100 ;

(h) area = 3.14f * r ** 2 ;

(i) volume = 3.14f * r ^ 2 * h ;

(j) k = ((a * b) + c) (2.5f * a + b) ;

(k) a = b = 3 = 4 ;

(l) count = count + 1 ;

(m) date = '2 Mar 11' ;

[C] Pick up the correct alternative for each of the following questions:

(a) Which of the following is the correct way to write a comment?

(1) // This is a comment
(2) / This is a comment
(3) /* This is a comment
(4) /* This is a /* comment */ */

(b) The maximum value that an integer constant can have is:

(1) -2147483647
(2) 2147483647
(3) 3.4×10^{38}
(4) -3.4×10^{38}

(c) A Java variable cannot start with:

(1) An alphabet
(2) A number
(3) A special symbol other than underscore
(4) Both (2) and (3) above

(d) Which of the following is odd one out?

(1) +
(2) -
(3) /
(4) **

[D] Answer the following:

(a) Assume a suitable value for Ramesh's basic salary. His dearness allowance is 40% of basic salary, and house rent allowance is 20% of basic salary. Write a Java program to calculate his gross salary.

(b) Assume a suitable value for distance between two cities (in km.). Write a Java program to convert and print this distance in meters, feet, inches and centimeters.

(c) Assume suitable values for marks obtained by a student in five different subjects are input through the keyboard. Write a Java program to find out the aggregate marks and percentage marks obtained by the student. Assume that the maximum marks that can be obtained by a student in each subject is 100.

(d) Assume a suitable value for temperature of a city in Fahrenheit degrees. Write a Java program to convert this temperature into Centigrade degrees and print both temperatures.

(e) Assume suitable values for length and breadth of a rectangle, and radius of a circle. Write a Java program to calculate the area and perimeter of the rectangle, and the area and circumference of the circle.

KanNotes

- Constants = Literals -> Cannot change
  Variables = Identifiers -> May change
- Data Types : 1) Primitives (value types) 2) Reference types
- Primtive types :
  - Char - 2 bytes
  - Integers - byte, short, int, long (sizes - 1, 2, 4, 8 bytes)
  - Real - float, double (sizes - 4, 8 bytes respectively)
  - Boolean - true / false (1 bit)
- Derived types (classes) :
  - Library : String, System, Exception, etc.
  - User-defined : CalOfSi, CalOfAvg, etc.
- Variable names are case-sensitive and should begin with an alphabet
- Total keywords = 48. Example : int, char, float
- A Java program is a collection of one or more packages
- Each package can contain multiple classes
- Each class may contain multiple functions
- A variable must belong to either a function or a class
- No global functions or variables in Java
- public class is accessible from outside the package
- public function is accessible from outside the class
- 3 types of comments :
  - Single line - //
  - Multiline - /* ... */
  - Documentation - /** .... */

3

Datatypes and Instructions

Well begun, is half done! Learn the basic building blocks of the language ...

Let Us JAVA
3rd Edition

Chapter Contents

In the last chapter we wrote programs with bare minimum knowledge of data types and instructions. As a result, the programs worked only for specific data. If they are to work with other data it would necessitate changes in the program, which is not a good idea. In this chapter we propose to rectify this situation. For that, we have to have more in-depth knowledge of data types and instructions. There is a lot of ground to cover here. Let us begin with the data types.

Data Types Revisited

So far we have used only an **int** to deal with integer values and **float** to deal with real values. However, Java provides many flavors of integers and reals. Let us begin with integers.

Integer Types

Java provides 4 types of integers—**byte**, **short**, **int** and **long** of sizes 1 byte, 2 bytes, 4 bytes and 8 bytes respectively. Figure 3.1 shows different types of integers available in Java along with their sizes and ranges.

Data Type	Range	Bytes	Default Value
byte	-128 to +127	1	0
short	-32768 to +32767	2	0
int	-2147483648 to +2147483647	4	0
long	-9223372036854775808 to +9223372036854775807	8	0

Figure 3.1

Let us now discuss some finer points associated with integer types.

(a) By default, number without a decimal point is treated as an **int**. During assignment, if the value being assigned exceeds the range of the variable, an error occurs. This is shown below.

```
byte a = 300 ; // error
short b = 40000 ; // error
int c = 2200000000 ; // error
```

(b) If we wish to treat an integer as a long integer, we have to add a suffix L or l at its end, as in

```
long int a = 365l * 1000 ;
```

(c) We can use underscores between digits in a number to improve the readability of our code, as shown below.

```
long creditCardNo = 1211_5178_9212_4231L ;
```

Note that we cannot use underscore at the beginning or at the end of a number, or prior to suffix L.

Real Types

Real numbers can be represented as **float** and **double**. The difference between them is the number of bytes occupied by each, their ranges and their precision. This is shown in Figure 3.2.

Data Type	Range	Default Value	Bytes
float	$\pm 1.5 \times 10^{-45}$ to $\pm 3.4 \times 10^{38}$	0.0f	4
double	$\pm 5.0 \times 10^{-324}$ to $\pm 1.7 \times 10^{308}$	0.0	8

Figure 3.2

There are some finer points associated with these real types. These are discussed below.

(a) By default, a number with a decimal point is treated as a **double**. If we wish to treat it as a **float**, we need to add a suffix **f** or **F** at the end of it to make it a **float**, as shown below.

```
float x = 3.5 ; // error
float y = 3.5f ; // correct
double d = 3.5f ; // correct
double e = 3.5 ; // correct
```

(b) If we want an integer number to be treated as double, use the suffix d or D, for example,

```
double a = 3d ;
```

(c) Any number of underscores can be used between digits in a number to improve the readability of your code, as shown below.

```
float pi = 3.14_28_57F;
```

Note that we cannot use underscore at the beginning or end of a number, prior to suffix F, or adjacent to decimal point.

(d) If the value of a **float / double** is too small or too large then instead of using the normal notation it is easier to specify the number in exponential notation. This is shown below.

```
float a = 0.0000341295f ;  // normal notation
double b = 3214.23221 ;  // normal notation
float c = 3.41295e-5f ; // exponential notation
double d = 3.21e3 ;  // exponential notation
```

(e) A real number is stored in a **float / double** it is stored in binary form. During conversion of decimal number into binary, some precision may be lost. So two real numbers that otherwise appear equal, when represented in binary numbers of different precisions, might turn out to be unequal. For example, 5.375 and 5.375f are not equal. When 5.375 is treated as double, it is represented as a 64-bit binary number, whereas when it is treated as a float, it is represented as a 32-bit binary number, resulting in some loss of precision.

char Data Type

A **char** data type represents a character expressed in Unicode format. The Unicode format has slowly replaced its predecessor, ASCII format. Characters in most of the known written languages used in the world can be represented using Unicode format.

In addition to the normal form, a character constant can also be specified using Unicode representation. This is shown below.

```
char ch = 'X' ;   // character literal
char dh = '\u0058' ;  // Unicode
```

Unicode representation can take a minimum value of '\u0000' (or decimal 0) and a maximum value of '\uffff' (or decimal 65535).

boolean Data Type

boolean data type can take Boolean values, true and false. A variable of the type **boolean** can either be assigned a Boolean value or an expression which evaluates to a Boolean value. This is shown below.

```
boolean a = false ;
System.out.println ( "a = " + a ) ;
```

```
boolean b = 4 > 2 ;
System.out.println ( "b = " + b ) ;
```

The output of this code snippet would be...

```
a = false
b = true
```

We should not use true / false as variable names. Lastly, unlike languages like C and C++, in Java true is not 1 and false is not 0. This is indicated in the following statements:

```
int a ; boolean b ;
a = 3 < 4 ; // error
b = 3 < 4 ; // works
```

Receiving Input

In the simple interest program of Chapter 2, we assumed the values of **p**, **n** and **r** to be 1000.5, 3 and 15.5. Every time we run this program we would get the same value for simple interest. To calculate simple interest for some other set of values, we would be required to replace the existing set with the new set of values, and again compile and execute the program. Thus, the program is not general enough to calculate simple interest for any set of values without being required to make a change in the program.

To make the program general, the program should ask the user to supply the values of **p**, **n** and **r** through the keyboard during execution. When the user supplies these values, they can be read by the program using the **readLine( )** function as illustrated in the program given below.

```
// Calculation of simple interest
package sibyreceivinginput ;
import java.io.* ;

public class SiByReceivingInput
{
    public static void main ( String[ ] args ) throws Exception
    {
        float p, r, si ;
        int n ;

        System.out.println ( "Enter values of p, n and r" ) ;
```

```
        BufferedReader br = new BufferedReader (
                              new InputStreamReader ( System.in ) ) ;
        p = Float.parseFloat ( br.readLine( ) ) ;
        n = Integer.parseInt ( br.readLine( ) ) ;
        r = Float.parseFloat ( br.readLine( ) ) ;
        si = ( p * n * r ) / 100 ;
        System.out.println ( "Simple interest = Rs. " + si ) ;
    }
}
```

Let us now see what happens when we execute this program. To begin with, the first **println( )** outputs the message 'Enter values of p, n, r' in the output window of NetBeans. In this window we are supposed to supply three numbers in three distinct lines separated by Enter key.

Our program should read each of these lines. To do this, we have to first create two objects of type **BufferedReader** and **InputStreamReader**, and then call the **readLine( )** function thrice. For now, we would just use the following lines mechanically:

```
BufferedReader br = new BufferedReader (
                      new InputStreamReader ( System.in ) ) ;
```

In Chapter 9 we would learn what objects are and how to create them. To be able to use the classes **BufferedReader** and **InputStreamReader**, we have to add the following statement at the beginning of our program, below the **package** statement:

```
import java.io.* ;
```

As mentioned earlier, the classes in Java library are organized in different packages. Through the above statement we are importing all (*) the classes present in the package **java.io**. This makes the classes **BufferedStreamReader** and **InputStreamReader** available for use.

If we supply wrong input to **readLine( )**, then conversion of this input into an **int / float** through **parseInt( ) / parseFloat( )** would result into an error during execution. There are different ways to take care of this possible error. Of these, we have chosen the easiest one—by writing **throws Exception** besides **main( )**. We would not get into the details of this and the other mechanisms to handle errors that occur during execution. These mechanisms are discussed in detail in Chapter 14.

The numeric values that we supply to the three **readLine( )** functions is treated as string of characters, rather than as numbers. So we need to convert the strings into numbers. This conversion is done by the **parseFloat( )** and **parseInt( )** functions. These functions belong to a library classes called **Float** and **Integer,** respectively. The converted values are then assigned to respective variables. Lastly, simple interest is calculated and printed out.

Command-line Arguments

In our simple interest program, instead of supplying the values to **readLine( )** functions during execution, we can provide the values at command-line itself. This would be another way of supplying input to the program. The modified program would look like this...

```
// Calculation of simple interest
package siusingcmdlineargs ;

public class SiUsingCmdLineArgs
{
    public static void main ( String[ ] args )
    {
        float p, r, si ;
        int n ;

        p = ( Float.valueOf ( args[ 0 ] ) ).floatValue( ) ;
        n = ( Integer.valueOf ( args[ 1 ] ) ).intValue( ) ;
        r = ( Float.valueOf (  args[ 2 ] ) ).floatValue( ) ;
        si = p * n * r / 100  ;
        System.out.println ( "Simple interest = Rs. " + si ) ;
    }
}
```

To supply the values of **p, n** and **r** as command-line arguments, Right click on the project name **siusingcmdlineargs** in the projects window of NetBeans and select 'Properties' from the menu that pops up. On doing so, the Project Properties window is displayed. In this window choose 'Run' from 'Categories' and type the values 1000.50f 3 15.5f in the 'Arguments' text box.

Now you can compile and execute the program as usual using F6. When we execute the program, the command-line arguments are available in **main( )** as an array (collection) of strings in **args**. From this collection we can access the individual strings using **args[0]**, **args[1]** and **args[2]**. These strings contain the values that we gave as command-line arguments. However, we cannot perform arithmetic on these strings. So it is necessary to first convert them into numbers. This conversion into **float** and **int** is done using the statements:

```
p = ( Float.valueOf ( args[ 0 ] ) ).floatValue( ) ;
n = ( Integer.valueOf ( args[ 1 ] ) ).intValue( ) ;
r = ( Float.valueOf (  args[ 2 ] ) ).floatValue( ) ;
```

The function **valueOf( )** returns a **Float** or **Integer** object. From these objects the actual float or integer value is obtained by calling the functions **floatValue( )** and **intValue( )** of **Float** and **Integer** class, respectively. The converted numbers are then assigned to **p**, **n** and **r**. Finally, simple interest is calculated and printed out.

Java Instructions

Now that we have written a few programs, let us look at the instructions that we have used in these programs. There are basically five types of instructions in Java. The purpose of each of these instructions is given in Figure 3.3.

Instruction	**Purpose**
Type declaration	To declare the type of variables used in a Java program
Arithmetic	To perform arithmetic operations between constants and variables
Control	To control the sequence of execution of various statements in a Java program
Exception Handling	To handle situations when errors occur during execution of a Java program
Advanced	Instructions for thread synchronization, for handling arithmetic overflow, etc.

Figure 3.3

Since, the elementary Java programs would usually contain only the type declaration and the arithmetic instructions; we would discuss only these two instructions at this stage. The other types of instructions would be discussed in detail in the subsequent chapters.

Type Declaration Instruction

This instruction is used to declare the type of each variable being used in the program. Any variable used in the program must be declared before using it in any statement.

Ex.:
```
int  bas ;
float  rs, grosssal ;
char  name, code ;
```

There are several subtle variations of the type declaration instruction. These are discussed below.

(a) While declaring the type of variable we can also initialize it as shown below.

```
int i = 10, j = 25 ;
float a = 1.5f, b = 1.99f + 2.4f * 1.44f ;
```

(b) The order in which we define the variables is sometimes important sometimes not. For example,

```
int  i = 10, j = 25 ;
```

is same as

```
int  j = 25, i = 10 ;
```

However,

```
float  a = 1.5f, b = a + 3.1f ;
```

is alright, but

```
float  b = a + 3.1f, a = 1.5f ;
```

is not. This is because here we are trying to use **a** even before defining it.

(c) The following statements would work:

```
int  a, b, c, d ;
a = b = c = 10 ;
```

However, the following statement would not work:

```
int  a = b = c = d = 10 ;
```

This is because we are trying to use **b** (to assign to **a**) before defining it.

Arithmetic Instruction

A Java arithmetic instruction consists of a variable name on the left hand side of =, and variable names and constants on the right hand side of =. The variables and constants appearing on the right hand side of = are connected using arithmetic operators like **+, -, *,** and **/**.

Ex.:
```
int budget ;
float alpha, beta ;
budget = 3200 ;
beta = 0.5f ;
alpha = beta + 3.2f * 2 / 5 - 3 ;
```

Here,

***, /, -, +** are the arithmetic operators
= is an assignment operator
2, 3, 5 and 3200 are integer constants
0.5f and 3.2f are float constants
budget is an integer variable
alpha, **beta** are float variables.

The variables and constants together are called 'operands'. While executing an arithmetic statement the operands on right hand side are operated upon by the 'arithmetic operators' and the result is then assigned, using the assignment operator, to the variable on left hand side.

A Java arithmetic statement could be of three types. These are as follows:

(a) Integer mode arithmetic statement - This is an arithmetic statement in which all operands are either integer variables or integer constants.

Ex.:
```
int i = 10, king, issac = 23, noteit = 45 ;
i = i + 1 ;
king = issac * 234 + noteit - 7689 ;
```

(b) Real mode arithmetic statement - This is an arithmetic statement in which all operands are either real constants or real variables.

```
Ex.: float  qbee, si, prin = 100.55f, noy = 1.5f, roi = 5.5f ;
     qbee = 23.123f / 4.5f * 0.3442f ;
     si = prin * noy * roi / 100.0f ;
```

(c) Mixed mode arithmetic statement - This is an arithmetic statement in which some operands are integers and some are real.

```
Ex.: float  si, prin = 100.55f, noy = 1.5f, roi = 5.5f, avg ;
     int  a = 10, b = 20, c =30, num = 40 ;
     si = prin * noy * roi / 100.0f ;
     avg = ( a + b + c + num + 10.5f ) / 5 ;
```

Though Arithmetic instructions look simple to use, one often commits mistakes in writing them. Let us take a closer look at these statements. Note the following points carefully:

(a) Java allows only one variable on left hand side of =. This means, **z = k * l** is legal, whereas **k * l = z** is illegal.

(b) In addition to the division operator Java also provides a modular division operator (%). This operator returns the remainder on dividing one operand with another. Thus the expression 10 / 2 yields 5, whereas, 10 % 2 yields 0. Note that on using %, the sign of the remainder is always same as the sign of the numerator. Thus -5 % 2 yields -1, whereas, 5 % -2 yields 1.

(c) Modular division can also be done on floats. If **a** and **b** are floats then **a % b** is computed as **a - n * b**, where **n** is the largest possible integer that is less than or equal to **a / b**. Thus **16.5f % 1.25f** yields **0.25**.

(d) An arithmetic instruction is at times used for storing character constants in character variables.

```
char  a, b ;
a = 'F' ;
b = '+' ;
```

When we do this, the Unicode values of the characters are stored in the variables.

(e) Arithmetic operations can be performed on **ints**, **floats** and **chars**. Thus the statements,

```
char  x = 'a', y = 'b' ;
```

```
int  z ;
z = x + y ;
```

are perfectly valid, since the addition is performed on the Unicode values of the characters and not on characters themselves. The Unicode values of 'a' and 'b' are 97 and 98, and hence they can be added.

(f) No operator is assumed to be present. It must be written explicitly. In the following example, the multiplication operator after **b** must be explicitly written:

```
a = c.d.b(xy)               usual arithmetic statement
b = c * d * b * ( x * y )   Java statement
```

(g) If we want to perform an exponentiation operation, we can get it done this way:

```
double  a ;
a = Math.pow ( 3.0, 2.0 ) ;
```

Here **pow( )** function is a function in the **Math** class. It is being used to raise 3.0 to the power of 2.0. Note that we should always use **double** values with **pow( )**.

There are many other mathematical functions in **Math** class, like **sqrt( ), abs( ), sin( ), cos( ), tan( ), log( ), log10( )**, etc.

Type Conversion in Arithmetic Instructions

In order to effectively develop Java programs, it is necessary to understand the rules that are used for the implicit conversion of real and integer values. These are mentioned below. Note them carefully.

(a) An arithmetic operation between an integer and integer always yields an integer result.

(b) An operation between a real and real always yields a real result.

(c) An operation between an integer and real always yields a real result. In this operation, the integer is first promoted to a real and then the operation is performed. Hence the result is real.

I think a few practical examples shown in Figure 3.4 would put the issue beyond doubt.

Operation	Result	Operation	Result
5 / 2	2	2 / 5	0
5.0 / 2	2.500000	2.0 / 5	0.400000
5 / 2.0	2.500000	2 / 5.0	0.400000
5.0 / 2.0	2.500000	2.0 / 5.0	0.400000

Figure 3.4

Here are a few more implicit conversion rules.

(a) An operation between any **byte**, **short**, **int** or chars results into an **int**. Hence, the result of these operations should always be assigned to an **int** variable. Otherwise, an error would be reported. The following code segment illustrates this:

```
byte a = 100, b = 50 ;
byte c = a + b ; // error, as resulting int cannot be assigned to a byte
int d = a + b ; // works
short l = 45, m = 20 ;
short n = l + m ; // error, as resulting int can't be assigned to a short
int p = l + m ; // works
char ch = 'A', dh = 'B' ;
char eh = ch + dh // error, resulting int can't be assigned to a char
int fh = ch + dh ; // works
```

(b) During assignment, the type on left hand side may not be same as type on right hand side. In such a case, if the value of right hand side is within the range of type on left hand side then no error results. The following code snippet illustrates this point:

```
byte s ;
s = 20 ; // though 20 is an int, it is within range of byte
short a ;
a = 100 ; // though 100 is an int, it is within range of short
```

If value of right hand side is not within the range of type on left hand side then an error is reported. For example,

```
byte s ;
s = 200 ; // error as 200 is not within range of byte
```

```
short a ;
a = 40000 ;  // error as 40000 is not within range of short
```

(c) A **char** can be implicitly converted to **short**, **int**, **long**, **float**, or **double**. However, there are no implicit conversions from other types to the **char** type. The following code snippet illustrates this:

```
float  a = 'A' ;  // works
char ch = a ;  // error
```

Explicit Conversion

At times we are required to explicitly convert one type into another. This is done using a type casting operation. Let us consider an example.

```
float  a, b ;
int  x = 6, y = 4 ;
a = x / y ;
b = ( float ) x / y ;
System.out.println ( "Value of a = " + a ) ;
System.out.println ( "Value of b = " + b ) ;
```

And here is the output...

```
Value of a = 1.0
Value of b = 1.5
```

Here **x** and **y** are both integers, hence **x / y** yields an integer, 1. If we don't want the quotient to be truncated, then we can use type casting as we have done in the next statement. Type casting involves putting a pair of ( ) around the data type. In our program the expression (**float**) causes the variable **x** to be converted from type **int** to type **float** before being used in the division operation.

Here is another example of type casting:

```
float  a = 6.35f ;
System.out.println ( "Value of a on type casting = " + ( int ) a ) ;
System.out.println ( "Value of a = " + a ) ;
```

And here is the output...

```
Value of a on type casting = 6
Value of a = 6.35
```

Note that the value of **a** doesn't change permanently as a result of typecasting. Rather, it is the value of the expression that undergoes type conversion when we do typecasting.

Hierarchy of Operations

While executing an arithmetic statement, which has two or more operators, we may have some problems as to how exactly does it get executed. For example, does the expression 2 * x - 3 * y correspond to (2x) - (3y) or to 2(x - 3y)? Similarly, does A / B * C correspond to A / (B * C) or to (A / B) * C? To answer these questions satisfactorily, one has to understand the 'hierarchy' of operations. Hierarchy decides the order in which the operations in an expression are performed. The hierarchy of commonly used operators is shown in Figure 3.5.

Priority	Operator	Description
1st	* / %	Multiplication, Division, Modular division
2nd	+ -	Addition, Subtraction
3rd	=	Assignment

Figure 3.5

Within parentheses the same hierarchy as mentioned in Figure 3.5 is operative. Also, if there are more than one set of parentheses, the operations within the innermost parentheses would be performed first, followed by the operations within the second innermost pair and so on.

An example would clarify the issue further.

Example 3.1: Determine the hierarchy of operations and evaluate the following expression, assuming that **i** is an integer variable:

i = 2 * 3 / 4 + 4 / 4 + 8 - 2 + 5 / 8

Stepwise evaluation of this expression is shown below.

```
i = 2 * 3 / 4 + 4 / 4 + 8 - 2 + 5 / 8
i = 6 / 4 + 4 / 4 + 8 - 2 + 5 / 8        operation: *
i = 1 + 4 / 4 + 8 - 2 + 5 / 8            operation: /
i = 1 + 1 + 8 - 2 + 5 / 8                operation: /
i = 1 + 1 + 8 - 2 + 0                    operation: /
i = 2 + 8 - 2 + 0                        operation: +
```

```
i = 10 - 2 + 0                     operation: +
i = 8 + 0                          operation : -
i = 8                              operation: +
```

Note that 6 / 4 gives 1 and not 1.5. This is because operations between two integers always evaluates to an integer. Similarly, 5 / 8 evaluates to zero, since 5 and 8 are integers.

Associativity of Operators

When an expression contains two operators of equal priority, the tie between them is settled using the associativity of the operators. All operators in Java have either Left to Right associativity or Right to Left associativity. Let us understand this with the help of a few examples.

Consider the expression a = 3 / 2 * 5 ;

Here there is a tie between operators of same priority, that is between / and *. This tie is settled using the associativity of / and *. Both enjoy Left to Right associativity. Therefore firstly / operation is done followed by *.

Consider one more expression.

a = b = 3 ;

Here both assignment operators have the same priority. So order of operations is decided using associativity of = operator. = associates from Right to Left. Therefore, second = is performed earlier than first =.

Consider yet another expression.

z = a * b + c / d ;

Here * and **/** enjoy same priority and same associativity (Left to Right). Compiler is free to perform * or **/** operation as per its convenience, since no matter which is performed earlier, the result would be same.

Note that the precedence and associativity of all operators is predetermined and we cannot change it.

Constant Variables

Many a times we have to use constant values in a program. For example, values of pi, Plank's constant or Avogadro's number. Suppose we need the value of pi at several places in a Java program. It would be a bad idea if we directly use the value 3.14 at all these places, as we might commit a typing error at one of the places and this error would go unnoticed by the compiler. To avoid this we can store the value 3.14 in a **float** variable **pi**, and then use this variable wherever we need the value of pi. This solution suffers from the limitation that being a variable, **pi** is liable to change. So if by mistake we assign a new value to this variable, the compiler would not be able to report this as an error.

A solution for this is to declare the variable as a constant variable using the keyword **final**. This is illustrated in the code snippet given below.

```
final float pi = 3.14f ;
float radius = 1.5f ;
float area = pi * radius * radius ;
```

Console Input/Output in Java

The screen and keyboard together are called a console. To receive input from keyboard and send output to screen there are functions **readLine( )** and **println( )**. There are lot of details associated with these functions. Let us begin with the **readLine( )** function.

readLine( ) Function

The **readLine( )** function reads a line of characters entered from the keyboard unless an Enter is hit. It returns these characters as a string. Hence, to receive anything other than a string using **readLine( )**, it is necessary to convert the received string into appropriate data type. The following program shows how these conversions can be carried out:

```
// Receiving different types of inputs
package receivingdifftypesofinput ;
import java.io.* ;

public class ReceivingDiffTypesOfInput
{
    public static void main ( String[ ] args ) throws Exception
    {
        byte b ;    short s ;
        int i ;     long l ;
        float f ;   double d ;    char c ;

        BufferedReader br = new BufferedReader (
                                   new InputStreamReader ( System.in ) ) ;
        System.out.println ( "Enter a byte value" ) ;
```

```
        b = Byte.parseByte ( br.readLine( ) ) ;
        System.out.println ( "Enter a short value" ) ;
        s = Short.parseShort ( br.readLine( ) ) ;
        System.out.println ( "Enter a int value" ) ;
        i = Integer.parseInt ( br.readLine( ) ) ;
        System.out.println ( "Enter a long value" ) ;
        l = Long.parseLong ( br.readLine( ) ) ;
        System.out.println ( "Enter a float value" ) ;
        f = Float.parseFloat ( br.readLine( ) ) ;
        System.out.println ( "Enter a double value" ) ;
        d = Double.parseDouble ( br.readLine( ) ) ;
        System.out.println ( "Enter a character value" ) ;
        c = ( char ) br.read( ) ;
    }
}
```

Having read each line of input, this program uses the parsing functions in classes **Byte**, **Short**, **Integer**, etc., to convert the string received using **readLine( )** into appropriate data type.

println( ) and *format( )* Functions

So far we have used **println( )** function to send output to the screen. Given below is an example of its usage.

```
int avg = 346 ;
float per = 69.5f ;
System.out.println ( "Output:" ) ;
System.out.println ( "Average = " + avg + "\n" + "Percentage = " + per ) ;
```

This code snippet would produce the following output:

```
Output:
Average = 346
Percentage = 69.5
```

In the first **println( )** we have merely printed the string **Output:**, whereas in the next we have converted the integer **avg** and float **per** into strings and then appended them at the end of **Average =** and **Percentage =**, respectively. We have also put a **\n** in between to display the strings in two different lines. Also note that the output of each **println( )** function appears on a new line because it prints the output and sends the cursor to the next line.

If we wish to control the format in which the output is displayed on the screen, we should use the **format( )** or **printf( )** function instead of **println( )** function. They can be used to control details like where the output appears on the screen, how many spaces are present between the two values, the number of places after the decimal points, etc. Its general form looks like this...

```
System.out.format ( "format string", list of variables ) ;
```

The different format specifiers that can be used in the format string of the **format( )** function are shown in Figure 3.7.

Format Specifier	Used for printing
%d	Integers in Decimal form
%e	Real numbers in Exponential form
%f	Real numbers in Fractional form
%o	Integers in Octal form
%X or %x	Integers in Hexadecimal form

Figure 3.7

We can also provide four optional specifiers with the above format specifications—width, zero, comma and sign. Their usage is shown in the following code snippet:

```
int num = 762432 ;
System.out.format ( "%10d\n", num ) ;
System.out.format ( "%010d\n", num ) ;
System.out.format ( "%+10d\n", num ) ;
System.out.format ( "%,10d\n", num ) ;
System.out.format ( "%+,10d\n", num ) ;
System.out.format ( "%10.2f\n", 5.05 ) ;
System.out.format ( "%10.2f\n", 413.25 ) ;
```

Here is the output of this code snippet.

```
0000762432
   +762432
   762,432
  +762,432
```

```
5.05
413.25
```

Width indicates the number of columns to be reserved for printing the number. For example, **%10d** indicates that the decimal integer be printed in 10 columns. If the number to be printed is smaller than the columns reserved for printing it, the number is right aligned. If we want to left-align the number we have to use **%-10d**. If width turns out to be smaller than what is required for printing the number, the width gets ignored.

The specifier **%010d** prints the number right-aligned in 10 columns with suitable number of zeros padded on the left. **%+10d** adds a **+** sign at beginning of the number. Had the number's value been negative a - sign would have been displayed. **%,10d** introduces comma in the number to make it more readable. Finally, **%+,10d** combines the effect of , and +.

The specifier **%10.2f** right aligns the double in 10 columns with 2 places beyond decimal point.

Control Instructions in Java

As the name suggests, the 'Control Instructions' enable us to specify the order in which the various instructions in a program are to be executed by the computer. In other words, the control instructions determine the 'flow of control' in a program. There are four types of control instructions in Java. They are:

(a) Sequence Control Instruction
(b) Selection or Decision Control Instruction
(c) Repetition or Loop Control Instruction
(d) Case Control Instruction

The Sequence control instruction ensures that the instructions are executed in the same order in which they appear in the program. Decision and Case control instructions allow the computer to take a decision as to which instruction is to be executed next. The Loop control instruction helps computer to execute a group of statements repeatedly. In the following chapters, we are going to learn these instructions in detail.

Exercise

[A] Evaluate the following expressions and show their hierarchy.

(a) g = big / 2 + big * 4 / big - big + abc / 3 ;
(abc = 2.5f, big = 2, assume **g** to be a single)

(b) on = ink * act / 2 + 3 / 2 * act + 2 + tig ;
(ink = 4, act = 1, tig = 3.2f, assume **on** to be an int)

(c) s = qui * add / 4 - 6 / 2 + 2 / 3 * 6 / god ;
(qui = 4, add = 2, god = 2, assume **s** to be an int)

(d) s = 1 / 3 * a / 4 - 6 / 2 + 2 / 3 * 6 / g ;
(a = 4, g = 3, assume **s** to be an int)

[B] Evaluate the result of the following statements.

(a) g = 10 / 5 /2 / 1 ;
(b) b = 3 / 2 + 5 * 4 / 3 ;
(c) a = b = c = 3 + 4 ;

[C] Convert the following equations into corresponding Java statements:

(a) $$Z = \frac{8.8(a+b)2/c - 0.5 + 2a/(q+r)}{(a+b)*(1/m)}$$

(b) $$X = \frac{-b + (b*b) + 2\ 4ac}{2a}$$

(c) $$R = \frac{2v + 6.22\ (c+d)}{g+v}$$

(d) $$A = \frac{7.7b\ (xy + a)/c - 0.8 + 2b}{(x+a)\ (1/y)}$$

[D] Match the following:

(a) Range of char	(1) 4 bytes
(b) Range of int	(2) 2 bytes
(c) Range of float	(3) -2147483648 to 2147483647
(d) Size of int	(4) -3.4e38 to +3.4e38
(e) Size of float	(5) 4 bytes
(f) Size of char	(6) 0 to 65535

[E] Fill in the blanks:

(a) Each character in Java is represented as a _________ character and not as a ASCII character.

(b) All trignometric functions like **sin( )**, **cos( )**, **tan( )**, etc. are present in _______ class.

(c) The result of an arithmetic operation between two **byte** values results into ______.

(d) Addition of a **byte** and a **short** results into a ______.

(e) A ______ can be implicitly converted to **short**, **int**, **long**, while performing arithmetic operation on it.

(f) In Java explicit conversion from one type into another can be done using a __________ operation.

[F] State which of the following statements are True or False:

(a) The output of the **println( )** function is always displayed on a fresh line.

(b) In **System.out.println( ), println( )** is a function of **PrintStream** class, and **out** is a **static** object defined in a **System** class.

(c) We can print values of four variables using the following statement:

```
System.out.println ( si, p, n, r ) ;
```

(d) All command-line arguments are received by **main( )** as strings.

(e) An integer value can be assigned to a **short** provided the value is within the range of **short**.

(f) It is not possible to implicitly convert a **float** to a **double**.

(g) The following two statements are same:

```
double a = ( double ) ( 2.5f + 3.5f ) ;
```

```
double a = ( double ) 2.5f + 3.5f ;
```

(h) Associativity of operators comes into play only when precedence of two operators is same.

(i) Following is the correct way to define a constant variable:

```
final float epsilon = 0.1241f ;
```

[G] Answer the following:

(a) Two numbers are input through the keyboard into two locations C and D. Write a Java program to interchange the contents of C and D.

(b) If a five-digit number is input through the keyboard, write a Java program to calculate the sum of its digits.

(c) If a five-digit number is input through the keyboard, write a Java program to reverse the number.

(d) In a town, the percentage of men is 52. The percentage of total literacy is 48. If total percentage of literate men is 35 of the total population, write a Java program to find the total number of illiterate men and women if the population of the town is 80,000.

(e) A cashier has currency notes of denominations 10, 50 and 100. If the amount to be withdrawn is input through the keyboard, write a Java program find the minimum number of currency notes of each denomination the cashier will have to give to the withdrawer.

kn KanNotes

- 2 ways to make the program general :
  - Receive input from keyboard
  - Receive input from command-line on starting program execution
- Procedure to receive input from command-line in Windows

```
C:\> javac myprogram.java
C:\> java myprogram.class cat dog parrot
```

- Procedure to receive input from command-line in Linux

```
# javac myprogram.java
# java myprogram.class cat dog parrot
```

- Procedure to receive input from command-line in NetBeans under Windows
  - Right click Project | Properties
  - From the dialog that pops up select "Run"
  - Enter "Arguments" as cat dog parrot
- Arguments are received from command-line as strings. If the strings contain numbers then these numeric strings should be converted to integer / float as show below :

```
int n = ( Integer.valueOf ( args[ 1 ] ) ).intValue() ; // method 1
int n = Integer.parseInt ( args[ 1 ] ) ; // method 2
float p = Float.parseFloat ( args[ 0 ] ) ; // method 1
float p = ( Float.valueOf ( args[ 0 ] ) ).floatValue() ; // method 2
```

- Integer type :
  - 4 types – byte, short, int, long. Most common – int
  - Number without a decimal point is byte, short, int, long depending on range in which it fits

    Ex.: 35 – byte 400 – short 45000 – int
  - Value being assigned should not exceed the range of the variable
- Real type :
  - 2 types – float, double. Most common – float

- double is used to deal with very big real values
- By default number with a decimal point is double
- Value being assigned should not exceed the range of the variable

- Boolean type :
  - Boolean can take a value true or false
  - Result of a Boolean expression is true / false
  - Do not use true / false as variable names
  - true is not 1 and false is not 0

- Arithmetic Instruction :
  - On LHS of = only variable can occur
  - + - * / % are Arithmetic Operators
  - No operator is assumed to be present
  - Do exponentiation using pow() function
    Ex. : double a = Math.pow (2.0, 5.0) ;
  - Other funs. - sqrt(), abs(), sin(), cos(), tan(), log(), ...
  - Widening conversions take place automatically
    Ex. : long l = 40000 * 2 ;
  - Narrowing conversions report errors. Ex. : short s = 40000 ;
  - Possible loss of precision is reported as error

Decision Control Instruction

4

All but the simplest of logics would involve decision making on the go. Learn how to make decisions in a Java program...

Chapter Contents

We all need to alter our actions in the face of changing circumstances. If the weather is fine, then I will go for a stroll. If the highway is busy, I would take a diversion. If the pitch takes spin, we would win the match. If she says no, I would look elsewhere. If you like this book, I would write the next edition. You can notice that all these decisions depend on some condition being met. Java language too must be able to perform different sets of actions depending on the circumstances. In this chapter, we will explore ways in which a Java program can react to changing circumstances.

Decisions! Decisions!

In the programs written in Chapters 2 and 3, the instructions in them got executed sequentially. However, in many programming situations, we want one set of instructions to get executed in one situation, and an entirely different set in another situation. Such situations are dealt with in Java programs using a decision control instruction. A decision control instruction can be implemented in Java using:

(a) The **if-else** statement
(b) The conditional operators

Now let us learn each of these and their variations in turn.

The *if-else* Statement

Like most languages, Java uses **if-else** to implement the decision control instruction. The general form of **if** statement looks like this:

```
if ( this condition is true )
{
    execute statement1 ;
    execute statement2 ;
}
else
{
    execute statement4 ;
    execute statement5 ;
}
```

The keyword **if** tells the compiler that what follows is a decision control instruction. The condition following the keyword **if** is always enclosed in a pair of parentheses. If the condition is true, then the statements 1, 2 are executed. If the condition is false, then statements 4, 5 are executed.

But how do we express the condition itself in Java? And how do we evaluate its truth or falsity? We express a condition using Java's 'relational' operators. They allow us to compare two values to see whether they are equal to each other, unequal, or whether one is greater than the other. Here's how they look and how they are evaluated in Java.

this expression	is true if
x == y	x is equal to y
x != y	x is not equal to y
x < y	x is less than y
x > y	x is greater than y
x <= y	x is less than or equal to y
x >= y	x is greater than or equal to y

Figure 4.1

The relational operators should be familiar to you except for the equality operator == and the inequality operator !=. Note that = is used for assignment, whereas, == is used for comparison of two quantities. Let us understand the usage of relational operators using a simple program based on Example 4.1.

Example 4.1: In a company an employee is paid as under:

If his basic salary is less than Rs. 1500, then HRA = 10% of basic salary and DA = 90% of basic salary. If his salary is either equal to or above Rs. 1500, then HRA = Rs. 1500 and DA = 98% of basic salary. If the employee's salary is input through the keyboard write a program to find his gross salary.

Now let us look at the program that implements this logic.

```
// Calculation of gross salary
package calofgrosssalary ;
import java.io.* ;

public class CalOfGrossSalary
```

```
{
    public static void main ( String[ ] args ) throws Exception
    {
        float  bs, gs, da, hra ;

        System.out.println ( "Enter basic salary " ) ;
        BufferedReader br = new BufferedReader (
                                    new InputStreamReader ( System.in ) ) ;
        bs = Float.parseFloat ( br.readLine( ) ) ;

        if ( bs < 1500 )
        {
            hra = bs * 10 / 100 ;
            da = bs * 90 / 100 ;
        }
        else
        {
            hra = 1200 ;
            da = bs * 98 / 100 ;
        }

        gs = bs + hra + da ;
        System.out.println ( "Gross salary = Rs. " + gs ) ;
    }
}
```

Here is some sample interaction with the program.

```
Enter basic salary
1200
Gross salary = Rs. 2400.0

Enter basic salary
2000
Gross salary = Rs. 4660.0
```

A few points worth noting...

(a) The group of statements in { } after the if is called an 'if block'. Similarly, the statements in { } after the else form the 'else block'.

(b) Notice that the **else** is written exactly below the **if**. The statements in the **if** block and those in the **else** block have been indented to the right. This formatting convention is followed throughout the book to enable you to understand the working of the program better.

(c) Had there been only one statement to be executed in the **if** block and only one statement in the **else** block we could have dropped the pair of braces.

(d) In the first run of the program, the condition evaluates to true, as 1200 (value of **bs**) is less than 1500. In this case the statements in the if block get executed. In the second run, the condition evaluates to false, as 2000 (value of **bs**) is greater than 1500. Now the statements in the else block get executed.

(e) It is perfectly all right if we write an entire **if-else** construct within an **if** block or else block. This is called 'nesting' of **if-else** statements.

(f) At times we may not wish to do anything if the condition in **if** fails. In such a case we should drop the **else** and the associated else block.

More Complex Decision Making

Sometimes the decision making becomes complex. We may wish to execute a set of statements if multiple conditions are true, or one out of multiple conditions is true. To deal with such situations Java provides logical operators, &&, || and !. These are to be read as 'AND' 'OR' and 'NOT', respectively.

The first two operators, **&&** and **||**, allow two or more conditions to be combined in an **if** statement. Let us see how they are used in a program. Consider the following example:

Example 4.2: The marks obtained by a student in 3 different subjects are input through the keyboard. The student gets a division as per the following rules:

Percentage above or equal to 60 - First division
Percentage between 50 and 59 - Second division
Percentage between 40 and 49 - Third division
Percentage less than 40 - Fail

Write a program to determine the division obtained by the student.

Here is the program that implements this logic.

```
// Determining student's division
package studentdiv ;
import java.io.* ;

public class StudentDiv
{
    public static void main ( String[ ] args ) throws Exception
    {
        int  m1, m2, m3, per ;

        System.out.println ( "Enter marks in three subjects" ) ;
        BufferedReader br = new BufferedReader (
                                new InputStreamReader ( System.in ) ) ;
        m1 = Integer.parseInt ( br.readLine( ) ) ;
        m2 = Integer.parseInt ( br.readLine( ) ) ;
        m3 = Integer.parseInt ( br.readLine( ) ) ;

        per = ( m1 + m2 + m3 ) * 100 / 300 ;

        if ( per >= 60 )
            System.out.println ( "First division" ) ;

        if ( ( per >= 50 ) && ( per < 60 ) )
            System.out.println ( "Second division" ) ;

        if ( ( per >= 40 ) && ( per < 50 ) )
            System.out.println ( "Third division" ) ;

        if ( per < 40 )
            System.out.println ( "Fail" ) ;
    }
}
```

As can be seen from the second **if** statement, the **&&** operator is used to combine two conditions. ‘Second division’ gets printed if both the conditions evaluate to true. If one of the conditions evaluates to false then the whole expression is treated as false.

We could have implemented the same logic without using logical operators, by using nested **if - else** statements. You may try doing this. If you do so you would observe that the program unnecessarily becomes lengthy.

The *else if* Clause

There is one more way in which we can write program for Example 4.1. This involves usage of **else if** blocks as shown below.

```
// else if ladder demo
package elseifladderdemo ;
import java.io.* ;

public class ElseIfLadderDemo
{
    public static void main ( String[ ] args ) throws Exception
    {
        int  m1, m2, m3, per ;

        System.out.println ( "Enter marks in three subjects" ) ;
        BufferedReader br = new BufferedReader (
                                    new InputStreamReader ( System.in ) ) ;
        m1 = Integer.parseInt ( br.readLine( ) ) ;
        m2 = Integer.parseInt ( br.readLine( ) ) ;
        m3 = Integer.parseInt ( br.readLine( ) ) ;
        per = ( m1 + m2 + m3 ) * 100 / 300 ;

        if ( per >= 60 )
            System.out.println ( "First division" ) ;
        else if ( per >= 50 )
            System.out.println ( "Second division" ) ;
        else if ( per >= 40 )
            System.out.println ( "Third division" ) ;
        else
            System.out.println ( "Fail" ) ;
    }
}
```

You can note that this program reduces the indentation of the statements. In this case, every **else** is associated with its previous **if**. The last **else** goes to work only if all the conditions fail. Also, if the first condition is satisfied, other conditions are not checked. Even in **else if** ladder, the last **else** is optional.

Another place where logical operators are useful is when we want to write programs for complicated logics that ultimately boil down to only two answers. This is shown in Example 4.2 given below.

Example 4.2: A company insures its drivers in the following cases:

- If the driver is married.
- If the driver is unmarried, male and above 30 years of age.
- If the driver is unmarried, female and above 25 years of age.

In all other cases, the driver is not insured. If the marital status, sex and age of the driver are the inputs, write a program to determine whether the driver is to be insured or not.

Here after checking a complicated set of instructions the final output of the program would be one of the two—either the driver should be ensured or the driver should not be ensured. Since these are the only two outcomes this problem can be solved using logical operators.

If we list down all those cases in which the driver is insured, then they would be:

(a) Driver is married.
(b) Driver is an unmarried male above 30 years of age.
(c) Driver is an unmarried female above 25 years of age.

Since all these cases lead to the driver being insured, they can be combined together using **&&** and **||** as shown in the program below.

```
// Insurance of driver - using logical operators
package driverinsurance ;
import java.io.* ;

public class DriverInsurance
{
    public static void main ( String[ ] args ) throws Exception
    {
        char sex, ms ;
        int age ;
        String str ;

        BufferedReader br = new BufferedReader (
                                new InputStreamReader ( System.in ) ) ;

        System.out.println ( "Enter age, sex, marital status" ) ;
```

```
        age = Integer.parseInt ( br.readLine( ) ) ;
        str = br.readLine( ) ;
        sex = str.charAt ( 0 ) ;
        str  = br.readLine( ) ;
        ms = str.charAt ( 0 ) ;

        if ( ( ms == 'M' ) || ( ms == 'U' && sex == 'M' && age > 30 )
                || ( ms == 'U' && sex == 'F' && age > 25 ) )
            System.out.println ( "Driver is insured" ) ;
        else
            System.out.println ( "Driver is not insured" ) ;
    }
}
```

In this program, it is important to note that:

- The driver will be insured only if one of the conditions enclosed in parentheses evaluates to true.
- For the second pair of parentheses to evaluate to true, each condition in the parentheses separated by **&&** must evaluate to true.
- Even if one of the conditions in the second parentheses evaluates to false, then the whole of the second parentheses evaluates to false.
- The last two of the above arguments apply to third pair of parentheses as well.

The & and | Operators

Consider the following code snippet:

```
int a = 1, b = 1, c = 5, d ;
if ( a > 3 && ( b = c + 4 ) > 1 )
    d = 35 ;
System.out.println ( b ) ;
```

On execution we would expect the output to be **9**. However, the output turns out to be 1. This so happens because the expression **(b = c + 4) > 1** doesn't get evaluated once **a > 3** fails. This is known as short-circuiting. This can be prevented by rewriting the **if** as follows:

```
if ( a > 3 & ( b = c + 4 ) > 1 )
    d = 35 ;
```

Note that we have used the operator & instead of &&. Using & ensures that both conditions are evaluated even if the first condition turns out to be false. Figure 4.2 summarizes the effects of using &&, ||, & and | operators.

Expression	Condition2 is evaluated
condition1 && condition2	Only if condition1 is true
condition1 & condition2	Always
condition1 || condition2	Only if condition1 is false
condition1 | condition2	Always

Figure 4.2

The ! Operator

So far we have used only the logical operators **&&** and **||**. The third logical operator is the NOT operator, written as **!**. This operator reverses the result of the expression it operates on. For example, if the expression evaluates to true, then on applying **!** operator to it results into a false. Vice versa, if the expression evaluates to false, then on applying **!** operator to it makes it true. Here is an example of the NOT operator applied to a relational expression.

```
! ( y < 10 )
```

This means "not **y** less than 10". In other words, if **y** is less than 10, the expression will be false, since **(y < 10)** is true. We can express the same condition as **(y >= 10)**.

The NOT operator is often used to reverse the logical value of a single **boolean** variable, as in the expression

```
if ( ! flag )
```

This is another way of saying

```
if ( flag == 0 )
```

Does the NOT operator sound confusing? Avoid it if you want, as the same thing can be achieved without using the NOT operator.

Figure 4.3 summarizes the working of all the three logical operators.

Operands		Results					
x	y	!x	!y	x &&y	x &y	x || y	x | y
false	false	true	true	false	false	false	false
false	true	true	false	false	false	true	true
true	false	false	true	false	false	true	true
true	true	false	false	true	true	true	true

Figure 4.3

Hierarchy of Operators Revisited

Since we have now added the logical operators to the list of operators we know, it is time to review these operators and their priorities. Figure 4.4 summarizes the operators we have seen so far. The higher the position of an operator is in the table, higher is its priority.

Operators	Type
!	Logical NOT
* / %	Arithmetic and modulus
+ -	Arithmetic
< > <= >=	Relational
== !=	Relational
&& &	Logical AND
|| |	Logical OR
=	Assignment

Figure 4.4

A Word of Caution

A common mistake while using the **if** statement is to write a semicolon (;) after the condition, as shown below.

```
if ( i == 5 ) ;
    System.out.println ( "Reached here" ) ;
```

The ; makes the compiler to interpret the statement as if you have written it in following manner:

```
if ( i == 5 )
    ;
System.out.println ( "Reached here" ) ;
```

Here, if the condition evaluates to true, the ; (null statement, which does nothing on execution) gets executed, following which the **println( )** gets executed. If the condition fails, then straightaway the **println( )** gets executed. Thus, irrespective of result of the condition, the **println( )** gets executed. Compiler would not point out this as an error, since as far as the syntax is concerned, nothing has gone wrong, but the logic has certainly gone awry. Moral is, beware of such a pitfall.

The Conditional Operators

The conditional operators **?** and **:** are sometimes called ternary operators since they take three arguments. In fact, they form a kind of foreshortened if-then-else. Their general form is,

expression 1 ? expression 2 : expression 3

What this expression says is: "if **expression 1** is true, then the value returned will be result of **expression 2**, otherwise the value returned will be result of **expression 3**". Let us understand this with the help of a few examples.

(a)
```
int x, y ;
y = x > 5 ? 3 + 4 : 4 + 7 ;
```

This statement will store 7 in **y** if **x** is greater than 5, otherwise it will store 11 in **y**.

(b)
```
int y ;
y = a >= 65 && a <= 90 ? 1 : 0 ;
System.out.println ( y ) ;
```

Here 1 would be assigned to **y** if **a >=65 && a <=90** evaluates to true, otherwise 0 would be assigned.

The following points may be noted about the conditional operators:

(c) If we use a function in ? part or in : part the function has to return a value, which can then be assigned to a variable. If we use a function that returns nothing (void) it would result in an error. This is illustrated in the following examples:

Ex.:
```
double j ;
j = ang > 45 ? Math.sin ( 0.5 ) : Math.cos ( 0.5 ) ;
```

This would work as the sine or cosine value returned would get assigned to **j**.

Ex.:
```
int x ;
x = act == 1 ? System.out.println ( "Amitabh" ) :
        System.out.println ( "All and sundry" ) ;
```

This would not work as **println( )** function doesn't return anything, so assignment to **x** cannot happen.

Ex.:
```
double j ;
System.out.println ( j = 3 > 4 ? 4.4 : 3.3 ) ;
System.out.println ( 3 > 4 ? 4.4 : 3.3 ) ;
```

These statements would work indicating that conditional operators can be used even inside **println( )** function.

(d) The conditional operators can be nested as shown below.

```
int big, a, b, c ;
big = a > b ? ( a > c ? 3: 4 ) : ( b > c ? 6: 8 ) ;
```

(e) Check out the following conditional expression:

```
a > b ? g = a : g = b ;
```

This would result in an error, because the result of the expression **g = a** or **g = b** on being returned is not being assigned to any variable. The error can be overcome by rewriting the statement as

```
g = a > b ? a : b ;
```

The limitation of the conditional operators is that after the **?** or after the **:**, only one statement can occur.

Exercise

[A] What will be the output of the following programs:

(a)
```
package sampleproject ;
public class SampleProject
{
    public static void main ( String[ ] args )
    {
        int a = 300, b = 0, c ;
        if ( a >= 400 )
            b = 300 ;
            c = 200 ;
        System.out.println ( b + " " + c ) ;
    }
}
```

(b)
```
package sampleproject ;
public class SampleProject
{
    public static void main ( String[ ] args )
    {
        int x = 10, y = 20 ;
        if ( x == y ) ;
            System.out.println ( x + " " + y ) ;
    }
}
```

(c)
```
package sampleproject ;
public class SampleProject
{
    public static void main ( String[ ] args )
    {
        int i = -4, j, num = -4 ;
        j = i < 0 ? 0 : num * num ;
        System.out.println ( j ) ;
    }
}
```

(d)
```
package sampleproject ;
public class SampleProject
{
    public static void main ( String[ ] args )
```

```
    {
        int k, num = 30 ;
        k = ( num > 5 ? ( num <= 10 ? 100 : 200 ) : 500 ) ;
        System.out.println ( k ) ;
    }
}
```

[B] Point out the errors, if any, in the following programs:

(a)
```
package sampleproject ;
public class SampleProject
{
    public static void main ( String[ ] args )
    {
        int  x = 10 ;
        if ( x >= 2 ) then
            System.out.println ( x ) ;
    }
}
```

(b)
```
package sampleproject ;
public class SampleProject
{
    public static void main ( String[ ] args )
    {
        int x = 10, y = 15 ;
        if ( x % 2 = y % 3 )
            System.out.println ( "Carpathians" ) ;
    }
}
```

(c)
```
package sampleproject ;
public class SampleProject
{
    public static void main ( String[ ] args )
    {
        char  spy = 'a', password = 'z' ;
        if ( spy == 'a' or password == 'z' )
            System.out.println ( "All the birds safe in the nest" ) ;
    }
}
```

(d)
```
package sampleproject ;
public class SampleProject
```

```
{
    public static void main ( String[ ] args )
    {
        int a = 5, b = 6 ;
        a == b ? System.out.println ( a ) ;
    }
}
```

(e)
```
package sampleproject ;
public class SampleProject
{
    public static void main ( String[ ] args )
    {
        int x = 10, y = 20 ;
        boolean ret ;
        ret = ( x == 20 && y != 10 ) ? true : false ;
        System.out.println ( ret ) ;
    }
}
```

[C] Attempt the following:

(a) If cost price and selling price of an item is input through the keyboard, write a program to determine whether the seller has made profit or incurred loss. Also determine how much profit he made or loss he incurred.

(b) Any integer is input through the keyboard. Write a program to find out whether it is an odd number or even number.

(c) Write a program to find the absolute value of a number that is entered through the keyboard.

(d) If the ages of Ram, Shyam and Ajay are input through the keyboard, write a program to determine the youngest of the three.

(e) Write a program to check whether a triangle is valid or not, when the three angles of the triangle are entered through the keyboard. A triangle is valid if the sum of all the three angles is equal to 180 degrees.

(f) If the three sides of a triangle are entered through the keyboard, write a program to check whether the triangle is valid or not. The triangle is valid if the sum of two sides is greater than the largest of the three sides.

(g) If the three sides of a triangle are entered through the keyboard, write a program to check whether the triangle is isosceles, equilateral, scalene or right angled triangle.

(h) Given the length and breadth of a rectangle, write a program to find whether the area of the rectangle is greater than its perimeter.

(i) Given the coordinates **(x, y)** of a center of a circle and its radius, write a program which will determine whether a point lies inside the circle, on the circle or outside the circle. (Hint: Use **Math.sqrt( )** and **Math.pow( )** functions)

(j) Given a point **(x, y)**, write a program to find out if it lies on the X-axis, Y-axis or on the origin, viz. (0, 0).

(k) Any year is entered through the keyboard, write a program (using logical operators) to determine whether the year is leap or not.

(l) What will be the result of the following expressions:

```
int a = 10, b = 20 ;
a > 5 && b != 5
a != 0 & b < 34
a > 45 || b > 45
a == 10 | b == 20
```

(m) Using conditional operators determine

(1) Whether the character entered through the keyboard is a lower case alphabet or not.

(2) Whether a character entered through the keyboard is a special symbol or not.

KanNotes

- Control instructions control the sequence of execution of instructions in a program
- 4 types of control instructions :

  1) Sequence 2) Decision 3) Repetition 4) Case
- Three forms of decision control instruction :

```
if ( condition )
    statement1 ;
else
    statement2 ;
```

{ } are optional here

```
if ( condition )
{
    statement1 ;
    statement2 ;
}
else
{
    statement3 ;
    statement4 ;
}
```

{ } are necessary

```
if ( condition1 )
    statement1 ;
else if ( condition2 )
    statement2 ;
else if ( condition3 )
    statement3 ;
else
    statement4 ;
```

else goes to work if the 3 ifs fail

- Condition is built using relational operators < > <= >= == !=
- a = b is assignment. a == b is comparison
- More complex decision making can be done using logical operators
- Logical operators are &&, ||, &, | and !
- Usage of Logical Operators :

  &&, ||, &, | - To combine two conditions (not numbers)

  ! - To negate the result of a condition (not number)
- Working of logical operators :

condition1 && condition2 - True only if both conditions are true
- condition2 goes to work only if condition1 is true

condition1 & condition2 - True only if both conditions are true
- Both conditions are always evaluated

condition1 || condition2 - True if any one condition is true
- condition2 goes to work only if condition1 is false

condition1 | condition2 - True if any one condition is true
- Both conditions are always evaluated

! condition - If condition is true ! condition is false
- If condition is false ! condition is true

- Hierarchy :
  !   * / %   + -   < > <= >=   && & || | =
- Unary operator - needs only 1 operand. Ex. !
- Binary operator - needs 2 operands. Ex. + - * / % < > <= >= == != && || & |
- ! (a <= b) is same as (a > b). ! (a >= b) is same as (a < b)
- Conditional operators ? : are ternary operators
- General form : result = condition ? value1 : value2
- value1 and value2 must be of same type
- ? : can have only 1 statement each
- ? : can be nested
- ? : always go together. : is not optional
- Always parenthesize assignment operation if used with ? :

Loop Control Instruction

5

If anything is worth doing, it is worth doing often. Learn how to repeat instructions in a Java program...

Chapter Contents

The programs that we have developed so far used either a sequential or a decision control instruction. These programs were of limited nature, because when executed, they always performed the same series of actions, in the same way, exactly once. In programming we frequently need to perform an action over and over, often with variations in the details each time. The mechanism, which meets this need, is the loop control instruction, and loops are the subject of this chapter.

Loops

The versatility of the computer lies in its ability to perform a set of instructions repeatedly. This involves repeating some portion of the program either a specified number of times or until a particular condition is being satisfied. There are three methods by way of which we can repeat a part of a program. They are:

(a) Using a **for** statement
(b) Using a **while** statement
(c) Using a **do-while** statement

Let us now understand each of these methods of looping.

The *while* Loop

It is often the case in programming that you want to do something a fixed number of times. Perhaps you want to calculate gross salaries of ten different persons, or you want to convert temperatures from Centigrade to Fahrenheit for 15 different cities. The **while** loop is ideally suited for such situations. Let us look at a simple program that uses a **while** loop.

```
// Calculation of simple interest for 3 sets of p, n and r
package siusingwhileloop ;
import java.io.* ;

public class SiUsingWhileLoop
{
    public static void main ( String[ ] args ) throws Exception
    {
        int p, n, count ;
        float r, si ;

        count = 1 ;
```

```
        while ( count <= 3 )
        {
            BufferedReader br = new BufferedReader ( new
                                InputStreamReader ( System.in ) ) ;
            System.out.println( "Enter values of p, n and r" ) ;
            p = Integer.parseInt ( br.readLine( ) ) ;
            n = Integer.parseInt ( br.readLine( ) ) ;
            r = Float.parseFloat ( br.readLine( ) ) ;
            si = p * n * r / 100 ;
            System.out.println ( "Simple interest = Rs. " + si ) ;
            count = count + 1 ;
        }
    }
}
```

And here are a few sample runs of this program...

```
Enter values of p, n and r
1000
5
13.5
Simple interest = Rs. 675.0
Enter values of p, n and r
2000
5
13.5
Simple interest = Rs. 1350.0
Enter values of p, n and r
3500
5
3.5
Simple interest = Rs. 612.5
```

The program executes all statements after the **while** 3 times. The logic for calculating the simple interest is written within a pair of braces immediately after the **while** keyword. These statements form what is called the 'body' of the **while** loop. The parentheses after the **while** contain a condition. So long as this condition remains true, all statements within the body of the **while** loop keep getting executed repeatedly. To begin with, the variable **count** is initialized to 1 and every time the simple interest logic is executed, the value of **count** is incremented by one. The variable **count** is often called a 'loop counter' or 'index variable'. When the value of **count** reaches 4, the condition in **while** fails and the loop is terminated.

Tips about *while*

Note the following points about **while**...

- The statements within the **while** loop would keep on getting executed till the condition being tested remains true. When the condition becomes false, the control passes to the first statement that follows the body of the **while** loop.
- The condition being tested may use relational or logical operators as shown in the following examples:

```
while ( i <= 10 )
while ( i >= 10 && j <= 15 )
while ( j > 10 && ( b < 15 || c < 20 ) )
```

- The statements within the loop may be a single line or a block of statements. In the first case, the braces are optional. Thus,

```
while ( i <= 10 )
    i = i + 1 ;
```

  is same as

```
while ( i <= 10 )
{
    i = i + 1 ;
}
```

- Almost always, the while must test a condition that will eventually become false, otherwise the loop would be executed forever, indefinitely.

```
int  i = 1 ;
while ( i <= 10 )
    System.out.println ( i ) ;
```

  This is an indefinite loop, since **i** remains equal to 1 forever. The correct form would be as under.

```
int  i = 1 ;
while ( i <= 10 )
{
```

```
    System.out.println ( i ) ;
    i = i + 1 ;
}
```

– Instead of incrementing a loop counter, we can even decrement it and still manage to get the body of the loop executed repeatedly. This is shown below.

```
int i = 5 ;
while ( i >= 1 )
{
    System.out.println ( "Make the computer literate!" ) ;
    i = i - 1 ;
}
```

– It is not necessary that a loop counter must only be an **int**. It can even be a **float**.

```
float a = 10.0f ;
while ( a <= 10.5f )
{
    System.out.println ( "Raindrops on roses..." ) ;
    System.out.println ( "...and whiskers on kittens" ) ;
    a = a + 0.1f ;
}
```

– Even floating-point loop counters can be decremented. Once again, the increment and decrement could be by any value, not necessarily 1.

– What will be the output of the following code snippet?

```
int i = 1 ;
while ( i <= 10 ) ;
{
    System.out.println ( i ) ;
    i = i + 1 ;
}
```

This is an indefinite loop, and it doesn't give any output at all. The reason is, we have carelessly given a **;** after the **while**. This would make the loop work like this...

```
while ( i <= 10 )
    ;
```

```
{
    System.out.println ( i ) ;
    i = i + 1 ;
}
```

Since the value of **i** is not getting incremented, the control would keep rotating within the loop, eternally. Note that enclosing **println( )** and **i = i +1** within a pair of braces is not an error. In fact we can put a pair of braces around any individual statement or a set of statements without affecting the execution of the program.

- Instead of incrementing a loop counter using the statement i = i + 1, we can use any of the following two forms to get the same result:

```
i++ ;
i = i += 1 ;
```

Note that the increment operator **++** increments the value of **i** by 1, every time the statement **i++** gets executed. Similarly, to reduce the value of a variable by 1, a decrement operator -- is also available. However, never use **n+++** to increment the value of **n** by 2, since Java doesn't have the operator **+++**.

+= is a compound assignment operator. It increments the value of **i** by 1. Similarly, **j = j + 10** can also be written as **j += 10**. Other compound assignment operators are **-=**, ***=**, **/** = and **%=**.

- The ++ and -- operators can be combined with some other operation like assignment, printing or testing of a condition. In such cases the the position of ++ decides the order of operations.

If ++ is used before the variable it is called pre-incrementation and iff it is present after the ++ then it is called post-incrementation. The following examples would clarify their usage:

```
int i = 1 ;
while ( i++ < 10 ) // first test the condition, then increment i
while ( ++i < 10 ) // first increment i, then test the condition
j = ++i ;  // first increment i, then assign to j
j = i++ ; // first assign i to j, then increment i
System.out.println ( ++i ) ; // first increment i, then print it
System.out.println ( i++ ) ; // first print i, then increment it
```

The *for* Loop

for is probably the most popular looping instruction. Unlike a **while** loop, the **for** loop allows us to initialize, test and increment the loop counter in a single line as shown below.

```
for ( initialize counter ; test counter ; increment counter )
{
    do this ;
    and this ;
    and this ;
}
```

Let us write down the simple interest program using **for**. Compare this program with the one, which we wrote using **while**.

```
// Calculation of simple interest for 3 sets of p, n and r
package siusingforloop ;
import java.io.* ;

public class SiUsingForLoop
{
    public static void main ( String[ ] args ) throws Exception
    {
        int p, n, count ;
        float r, si ;

        BufferedReader br = new BufferedReader (
                                new InputStreamReader ( System.in ) ) ;

        for ( count = 1 ; count <= 3 ; count = count + 1 )
        {
            System.out.println ( "Enter values of p, n and r" ) ;
            p = Integer.parseInt ( br.readLine( ) ) ;
            n = Integer.parseInt ( br.readLine( ) ) ;
            r = Float.parseFloat ( br.readLine( ) ) ;
            si = p * n * r / 100 ;
            System.out.println ( "Simple Interest = Rs. " + si ) ;
        }
    }
}
```

Let us now examine how the **for** statement gets executed:

- When the **for** statement is executed for the first time, the value of **count** is set to an initial value 1.
- Now the condition **count <= 3** is tested. Since **count** is 1, the condition is satisfied and the body of the loop is executed for the first time.
- Upon reaching the closing brace of **for**, control is sent back to the **for** statement, where the value of **count** gets incremented by 1.
- Again the test is performed to check whether the new value of **count** exceeds 3.
- If the value of **count** is less than or equal to 3, the statements within the braces of **for** are executed again.
- The body of the **for** loop continues to get executed till **count** doesn't exceed the final value 3.
- When **count** reaches the value 4, the control exits from the loop and is transferred to the statement (if any) immediately after the body of **for**.

It is important to note that the initialization and incrementation part of a **for** loop can be replaced by any valid expression. Thus the following **for** loops are perfectly OK.

```
for ( i = 1 ; i <=10 ; System.out.println ( i++ ) )
    ;

BufferedReader br ;
br = new BufferedReader ( new InputStreamReader ( System.in ) ) ;
for ( i = Integer.parseInt ( br.readLine( ) ) ; i <= 10 ; i++ )
    System.out.println ( i ) ;
```

Partial *for* Loops

We can drop the initialization, test (condition) or incrementation part of a **for** loop. Thus all the following loops would be correct and would print numbers from 1 to 10.

```
// Method 1 - Normal for loop
int i ;
for ( i = 1 ; i <= 10 ; i = i + 1 )
    System.out.println ( i ) ;
```

```
// Method 2 - Drop initialization
int i = 1 ;
for ( ; i <= 10 ; i++ )
    System.out.println ( i ) ;

// Method 3 - Drop initialization and incrementation
int i = 1 ;
for ( ; i <= 10 ; )
{
    System.out.println ( i ) ;
    i++ ;
}

// Method 4 - Drop initialization, incrementation and test
int i = 1 ;
for ( ; ; )
{
    System.out.println ( i ) ;
    i++ ;
    if ( i > 10 )
        break ;
}
```

Note that in spite of dropping initialization / incrementation / test, the two semicolons in the **for** loop are always necessary.

The **for** loop in Method 4 behaves like an infinite loop. Hence we have checked the value of **i** against 10. If it goes beyond 10, we terminate the **for** loop using the **break** statement.

Nesting of Loops

The way **if** statements can be nested, similarly **while**s and **for**s can also be nested. To understand how nested loops work, look at the program given below.

```
// Demonstration of nested loops
package nestedforloopsdemo ;

public class NestedForLoopsDemo
{
    public static void main ( String[ ] args )
```

```
    {
        int r, c, sum ;
        for ( r = 1 ; r <= 3 ; r++ ) // outer loop
        {
            for ( c = 1 ; c <= 2 ; c++ ) // inner loop
            {
                sum = r + c ;
                System.out.println ( "r = " + r + " c = " + c +
                                            " sum = " + sum ) ;
            }
        }
    }
}
```

When you run this program, you will get the following output:

```
r = 1 c = 1 sum = 2
r = 1 c = 2 sum = 3
r = 2 c = 1 sum = 3
r = 2 c = 2 sum = 4
r = 3 c = 1 sum = 4
r = 3 c = 2 sum = 5
```

Here, for each value of **r**, the inner loop is cycled through twice, with the variable **c** taking values from 1 to 2. The inner loop terminates when the value of **c** exceeds 2, and the outer loop terminates when the value of **r** exceeds 3.

Multiple Initializations in the *for* Loop

The initialization expression of the **for** loop can contain more than one statement separated by a comma (,). For example,

```
for ( i = 1, j = 2 ; j <= 10 ; j++ )
```

Multiple statements can also be used in the incrementation expression of **for** loop; i.e., you can increment (or decrement) two or more variables at the same time. However, only one statement is allowed in the test expression. This expression may contain several conditions linked together using logical operators.

Use of multiple statements in the initialization expression also demonstrates why semicolons are used to separate the three expressions in the **for** loop. Had commas been used, they could not also have been used to separate multiple statements in the initialization expression, without confusing the compiler.

The *do-while* Loop

The **do-while** loop looks like this:

```
do
{
    this ;
    and this ;
    and this ;
} while ( this condition is true ) ;
```

There is a minor difference between the working of **while** and **do-while** loops. This difference is the place where the condition is tested. The **while** tests the condition before executing any of the statements within the **while** loop. As against this, the **do-while** tests the condition after having executed the statements within the loop.

This means that **do-while** would execute its statements at least once, even if the condition fails for the first time. The **while**, on the other hand will not execute its statements if the condition fails for the first time.

The *break* Statement

We often come across situations where we want to jump out of a loop instantly, without waiting to get back to the conditional test. The keyword **break** allows us to do this. When **break** is encountered inside any loop, control automatically passes to the first statement after the loop. A **break** is usually associated with an **if**. Let's consider an example where **break** statement would make sense.

Example 5.1: Write a program to determine whether a number is prime or not. A prime number is one, which is divisible only by 1 or itself.

All we have to do to test whether a number is prime or not, is to divide it successively by all numbers from 2 to one less than itself. If remainder of any of these divisions is zero, the number is not a prime. If no division yields a zero then the number is a prime number. Following program implements this logic:

```
// Prime number or not
package primenumberproject ;
```

```
import java.io.* ;

public class PrimeNumberProject
{
    public static void main ( String[ ] args ) throws Exception
    {
        int  num, i ;

        BufferedReader br = new BufferedReader (
                                new InputStreamReader ( System.in ) ) ;
        System.out.println ( "Enter a number " ) ;
        num = Integer.parseInt ( br.readLine( ) ) ;

        i = 2 ;
        while ( i <= num - 1 )
        {
            if ( num % i == 0 )
            {
                System.out.println ( "Not a prime number" ) ;
                break ;
            }
            i++ ;
        }

        if ( i == num )
            System.out.println ( "Prime number" ) ;
    }
}
```

In this program, the moment **num % i** turns out to be zero, (i.e., **num** is exactly divisible by **i**), the message "Not a prime number" is printed and the control breaks out of the **while** loop.

Why does the program require the **if** statement after the **while** loop at all? Well, there are two ways the control could have reached outside the **while** loop:

(a) It jumped out because the number proved to be not a prime.
(b) The loop came to an end because the value of **i** became equal to **num**.

When the loop terminates in the second case, it means that there was no number between 2 to **num - 1** that could exactly divide **num**. That is, **num** is indeed a prime. If this is true, the program should print out the message "Prime number".

The keyword **break**, breaks the control only from the **while** in which it is placed. So in case of nested loops if we use **break** in the inner loop, the inner loop would be terminated. What if we wish to break out of the outer loop? Well, we just have to name the outer loop and use **break** to take the control out of the named loop. The following program illustrates how this can be done:

```
first : while ( i++ <= 100 )
{
    while ( j++ <= 200 )
    {
        if ( j == 150 )
            break first ;
        else
            System.out.println ( i + " " + j ) ;
    }
}
```

Note that we have now given a name to the out **while** loop—first. When the condition **j == 150** is satisfied the statement **break first** gets executed. As a result, control goes outside the loop named **first**, i.e., the outer **while** loop.

The *continue* Statement

In some programming situations, we want to take the control to the beginning of the loop, bypassing the statements inside the loop, which have not yet been executed. The keyword **continue** allows us to do this. When **continue** is encountered inside any loop, control automatically passes to the beginning of the loop.

A **continue** is usually associated with an **if**. As an example, let's consider the following program.

```
// Demo of usage of continue keyword
package continuedemoproject ;

public class ContinueDemoProject
```

```
{
    public static void main ( String[ ] args )
    {
        int  i, j ;

        for ( i = 1 ; i <= 2 ; i++ )
        {
            for ( j = 1 ; j <= 2 ; j++ )
            {
                if ( i == j )
                    continue ;

                System.out.println ( i + " " + j ) ;
            }
        }
    }
}
```

The output of the above program would be...

```
1 2
2 1
```

Note that when the value of **i** equals that of **j**, the **continue** statement takes the control to the **for** loop (inner) bypassing the rest of the statements pending execution in the **for** loop (inner).

The way while working in nested loops we can break the control out of the desired loop by naming a loop, likewise, we can use **continue** with named loops. This is shown below.

```
first : while ( i++ <= 100 )
{
    while ( j++ <= 200 )
    {
        if ( j == 150 )
            continue first ;
        else
            System.out.println ( i + " " + j ) ;
    }
}
```

When **continue first** goes to work, the control is transferred to **while (i++ <= 100)**.

break and **continue** can also be used with **do-while** just as they would be in a **while** or a **for** loop. A **break** takes you out of the **do-while** bypassing the conditional test. A **continue** sends you straight to the test at the end of the loop.

Common Usage

In principle, what can be achieved using one loop can always be achieved using the other two loops. However, in practice people use the three loops for following purposes:

(a) Repeat logic unknown number of times - **while** loop
(b) Repeat logic finite number of times - **for** loop
(c) Repeat logic at least once - **do - while** loop

If you also follow the same practice then while reading a program you can recognize the purpose of the loop just by looking at the type of the loop used.

Exercise

[A] What will be the output of the following programs:

(a)
```
package sampleproject ;
public class SampleProject
{
    public static void main ( String[ ] args )
    {
        int i = 1 ;
        while ( i <= 10 ) ;
        {
            System.out.println ( i ) ;
            i++ ;
        }
    }
}
```

(b)
```
package sampleproject ;
public class SampleProject
{
    public static void main ( String[ ] args )
    {
        int x = 4, y, z ;
        y = --x ;
        z = x-- ;
        System.out.println ( x + " " + y + " " + z ) ;
    }
}
```

(c)
```
package sampleproject ;
public class SampleProject
{
    public static void main ( String[ ] args )
    {
        int x = 4, y = 3, z ;
        z = x-- - y ;
        System.out.println ( x + " " + y + " "+ z ) ;
    }
}
```

(d)
```
package sampleproject ;
public class SampleProject
```

```
{
    public static void main ( String[ ] args )
    {
        int x = 4, y = 0, z ;
        while ( x >= 0 )
        {
            if ( x == y )
                break ;
            else
                System.out.println ( x + " " + y ) ;
            x-- ;
            y++ ;
        }
    }
}
```

(e)
```
package sampleproject ;
public class SampleProject
{
    public static void main ( String[ ] args )
    {
        int i ;
        for ( i = 1 ; i <= 5 ; System.out.println ( i ) ) ;
            i++ ;
    }
}
```

[B] Answer the following:

(a) An expression contains relational operators, assignment operators, and arithmetic operators. In the absence of parentheses, they will be evaluated in which of the following order:

1. assignment, relational, arithmetic
2. arithmetic, relational, assignment
3. relational, arithmetic, assignment
4. assignment, arithmetic, relational

(b) The **break** statement is used to exit from

1. an **if** statement
2. a **for** loop
3. a program
4. the **main( )** function

(c) In what sequence the initialization, testing and execution of body is done in a **do-while** loop:

1. Initialization, execution of body, testing
2. Execution of body, initialization, testing
3. Initialization, testing, execution of body
4. None of the above

(d) Which of the following statement is used to take the control to the beginning of the loop?

1. exit
2. break
3. continue
4. goto

(e) Which of the following statement is true about a **for** loop used in a Java program?

(1) **for** loop works faster than a **while** loop.
(2) All things that can be done using a **for** loop can also be done using a **while** loop.
(3) **for (; ;)** implements an infinite loop.
(4) **for** loop can be used if we want statements in a loop to get executed at least once.

[C] Attempt the following:

(a) Write a program to find the factorial value of any number entered through the keyboard.

(b) Two numbers are entered through the keyboard. Write a program to find the value of one number raised to the power of another.

(c) Write a program to print out all Armstrong numbers between 1 and 500. If sum of cubes of each digit of the number is equal to the number itself, then the number is called an Armstrong number. For example, 153 = (1 * 1 * 1) + (5 * 5 * 5) + (3 * 3 * 3)

(d) Write a program to print all prime numbers from 1 to 300. (Hint: Use nested loops, **break** and **continue**).

(e) Write a program to generate all combinations of 1, 2 and 3 using **for** loops.

(f) According to a study, the approximate level of intelligence of a person can be calculated using the following formula:

i = 2 + (y + 0.5 x)

Write a program that will produce a table of values of **i**, **y** and **x**, where **y** varies from 1 to 6, and, for each value of **y**, **x** varies from 5.5 to 12.5 in steps of 0.5.

(g) Write a program to print the multiplication table of the number entered by the user. The table should get displayed in the following form:

29 * 1 = 29
29 * 2 = 58
...

(h) When interest compounds **q** times per year at an annual rate of **r** % for **n** years, the principle **p** compounds to an amount **a** as per the following formula:

$a = p (1 + r / q)^{nq}$

Write a program to read 10 sets of **p, r, n** & **q** and calculate the corresponding **a**s.

(i) Write a program to add first seven terms of the following series using a **for** loop:

$$\frac{1}{1!} + \frac{2}{2!} + \frac{3}{3!} + \ldots\ldots$$

(j) The natural logarithm can be approximated by the following series.

$$\frac{x-1}{x} + \frac{1}{2}\left(\frac{x-1}{x}\right)^2 + \frac{1}{2}\left(\frac{x-1}{x}\right)^3 + \frac{1}{2}\left(\frac{x-1}{x}\right)^4 + \ldots.$$

If **x** is input through the keyboard, write a program to calculate the sum of first seven terms of this series.

kn KanNotes

- Repetition control instruction is used to repeat a set of statements in a program
- It is also called a loop control instruction
- It is implemented using 1) while loop 2) for loop 3) do-while loop
- What can be done using one loop can always be done using the other two
- Usual usage :

  while - to repeat something an unknown number of times
  for - to repeat something a fixed number of times
  do - while - to repeat something at least once

- Equivalent forms of 3 loops :

```
i = 1 ;
while ( i <= 10 )
{
    statement1 ;
    statement2 ;
    i++ ;
}
```

```
for( i = 1 ; i <= 10 ; i++)
{
    statement1 ;
    statement2 ;
}
```

```
i = 1 ;
do
{
    statement1 ;
    statement2 ;
    i++ ;
} while ( i <= 10 ) ;
```

- To create infinite loops use :

```
for ( ; ; )
```

```
while ( true )
```

```
do
{
    ..
} while ( true )
```

- Multiple initializations, conditions and incrementations in a for loop are acceptable. Ex. :

```
for ( i = 1 , j = 2 ; i <= 10 && j <= 24 ; i++, j += 3 )
{
    statement1 ;    statement2 ;
}
```

- break - terminates the execution of the loop

  continue - abandons rest of the instructions in the loop and goes for the next iteration of the loop
- Usually break and continue are used in this form :

```
while ( condition1 )
{
    if ( condition2 )
        break ;
    statement1 ;
    statement2 ;
}
```

```
while ( condition1 )
{
    if ( condition2 )
        continue ;
    statement1 ;
    statement2 ;
}
```

- i++ increments vale by 1

  i-- decrements value of i by 1

  There are no ** // and %% operators
- The expressions i = i + 1, i++ and ++i are all same
- j = ++i ; first increments i, then assigns the incremented value to j
- j = i++ ; first assigns current value of i to j, then increments i
- while (++i < 10) first increments i, then checks condition
- while (i++ < 10) first checks condition, then increments i
- i = i + 5 is same as i += 5
- Compound assignment operators : += -= *= /= %=

6

Case Control Instruction

Often one is faced with multiple choices. Learn how to deal with such situations using a switch...

Let Us JAVA 3rd Edition

Chapter Contents

In real life, we are often faced with situations where we are required to make a choice between a number of alternatives rather than only one or two. For example, which school to join, or which hotel to visit, or which movie to see, etc. Serious Java programming is same; the choice we are asked to make is more complicated than merely selecting between two alternatives. Java provides a case control instruction that allows us to handle such cases effectively; rather than using a series of **if** statements. Case control instruction is, in fact, the topic of this chapter.

Decisions using *switch*

The control instruction that allows us to make a decision from the number of choices is called a **switch**, or more correctly a **switch-case-default**, since these three keywords go together to make up this control instruction. They most often appear as follows:

```
switch ( expression )
{
    case constant 1 :
        do this ;
        break ;
    case constant 2 :
        do this ;
        break ;
    case constant 3 :
        do this ;
        break ;
    default :
        do this ;
        break ;
}
```

The expression following the keyword **switch** is any Java expression that will yield an integer value or boolean value. The keyword **case** is followed by an integer, boolean or a character constant. Each constant in each **case** must be different from all the others. The "do this ;" lines in the above form of **switch** represent any valid Java statement.

What happens when we run a program containing a **switch**? First, the expression following the keyword **switch** is evaluated. The value it gives is then matched, one-by-one, against the constant values that follow the **case** statements. When a match is found, the program executes the statements following that **case** until a **break** is encountered. On encountering **break** the control goes outside the **switch**. If no match is found with any of the **case** statements, then the statements following the **default** are executed. Let us now look at a program that uses this control instruction.

```
// Demo of usage of switch
package switchdemoproject ;

public class SwitchDemoProject
{
    public static void main ( String[ ] args )
    {
        int i = 2 ;

        switch ( i )
        {
            case 1 :
                System.out.println ( "I am in case 1" ) ;
                break ;
            case 2 :
                System.out.println ( "I am in case 2" ) ;
                break ;
            case 3 :
                System.out.println ( "I am in case 3" ) ;
                break ;
            default :
                System.out.println ( "I am in default" ) ;
                break ;
        }
    }
}
```

The output of this program would be:

```
I am in case 2
```

The output is as expected. Note that usage of **break** is mandatory in each case including the **default** case.

The Tips and Traps

Let us now note down a few useful tips about the usage of **switch** and a few pitfalls that should be avoided.

(a) Cases in a **switch** can be written in any order.

(b) Even if there are multiple statements to be executed in each **case**, there is no need to enclose them within a pair of braces.

(c) Every statement in a **switch** must belong to some **case** or the other. If a statement doesn't belong to any **case**, the compiler would report an error.

(d) If we have no **default** case and no other case is satisfied, then the program simply falls through the entire **switch** and continues with the next instruction (if any,) that follows the closing brace of **switch**.

(e) **switch** cannot have a case looks like:

```
case i <= 20 :
```

All that we can have after the case is a **byte**, **short**, **int** or **char** constant or an expression that evaluates to one of these constants. Even a **float**, **double**, **long** or **boolean** is not allowed.

(f) From JDK 7 onwards strings can also be checked using **switch**.

(g) The advantage of **switch** over **if** is that it leads to a more structured program and the level of indentation is manageable, more so, if there are multiple statements within each **case** of a **switch**.

(h) We can check the value of any expression in a **switch**. Thus, the following **switch** statements are legal:

```
switch ( i + j * k )
switch ( 23 + 45 % 4 * k )
```

(i) Expressions can also be used in cases provided they are constant expressions. Thus **case 3 + 7** is correct, however, **case a + b** is incorrect.

(j) The **break** statement when used in a **switch** takes the control outside the **switch**. However, use of **continue** will not take the control to the beginning of **switch** as one is likely to believe. This is because **switch** is not a looping statement, unlike **while**, **for** or **do-while**.

(k) In principle, a **switch** may occur within another, but in practice, it is rarely done. Such statements would be called nested **switch** statements.

(l) The **switch** statement is very useful while writing menu driven programs. This aspect of **switch** is discussed in the exercise of this chapter.

(m) At times we may want to execute a common set of statements for multiple **case**s. How this can be done is shown in the following example:

```
package switchformsproject ;
import java.io.IOException ;

public class SwitchFormsProject
{
    public static void main ( String[ ] args ) throws Exception
    {
        char ch ;

        System.out.println( "Enter an alphabet a, or b " ) ;
        ch = ( char ) System.in.read( ) ;

        switch ( ch )
        {
            case 'a' :
            case 'A' :
                System.out.println ( "a as in ashar" ) ;
                break ;
            case 'b' :
            case 'B' :
                System.out.println ( "b as in brain" ) ;
                break ;
            default :
                System.out.println ( "wish you knew alphabets" ) ;
                break ;
        }
    }
}
```

Here, we are making use of the fact that once an empty **case** is satisfied; the control simply falls through to the next **case** till it doesn't encounter a **break** statement. That is why if an alphabet **a** is entered, the **case 'a'** is satisfied and since there are no statements to be executed in this **case**, the control automatically reaches the next **case**, i.e., **case 'A'** and executes all the statements in this **case**.

Also note that any non-empty case has to have a **break** statement at the end of it.

Also observe the way we have read the character from the keyboard. Instead of using the usual **InputStreamReader** and **BufferredReader**, we are using the **System.in.read( )** and converting its return value into a **char**.

switch Versus *if-else* Ladder

There are some things that you simply cannot do with a **switch**. These are:

(a) A **float**, **double**, **boolean**, or **long** expression cannot be tested using a **switch**.

(b) Cases can never have variable expressions (for example it is wrong to say **case a + 3 :**).

(c) Multiple cases cannot use same expressions. Thus a **switch** containing **case 3** : and **case 1 + 2** : is illegal:

(a), (b) and (c) above may lead you to believe that these are obvious disadvantages with a **switch**, especially since there weren't any such limitations with **if-else**. Then why use a **switch** at all? For speed—**switch** works faster than an equivalent **if-else** ladder. How? Well, this is because the compiler generates a jump table for a **switch** during compilation. As a result, during execution it simply refers the jump table to decide which case should be executed, rather than actually checking which case is satisfied.

Note that a lookup in the jump table is faster than evaluation of a condition, especially if the condition is complex.

Exercise

[A] Which of the following case statements are correct:

(a) case 4 / 3 :
(b) case ch :
(c) case a + b :
(d) case 1.5f :
(e) case true :
(f) case 8 % 5 + c / d :
(g) case (temp <= 20) :
(h) case a || b :

[B] Write a menu driven program which has following options:

1. Factorial of a number
2. Prime or not
3. Odd or even
4. Exit

Once a menu item is selected the appropriate action should be taken and once this action is finished, the menu should reappear. Unless the user selects the 'Exit' option the program should continue to work.

(Hint: Make use of an infinite **while** and a **switch** statement).

KanNotes

- One more form of decision making can be done using switch - case - default
- This should be used when we are to find out whether a variable or an expression has one of the several possible values
- switch should not be used for checking ranges or for solving a yes / no problem
- General form :

```
switch ( expression )   // expression can be constant / variable
{
        case constant expression :
                ...
                break ;
        case constant expression :
                ...
                break ;
        default :
                ...
}
```

- If a case fails, control jumps to the next case
- If a case is satisfied, then all statements below it up to } of switch are executed
- Even though there are multiple statements in a case there is no need to enclose them within { }
- Usually a break is used at the end of statements in each case
- break takes the control out of the switch
- continue DOES NOT take the control to the beginning of the switch
- Order in which cases are written does not matter

- Default case is optional
- cases in a switch must always be unique
- switch can be used with byte, short, int, long, char

  switch cannot be used with float, double
- switch works faster than a series of ifs
- switch is popularly used in menu driven programs to check which choice from the menu has been made by the user

Functions

7

Learn how to improve functionality of a Java program using Functions...

Let Us JAVA

3rd Edition

Chapter Contents

A computer program (except for the simplest one) finds cannot handle all the tasks by itself. Instead, it requests other program-like entities, called 'functions' to get its tasks done. So far our programs had only one function **main( )**. In this chapter we will study how to create multiple function, how to use them and how to carry out communication between them.

What is a Function?

A function is a self-contained block of statements that perform a coherent task of some kind. Every Java program has one or more functions in it. Let us now look at a simple program containing two functions.

```
// Function call and function definition
package functiondemoproject ;

public class FunctionDemoProject
{
    public static void main ( String[ ] args )
    {
        message( ) ; /* function call */
        System.out.println ( "Cry, and you stop the monotony!" ) ;
    }
    static void message( )  /* function definition */
    {
        System.out.println ( "Smile, and the world smiles with you..." ) ;
    }
}
```

On execution, the program produces the output given below.

```
Smile, and the world smiles with you...
Cry, and you stop the monotony!
```

Here, we have defined two functions—**main( )** and **message( )**. In fact we have used the word **message** at two places in the program. Let us understand the meaning of each.

The first usage of **message** is...

```
static void message( )
{
```

```
    System.out.println ( "Smile, and the world smiles with you..." ) ;
}
```

This is the function definition. In this definition right now we are merely printing a string.

The second usage is...

```
message( ) ;
```

Here the function **message( )** is being called from **main( )**. What do we mean when we say that **main( )** 'calls' the function **message( )**? We mean that the control passes to the function **message( )**. The activity of **main( )** is temporarily suspended; it falls asleep while the **message( )** function wakes up and goes to work. When the **message( )** function runs out of statements to execute, the control returns to **main( )**, which comes to life again and begins executing its code at the exact point where it left off. Thus, **main( )** becomes the 'calling' function, whereas **message( )** becomes the 'called' function.

If you have grasped the concept of 'calling' a function you are prepared for a call to more than one function. Consider the following program:

```
// Calling and defining multiple functions
package multiplefunctionproject ;

public class MultipleFunctionProject
{
    public static void main ( String[ ] args )
    {
        System.out.println ( "I am in main" ) ;
        italy( ) ;
        brazil( ) ;
        argentina( ) ;
    }
    static void italy( )
    {
        System.out.println ( "I am in italy" ) ;
    }
    static void brazil( )
    {
        System.out.println ( "I am in brazil" ) ;
    }
    static void argentina( )
```

```
    {
        System.out.println ( "I am in argentina" ) ;
    }
}
```

The output of the above program when executed would be as under:

```
I am in main
I am in italy
I am in brazil
I am in argentina
```

A number of conclusions can be drawn from this program:

- A Java program can contain one or more classes. Each class can contain one or more functions.

- One of the classes in a Java program has to be marked as the 'Main class'. When we create Java project in NetBeans in the 'New Java Application' window there is a check box titled 'Create Main Class'. This check box is by default checked. So the skeleton code for **Main** class is created for us by NetBeans. This class has the same name as the name of the project. This class is also marked as the class from which execution of the program would begin.

  If we uncheck the check box during project creation, we can later mark any class in our program as **Main** class. To do this, we have to right click on the project name and select 'Properties' from the menu that pops up. On doing this the 'Project Properties' window appears. Select 'Run' from this window and in the 'Main Project' text box mention the class name in the syntax **packagename.classname**. For example, for the current project this name would be **multiplefunctionproject.MultipleFunctionProject**.

- Execution always begins with **main( )** function present in the class that has been marked as **Main** class.

- If the class marked as **Main** class contains only one function, it must be **main( )**.

- If the class marked as **Main** class contains more than one function, then one (and only one) of these functions must be **main( )**. This is because program execution always begins with **main( )**.

- There is no limit on the number of functions that might be present in a Java class.
- Each function in a program is called in the sequence specified by the function calls in **main( )**.
- After each function has done its thing, control returns to **main( )**. When **main( )** runs out of statements and function calls, the program ends.

As we have noted earlier, the program execution always begins with **main( )** present in the class marked as **Main** class. Except for this fact, all Java functions enjoy a state of perfect equality. No precedence, no priorities, nobody is nobody's boss. One function can call another function it has already called but has in the meantime left temporarily in order to call a third function which will sometime later call the function that has called it, if you understand what I mean. No? Well, let me illustrate with an example.

```
// Multiple function calls
package functioncallsproject ;

public class FunctionCallsProject
{
    public static void main ( String[ ] args )
    {
        System.out.println ( "I am in main" ) ;
        italy( ) ;
        System.out.println ( "I am finally back in main" ) ;
    }
    static void italy( )
    {
        System.out.println ( "I am in italy" ) ;
        brazil( ) ;
        System.out.println ( "I am back in italy" ) ;
    }
    static void brazil( )
    {
        System.out.println ( "I am in brazil" ) ;
        argentina( ) ;
    }
    static void argentina( )
    {
```

```
        System.out.println ( "I am in argentina" ) ;
    }
}
```

And the output would look like...

```
I am in main
I am in italy
I am in brazil
I am in argentina
I am back in italy
I am finally back in main
```

Here, **main( )** calls other functions, which in turn call still other functions. Trace carefully the way control passes from one function to another. Since execution always begins with **main( )**, every function in a program must be called directly or indirectly by **main( )**. In other words, the **main( )** function drives other functions.

Let us now summarize what we have learnt so far.

(a) A function gets called when the function name is followed by a semicolon (;).

(b) A function is defined when function name is followed by a pair of braces in which one or more statements may be present.

(c) Any function can be called from any other function. Even **main( )** can be called from other functions.

(d) A function can be called any number of times.

(e) The order in which the functions are defined in a program and the order in which they get called need not necessarily be same.

(f) A function can call itself. Such a process is called 'recursion'. We would discuss this aspect of Java functions later in this chapter.

(g) A function can be called from another function, but a function cannot be defined in another function.

(h) There are basically two types of functions:
Library functions Ex. **readLine( )**, **println( )**, etc.
User-defined functions Ex. **argentina( )**, **brazil( )**, etc.

Library functions are commonly required functions grouped together in different classes and stored in as Java API Library. The procedure of calling both types of functions is exactly same.

Why use Functions?

Why write separate functions at all? Why not squeeze the entire logic into one function, **main( )**? It is a very bad style of programming. Instead, break a program into small units and write functions for each of these isolated subdivisions. Don't hesitate to write functions that are called only once. What is important is that these functions perform some logically isolated task.

Passing Values between Functions

The functions that we have used so far haven't been very flexible. We called them and they did what they were designed to do. It would be nice to have communication between the 'calling' and the 'called' functions.

Consider the following program. In this program, in **main( )** we receive the values of **a**, **b** and **c** through the keyboard and then output the sum of **a**, **b** and **c**. However, the calculation of sum is done in a different function called **calSum( )**. Since sum is to be calculated in **calSum( )** and values of **a**, **b** and **c** are received in **main( )**, we must pass on these values to **calSum( )**, and once **calSum( )** calculates the sum, we must return it from **calSum( )** back to **main( )**.

```
// Communication between functions
package functioncommunicationproject ;
import java.io.* ;

public class FunctionCommunicationProject
{
    public static void main ( String[ ] args ) throws Exception
    {
        int a, b, c, sum ;

        BufferedReader br = new BufferedReader (
                              new InputStreamReader ( System.in ) ) ;
        System.out.println ( "Enter any three numbers" ) ;
        a = Integer.parseInt ( br.readLine( ) ) ;
        b = Integer.parseInt ( br.readLine( ) ) ;
```

```
        c = Integer.parseInt ( br.readLine( ) ) ;
        sum = calSum ( a, b, c ) ;
        System.out.println ( "Sum = " + sum ) ;
    }
    static int calSum ( int x, int y, int z )
    {
        int d ;
        d = x + y + z ;
        return ( d ) ;
    }
}
```

And here is the output...

```
Enter any three numbers
10
20
30
Sum = 60
```

There are a number of things to note about this program:

(a) To pass the values of **a**, **b** and **c** to the function **calSum( )**, while making a call to the function **calSum( )** we have mentioned **a**, **b** and **c** in the parentheses:

```
sum = calSum ( a, b, c ) ;
```

In the **calSum( )** function these values get collected in three variables **x**, **y** and **z**:

```
int calSum ( int x, int y, int z )
```

(b) The variables **a**, **b** and **c** are called 'actual arguments', whereas the variables **x**, **y** and **z** are called 'formal arguments'. Actual arguments are often called just arguments, whereas formal arguments often called parameters. The type, order and number of the actual and formal arguments must always be same.

Instead of using different variable names **x**, **y** and **z**, we could have used the same variable names **a**, **b** and **c**. But the compiler would still treat them as different variables since they are in different functions.

(c) Since the function **calSum( )** is going to return an **int** we have replaced the usual **void** with **int** while defining **calSum( )**.

(d) In the earlier programs, the moment closing brace (}) of the called function was encountered, the control returned to the calling function. No separate **return** statement was necessary to send back the control.

This approach is fine if the called function is not going to return any meaningful value to the calling function. In the above program, however, we want to return the sum of **x**, **y** and **z**. Therefore, it is necessary to use the **return** statement.

(e) The return statement serves two purposes:

(1) On executing the **return** statement, it immediately transfers the control back to the calling function.

(2) It returns the value present in the parentheses after **return**, to the calling function. In the above program, the value of sum of three numbers is being returned.

(f) There is no restriction on the number of **return** statements that may be present in a function. Also, the **return** statement need not always be present at the end of the called function.

(g) Whenever the control returns from a function, the sum being returned is collected in the calling function by equating the called function to some variable. For example,

```
sum = calSum ( a, b, c ) ;
```

(h) All the following are valid **return** statements:

```
return ( a ) ;
return ( 23 ) ;
return ( a + b + c ) ;
return ;
```

The last statement can be used when we wish to return the control to the calling function without returning a value. Note that, in this case, the parentheses after **return** are dropped. In the other **return** statements too, the parentheses can be dropped.

(i) A function can return only one value at a time. Thus, the following statements are invalid:

```
return ( a, b ) ;
return ( x, 12 ) ;
```

(j) If the value of a formal argument is changed in the called function, the corresponding change does not take place in the calling function. For example,

```
// Effect of changing formal arguments
package formalargchangeproject ;

public class FormalArgChangeProject
{
    public static void main ( String[ ] args )
    {
        int a = 30 ;
        fun ( a ) ;
        System.out.println ( a ) ;
    }
    static void fun ( int b )
    {
        b = 60 ;
        System.out.println ( b ) ;
    }
}
```

The output of the above program would be:

```
60
30
```

Thus, even though the value of **b** is changed in **fun( ),** the value of **a** in **main( )** remains unchanged. This means that when values are passed to a called function, the values present in actual arguments are not physically moved to the formal arguments; just a photocopy of values in actual argument is made into formal arguments.

(k) Actual arguments can be constants / variables / expressions, whereas formal arguments must always be variables. Thus the following calls would work without any problem:

```
sum = calSum  ( a, 25, c ) ;
sum = calSum  ( 10 + 2, 25 % 3, a ) ;
```

(l) Nested calls are legal, so also are calls within an expression. Thus the following calls would work fine:

```
sum = calSum ( a, calSum ( 25, 10, 4 ), b ) ;
sum = calSum ( a, 25, c ) * calSum ( a, 25, c ) + 23 ;
```

Exercise

[A] What will be the output of the following programs:

(a)
```
package sampleproject ;
public class SampleProject
{
    public static void main ( String[ ] args  )
    {
        int a = 10, b = 20 ;
        modify( ) ;
        System.out.println ( a + "  " + b ) ;
    }
    static void modify ( int a, int b )
    {
        a++ ; b++ ;
    }
}
```

(b)
```
package sampleproject ;
public class SampleProject
{
    public static void main ( String[ ] args )
    {
        int i = 45, c ;
        c = check ( i ) ;
          System.out.println ( c ) ;
     }
     static int check ( int ch )
     {
          if ( ch >= 45 )
               return ( 100 ) ;
          else
               return ( 10 ) ;
     }
}
```

(c)
```
package sampleproject ;
public class SampleProject
{
     public static void main ( String[ ] args  )
```

```
    {
        float area ;
        int radius = 1 ;
        area = areaOfCircle ( radius ) ;
        System.out.println ( area ) ;
    }
    static float areaOfCircle ( int r )
    {
        float a ;
        a = 3.14f * r * r ;
        return ( a ) ;
    }
}
```

[B] Point out the errors, if any, in the following programs:

(a)
```
package sampleproject ;
public class SampleProject
{
    public static void main ( String[ ] args  )
    {
        int i = 3, j = 4, k, l ;
        k = addMult ( i, j ) ;
        l = addMult ( i, j ) ;
        System.out.println ( k + " " + l ) ;
    }
    static int addMult ( int  ii, int  jj )
    {
        int  kk, ll ;
        kk = ii + jj ;
        ll = ii * jj ;
        return ( kk, ll ) ;
    }
}
```

(b)
```
package sampleproject ;
public class SampleProject
{
    public static void main ( String[ ] args  )
    {
        message( ) ;
        message( ) ;
```

```
    }
    public void message( ) ;
    {
        System.out.println ( "Praise worthy effort!" ) ;
    }
}
```

(c)
```
package sampleproject ;
public class SampleProject
{
    public static void main ( String[ ] args  )
    {
        LetUsJava( )
        {
            System.out.println ( "Java is a Cimple  !" ) ;
            System.out.println ( "Others are no match !" ) ;
        }
    }
}
```

[C] State whether the following statements are True or False:

(a) The variables commonly used in Java functions are available to all the functions in a program.

(b) To return the control back to the calling function we must use the keyword return.

(c) The same variable names can be used in different functions without any conflict.

(d) Every called function must contain a return statement.

(e) A function may contain more than one return statement.

(f) Each return statement in a function may return a different value.

(g) A function can still be useful even if you don't pass any arguments to it and the function doesn't return any value back.

(h) A function may be called more than once from any other function.

(i) It is necessary for a function to return some value.

(j) Function definitions cannot be nested; however, function calls can be nested.

[D] Answer the following:

(a) Write a function to calculate the factorial value of any integer entered through the keyboard.

(b) Write a function **power (a, b)**, to calculate the value of **a** raised to **b**.

(c) Any year is entered through the keyboard. Write a function to determine whether the year is a leap year or not.

(d) Write a function which receives a **float** and an **int** from **main( )**, finds the product of these two and returns the product which is printed through **main( )**.

(e) If the lengths of the sides of a triangle are denoted by **a**, **b**, and **c**, then area of triangle is given by

$$area = \sqrt{S(S-a)(S-b)(S-c)}$$

where, S = (a + b + c) / 2

(f) If a function **fun( )** is to receive an **int**, a **float** & a **double** and it is to return a **decimal** then how will you define this function?

KanNotes

- Functions are a group of instructions achieving some intended goal
- Why create functions :
  1) Better complexity management - Easy to Design, Easy to Debug
  2) Provide reuse mechanism - Avoids rewriting same code repeatedly
- Types of functions :
  1) Library – println(), printf(), pow(), parseInt()
  2) User-defined – main()
- Rules for building both are same
- Two things should be done while creating a function :
  1) Function definition
  2) Function call
- General form of a function definition :

```
return-type function-name ( type arg1, type arg2, type arg3 )
{
    statement1 ;  statement2 ;
    return ( variable/constant/expression ) ; // can return only 1 value
}
```

- A function can be called any number of times
- Functions can be defined in any order
- Execution of any Java program always begins with main() present in primary class
- More the function calls, slower the execution
- Communication between functions is done using arguments and return values

- While calling function any number of arguments can be passed, whereas only 0/1 value can be returned. If no value is returned the return type of the function must be void
- Actual & Formal arguments must match in Number, Order and Type
- Actual arguments can be constants / variables / expressions
- Formal arguments can only be variables
- Nested calls are legal
  Ex. : a = Math.sin (Math.cos (b)) ;
- Call within an expression is legal
  Ex. : a = Math.sin (b) + Math.cos (c) ;
- return (s) ; - Return control & value
- return ; - Returns only control. Return type of function must be void
- If values are passed to a function, the function must collect them while defining it
- If value is returned from a function, we can choose to ignore it

Advanced Features of Functions

8

Functions are more mature in Java. You can appreciate this maturity in this chapter...

Let Us JAVA 3rd Edition

Chapter Contents

Functions in Java offers some advanced features which come in quite handy while doing programming. These include functions overloading, defining functions that receive variable number of arguments and recursive functions. This chapter is devoted to discussing these advanced features. Let us being with function overloading.

Function Overloading

With the facility of function overloading we can have multiple functions in a class with the same name. For example, if we wish to write functions that return the absolute value of a numeric argument we can consider writing a separate function for each numeric data type—one that returns absolute value of an **int**, another which returns absolute value of a **long** and yet another which returns absolute value of a **double**.

Since all these functions basically do the same thing, it seems unnecessary to have three different function names. Java overcomes this situation by allowing the programmer to create three different functions with the same name. These functions are called overloaded functions. The following program illustrates how to implement them:

```
// Overloading functions to do different but similar jobs
package functionoverloadingproject ;

public class FunctionOverloadingProject
{
    public static void main ( String[ ] args )
    {
        int i = -25, j ;
        long l = -100000, m ;
        double d = -12.34, e ;

        j = abs ( i ) ;
        m = abs ( l ) ;
        e = abs ( d ) ;
        System.out.println ( "j = " + j + " m = " + m + " e = "+ e ) ;
    }
    static int abs ( int ii )
    {
        return ( ii > 0 ? ii : ii * -1 ) ;
    }
    static long abs ( long ll )
```

```
    {
        return ( ll > 0 ? ll : ll * -1 ) ;
    }
    static double abs ( double dd )
    {
        return ( dd > 0 ? dd : dd * -1 ) ;
    }
}
```

The output of the program would be:

```
j = 25  m = 100000 e = 12.34
```

How does the Java compiler know which of the **abs( )**s should be called when a call is made? It decides that from the type of the argument being passed during the function call. For example, if an **int** is being passed the integer version of **abs( )** gets called, if a **double** is being passed then the double version of **abs( )** gets called and so on. That's quite logical, you would agree.

Overloaded functions must at least differ in the type, number or order of parameters they accept. Just having different return types is not enough to differentiate them.

It's a bad programming idea to create overloaded functions that perform different types of actions; functions with the same name should have the same general purpose. For example, if we write an **abs( )** function that returns the square root of a number, it would be both silly and confusing. We must use overloaded functions judiciously. Their purpose is to provide a common name for several similar but slightly divergent functions. Overusing overloaded functions can make a program unreadable.

Functions with Variable Number of Arguments

The functions that we have used so far used to receive a fixed number of arguments. These include the following functions:

```
System.out.println ( "a = " + a ) ;
y = Math.pow ( 2.0, 5.0 ) ;
s = calSum ( a, b, c ) ;
```

Java also permits functions to receive variable number of arguments. For example,

```
System.out.printf ( "%d %d", a, b ) ;
System.out.printf ( "%d %d %f %f", a, b, c, d ) ;
```

Here, in the first call to **printf( )** we are passing 3 arguments, whereas, in the second call we are passing 5 arguments.

Even we can define functions that can receive variable number of arguments. The following program illustrates this:

```
package varargsproject ;
public class VarArgsProject
{
    public static void main ( String args[ ] )
    {
        double d1 = 10.0 ;  double d2 = 20.0 ;
        double d3 = 30.0 ;  double d4 = 40.0 ;

        System.out.printf ( "Avg = %f\n", average ( d1, d2 ) ) ;
        System.out.printf ( "Avg = %f\n", average ( d1, d2, d3 ) ) ;
        System.out.printf ( "Avg = %f\n", average ( d1, d2, d3, d4 ) ) ;
    }

    static double average ( double... numbers )
    {
        double total = 0.0 ;
        for ( double d : numbers )
            total = total + d ;

        double avg ;
        avg =  total / numbers.length ;
        return avg ;
    }
}
```

Here we are passing different number of arguments to average( ) function in each call. To make **average( )** capable such variable number of arguments, a special syntax is used while defining its parameters.

```
static double average ( double... numbers )
{
    ..
}
```

Here **double** is followed by ellipsis (...), meaning that this function is going to receive different number of doubles in each call. **numbers** is treated as an array. So while finding the average value, we need to iterate through the array elements. To do this, a special **for** loop syntax has been evolved.

Each time through this **for** loop, **d** takes the next value from the **numbers** array. The number of values present in the array can be obtained using the **length** property of the array. This aspect of array would be discussed in detail in Chapter 12.

Sometime we might be required to define a function that receives fixed arguments as well as variable arguments. While defining such function we have to ensure that the fixed arguments precede the variable arguments while making the call to such functions.

Recursion

In Java, it is possible for the functions to call themselves. A function is called 'recursive' if a statement within the body of a function calls the same function. Sometimes called 'circular definition', recursion is thus the process of defining something in terms of itself.

Let us now see a simple example of recursion. Suppose we want to calculate the factorial value of an integer. As we know, the factorial of a number is the product of all the integers between 1 and that number. For example, 4 factorial is 4 * 3 * 2 * 1. This can also be expressed as 4! = 4 * 3!, where '!' stands for factorial. Thus factorial of a number can be expressed in the form of itself. Hence, this logic can be programmed using recursion as shown below.

```
// Calculating factorial using recursive function
package recursivefactorialproject ;
import java.io.* ;

public class Main
{
    public static void main ( String[ ] args ) throws Exception
    {
        int a, fact ;

        BufferedReader br = new BufferedReader (
                                  new InputStreamReader ( System.in ) ) ;
```

```
        System.out.println ( "Enter any number " ) ;
        a = Integer.parseInt ( br.readLine( ) ) ;

        fact = rec ( a ) ;
        System.out.println ( "Factorial value = " + fact ) ;
    }

    static int rec ( int x )
    {
        int f ;

        if ( x == 1 )
            return ( 1 ) ;
        else
            f = x * rec ( x - 1 ) ;

        return ( f ) ;
    }
}
```

And here is the output for sample run of the program...

```
Enter any number 3
Factorial value = 6
```

Let us understand this recursive factorial function thoroughly. When value of **a** is 3, **main( )** would call **rec( )** with 3 as its actual argument, and **rec( )** will send back the computed value. But before sending the computed value, **rec( )** calls **rec( )** and waits for a value to be returned. It is possible for the **rec( )** that has just been called to call yet another **rec( )**, the argument **x** being decreased in value by 1 for each of these recursive calls. These recursive invocations end finally when the last invocation gets an argument value of 1, which the preceding invocation of **rec( )** now uses to calculate its own **f** value and so on up the ladder. So we might say what happens is,

```
rec ( 3 ) returns ( 3 times rec ( 2 ),
    which returns ( 2 times rec ( 1 ),
        which returns ( 1 ) )
```

Foxed? Well, that is recursion for you in its simplest garbs. I hope you agree that it's difficult to visualize how the control flows from one function call to another. Possibly Figure 8.1 would make things a bit clearer.

Assume that the number entered through **readLine( )** is 3. Using Figure 8.1 let us visualize what exactly happens when the recursive function **rec( )** gets called. The first time when **rec( )** is called from **main( )**, **x** collects 3. From here, since **x** is not equal to 1, the **if** block is skipped and **rec( )** is called again with the argument **(x – 1)**, i.e. 2. This is a recursive call. Since **x** is still not equal to 1, **rec( )** is called yet another time, with argument (2 - 1). This time as **x** is 1, control goes back to previous **rec( )** with the value 1, and **f** is evaluated as 2.

Similarly, each **rec( )** evaluates its **f** from the returned value, and finally 6 is returned to **main( )**. The sequence would be grasped better by following the arrows shown in Figure 8.1. Let it be clear that while executing the program, there do not exist so many copies of the function **rec( )**. These have been shown in Figure 8.1 just to help you keep track of how the control flows during successive recursive calls.

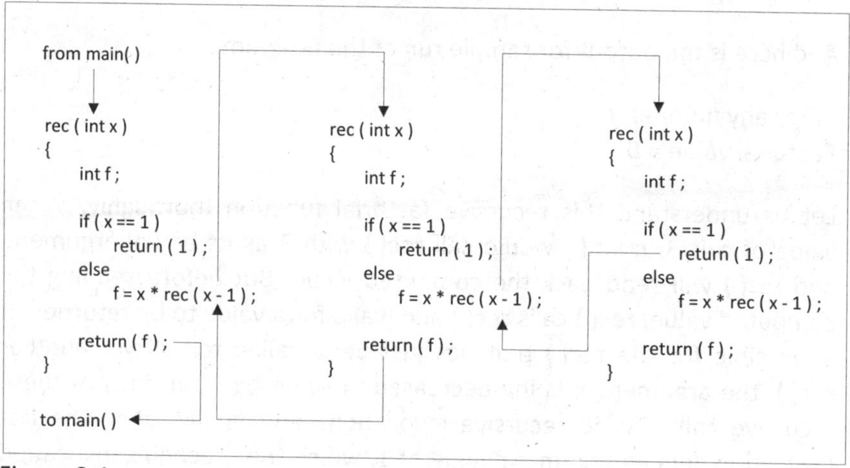

Figure 8.1

Recursion may seem strange and complicated at first glance, but it is often the most direct way to code an algorithm, and once you are familiar with recursion, the clearest way of doing so.

Exercise

[A] Answer the following:

(a) Define an overloaded **max( )** function which returns maximum out of two integers / floats / doubles.

(b) Define a function **min( )** that can find out and return minimum out of variable number of integers passed to it.

(c) A 5-digit positive integer is entered through the keyboard, write a recursive function to calculate sum of digits of the 5-digit number.

(d) A positive integer is entered through the keyboard, write a program to obtain the prime factors of the number using a recursive function.

(e) Write a recursive function to obtain the first 25 numbers of a Fibonacci sequence. In a Fibonacci sequence the sum of two successive terms gives the third term. Following are the first few terms of the Fibonacci sequence:

1 1 2 3 5 8 13 21 34 55 89...

(f) A positive integer is entered through the keyboard, write a function to find the binary equivalent of this number using recursion.

(g) Write a recursive function to obtain the running sum of first 25 natural numbers.

(h) Write the function **Fun( )** which finds the minimum number from the variable arguments list passed to it.

```
package sampleproject ;
public class Main
{
    public static void main ( String[ ] args )
    {
        int a = 5, b = 4, res ;
        res = Fun ( a, b ) ;
        System.out.println ( res ) ;
        res = Fun ( 1, 5, a, b, 7, 99, 100 ) ;
        System.out.println ( res ) ;
    }
    // Add code here
}
```

KanNotes

- Function names in a class can be same. Such functions are known as Overloaded Functions
- If function names are same then their arguments must differ in Number, Order or Type
- Usually overloaded functions carry out similar jobs. Ex. Getting absolute value of different data types
- Functions can receive variable number of arguments.
- If a function receives fixed as well as variable number of arguments, then fixed arguments must be at the beginning and variable number of arguments at the end of argument-list
- Variable number of arguments are received in an array. This array can be processed using a special for loop :

```
static void fun ( int, a, float b, double... numbers )
{
    for ( double d : numbers )
        System.out.println ( d ) ;
}
```

- A function that calls itself is called a recursive function
- Any function, including main() can become a recursive function
- Recursive call always leads to an infinite loop. So a provision must be made to get outside this infinite loop
- The provision is done by making the recursive call either in the if block or in the else block
- If recursive call is made in the if block, else block should contain the end condition logic

- If recursive call is made in the else block, if block should contain the end condition logic
- Fresh set of variables are born during each function call - normal call and recursive call
- Variables die when control returns from a function
- Recursive function may or may not have a return statement
- Recursion is an alternative for loop in logics which are expressible in the form of themselves
- Recursive calls are slower than an equivalent while / for / do-while loop
- If stuck in a infinite loop while using recursion stack overflow would occur and the program execution would come to an end

9

Introduction to OOP

Paradigm shift! This chapter would change your thinking about how to organize a program ...

Let Us JAVA
3rd Edition

Chapter Contents

Data types, control instructions and functions are the basic building blocks of any Java program. With all these topics under our belt it is time to move on to something more complex, namely, Object Oriented Programming.

Java is an Object–Oriented Programming (OOP) language. Many programmers tend to use object-oriented features of Java mechanically. Though this might make the program work, the real advantages of object-oriented programming do not accrue unless you understand the concept of object-oriented programming and what features it offers. Hence, in this chapter we would not write a single program. Instead we would concentrate on understanding what is OOP and why do we need it.

This chapter addresses these issues and provides an overview of the features to be discussed in the rest of the book. What we say here will necessarily be general and brief. Don't worry if you don't catch everything in this chapter on the first pass; OOP is a bit complex and understanding it takes time. We will be going over these features again in subsequent chapters. There's lot of ground to cover here, so let's get started.

The purpose of a programming language is to express the solution to a problem with the help of an algorithm (step-by-step procedure). The success of the solution depends on how the solution models (represents) the problem. Different approaches have evolved over the years to model solutions to problems. The primary amongst them are Structured programming model (also called Procedural programming model) and Object-oriented programming model. These models are often called programming paradigms, i.e. principle of program organization. To understand these models we need to begin by taking a peek at the history of programming models.

The Beginning...

The earliest computers were programmed in binary. Mechanical switches were used to load programs. With the advent of mass storage devices and larger and cheaper computer memories, the first high-level computer programming languages came into existence. With their arrival, instead of thinking in terms of bits and bytes, programmers could write a series of English-like instructions that a compiler could translate into the binary language of computers.

These languages were simple in design and easy to use because programs at that time were primarily concerned with relatively simple tasks like calculations. As a result, programs were pretty short, limited to about a few hundred lines of instructions.

As the computers' capacity and capability increased, so also did the ability to develop more complex computer programs. However, the earlier programming languages were found wanting in performing the complex programming tasks. These languages suffered from following limitations:

(a) There were no facilities to reuse existing program code. Wherever the same piece code was required, it was simply duplicated.

(b) The control of execution within a program was transferred via the dangerous **goto** statement. As a result, there was too much jumping around in the program, often without any clear indication of how, where and why the control is flowing.

(c) All variables in the program were global. Tracking down spurious changes in global data in long convoluted programs was a very tedious job.

(d) Writing, understanding and maintaining long programs became a programmer's nightmare.

In short, we can call this methodology of developing programs as **Unstructured** programming.

Structured Programming

To overcome the limitations mentioned above, a quest began to develop new languages with new features that would help to create more sophisticated applications. The breakthrough occurred in late 1960's and early 1970's with the introduction of structured programming. The long programs that the programmer found difficult to comprehend could now be broken down into smaller units of few hundred statements. Functions/subroutines/procedures were introduced in these languages to make the programs more comprehensible to their human creators. A program was now divided into functions, with each function having a clearly defined purpose.

How structured programming overcame the limitations experienced in unstructured programming is given below.

(a) Reuse of existing program code – Wherever the same piece code is required at multiple places in a program, the function containing that code was used. As a result, there was no need to repeat the same code at multiple places.

(b) Excessive use of **goto** statement – This was minimized by introducing powerful control instructions that could transfer the control within the program in an easy-to-understand manner.

(c) Unexpected changes in global variables – With introduction of functions, need for global variables were minimized.

(d) Complexity of programs – Complexity became more manageable as structured programming permitted better organization of the program.

A structured program is built by breaking down a solution into smaller pieces that then become functions within that program. Each function can have its local variables and logic. The execution begins with one function and then all other functions are called directly or indirectly from this function. This is shown in Figure 9.1.

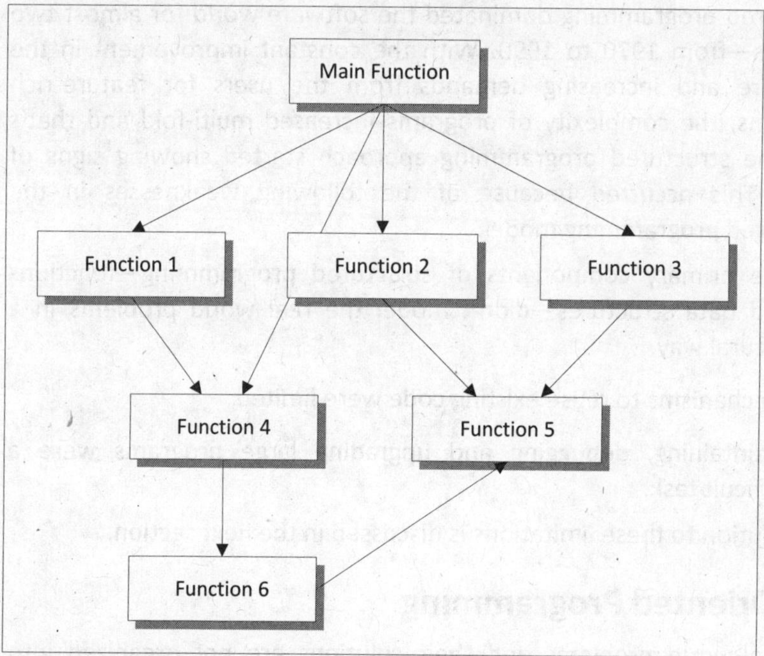

Figure 9.1

In structured programming, there is less need of global variables, which are now replaced by local variables that have a smaller and more controllable scope. Information is passed between functions using parameters and functions can have local variables that cannot be accessed outside the function's scope.

By isolating processes within functions, a structured program minimizes the chance that one function will affect another. This also makes it easier to locate problems, if any. Structured programming helps in writing cleaner code and in maintaining control over each function. All this makes the development and maintenance of code easier as well as efficient.

A new concept came into existence with structured programming—**Abstraction**. Abstraction permits the programmer to look at something without being concerned with is internal details. In a structured program, it is enough to know which task is performed by function. It does not matter to the programmer how that task is performed so long as the function does it reliably. This is called functional abstraction and is the corner-stone of structured programming.

Structured programming dominated the software world for almost two decades—from 1970 to 1990. With the constant improvement in the hardware and increasing demands from the users for feature-rich programs, the complexity of programs increased multi-fold and that's the time structured programming approach started showing signs of strain. This occurred because of the following weaknesses in the structured programming model:

(a) The primary components of structured programming—functions and data structures—didn't model the real world problems in a natural way.

(b) Mechanisms to reuse existing code were limited.

(c) Maintaining, debugging and upgrading large programs were a difficult task.

The solution to these limitations is discussed in the next section.

Object-Oriented Programming

The real-world problems and their solutions are not organized into values and procedures separate from one another. Instead, they are perceived as objects containing values and procedures that either access or manipulate these values. The world is full of objects and the OOP methodology helps us expresses computer programs in ways that model how people perceive the world.

The fundamental change in OOP is that a program is designed around the data being operated upon, rather than around the operations themselves. This is to be expected once we appreciate that the prime purpose of the program is to access or manipulate data. The basic idea behind object-oriented language is to combine into a single unit, both, the data and the functions that operate on the data. Such a unit is called an object.

An object's functions, called member functions or methods, typically provide the only way to access its data. If you want to access a data item in an object, you call a member function in the object. It will read the item and return the value to you. You can't access the data directly.

If you want to modify the data in an object, you call the member functions in the object. No other functions can access the data. This simplifies writing, debugging, and maintaining the program.

A Java program typically consists of a number of objects which communicate with each other by calling one another's member functions. The organization of a Java program is shown in Figure 9.2.

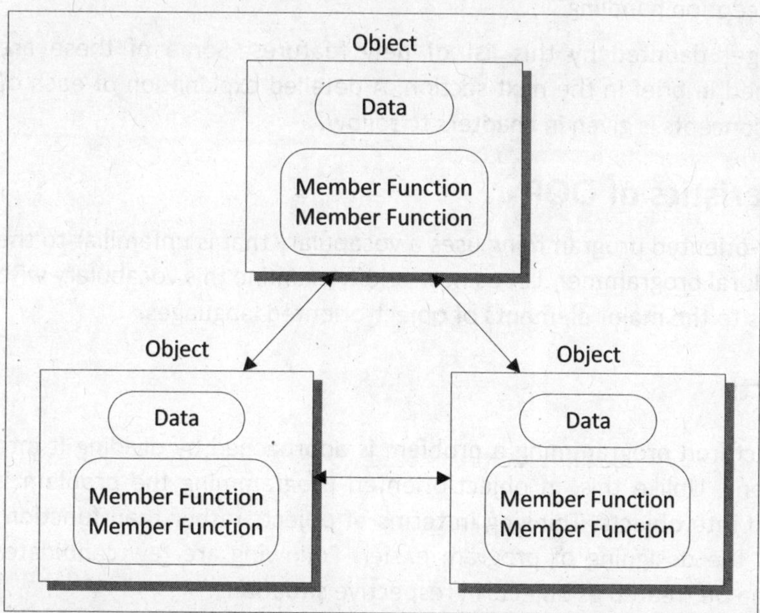

Figure 9.2

When you approach a programming problem in an object-oriented manner, you no longer ask how the problem will be divided into functions, but rather how it will be divided into objects. Thinking in terms of objects, rather than functions, has a surprisingly helpful effect on how easily programs can be designed. This results from the close match between objects in the programming world and objects in the real world.

The match between programming objects and real world objects is the happy result of combining data and functions. The resulting objects offer a revolution in program design. No such close match between programming constructs and the concepts being modeled exists in a procedural language.

There is more to OOP than just binding the data and functions together. Given below are some of the new concepts introduced in OOP.

(a) Data hiding
(b) Encapsulation
(c) Inheritance
(d) Containership
(e) Polymorphism
(f) Templates
(g) Exception handling

Don't get daunted by this list of new features. Some of these are explained in brief in the next section. A detailed explanation of each of these concepts is given in chapters to follow.

Characteristics of OOP

Object-oriented programming uses a vocabulary that is unfamiliar to the procedural programmer. Let us now briefly examine this vocabulary with regards to the major elements of object-oriented languages.

Objects

In structured programming a problem is approached by dividing it into functions. Unlike this, in object-oriented programming the problem is divided into objects. Thinking in terms of objects rather than functions makes the designing of program easier. Following are few candidates that can be treated as objects in respective situations:

- Employees in a Payroll processing system
- GUI elements like windows, menus, icons, etc.

– Elements in computer games like cannons, guns, animals, etc.
– Customers, sales persons in a sales tracking system

Classes

Most languages offer primitive data types like **int**, **long** and **float**. Their data representation and response to arithmetic, assignment and relational operators are defined as part of the language. However, not all the information about real world objects can be represented using these limited built-in data types. The programmer often needs to create his own data types by defining a **class** for it.

For example, there can be a user-defined data type to represent dates. Programmers have to define the behavior of dates by designing a **Date** class. This class expresses the format of a date and the operations that can be performed on it. The way we can declare many variables of the primitive type **int**, we can define many objects of the **Date** class. A class serves as a blueprint or a plan or a template. It specifies what data and what functions will be included in objects of that type. Defining a class doesn't create any objects, just as the mere existence of a type **int** doesn't create any variables.

Inheritance

OOP permits you to create your own data types (classes) just like the types built into the language. However, unlike the built-in data types, the user-defined classes can use other classes as building blocks. Using a concept called **inheritance**; new classes can be built on top of the old ones. The new class referred to as a **derived** class, can inherit the data and functions of the original, or the **base** class. The new class can add its own data elements and functions in addition to those it inherits from its base class.

For example, we can build a set of classes that describe a library of publications. There are two primary types of publications— periodicals and books. We can create a general **Publication** class by defining data items for the publisher name, the number of pages and the accession number. Publications can be retrieved, stored and read. These would be the functions of **Publication** class.

Next we can define two classes named **Periodical** and **Book**. Both these classes can be derived from the base class **Publication**. This is natural because a periodical as well as a book would have properties like publisher name, number of pages and the accession number.

In addition to this, a periodical also has a volume and issue number and contains articles written by different authors. Data items for these should be included in the definition of the **periodical** class. The **Periodical** class will also need a function, subscribe.

Data items for the **Book** class will include the names of its author a cover type (hard or soft) and its ISBN (International Standard Book Number). This class would also have a function called **subscribe**. As you can see, the **Book** class and the **Periodical** class share the characteristics of **Publication** class while having their own unique attributes. This entire scenario is depicted in Figure 9.3.

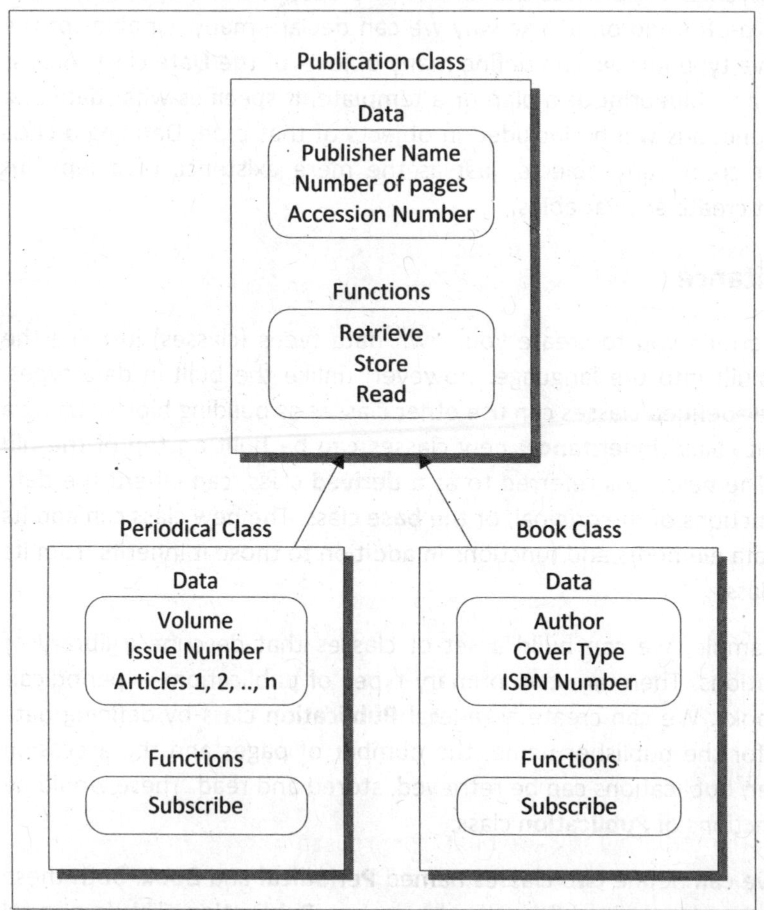

Figure 9.3

Polymorphism

Extending the same example of the Publication, Periodical and Book, let us now understand another important concept. Our base class, Publication, defines methods for storing and retrieving data. A periodical may be stored in a binder, while a book is usually placed on a shelf. Furthermore, the way to find a specific periodical is different from finding a book. Periodicals are located through a guide to periodical literature, while books are found using a card catalog system. Based on this we can design a 'find through periodical literature' function for a periodical and a 'find through card catalog' function for a book.

OOP provides an elegant facility called **polymorphism** to handle such situations. In our example, the retrieval method for a periodical is different from the retrieval method for a book, even though the end result is same. Polymorphism permits us to define a function for retrieving a publication that can work for both periodicals and books. When a periodical is retrieved, the retrieve function that is specific to a periodical is used, but when a book is retrieved, the retrieve function associated with a book is used. The end result is that a single function name can be used for the same operation performed on related derived classes even if the implementation of that function varies from class to class. This concept of polymorphism (one thing with several distinct forms) can be extended even to operators, as we would see in later chapters.

Containership

In a typical super-market, each item on sale can be represented using a class. These items in turn belong to different categories like cosmetics, food, cold-drink, clothes, books, electronics, etc. Such relationships can be represented using containership. For example objects like cold-cream, face-wash, shampoo are contained inside a category object called cosmetics. You will be able to observe this containership relationship in many real-world problems.

Reusability

Object-oriented programs are built from reusable software components. Once a class is completed and tested, it can be distributed to other programmers for use in their own programs. This is called reusability. If those programmers want to add new features or change the existing ones, new classes can be derived from existing ones. The tried and tested capabilities of base classes do not need to be redeveloped. Programmers can devote time to writing new code instead of wasting time in rewriting existing code. This way software becomes easier to test, since programming errors can be isolated within the new code of derived classes.

For example, you might have written (or purchased from someone else) a class that creates a menu system. You are happy with the working of this class and you don't want to change it, but you want to add the capability of displaying *help* for each menu item. To do this, you simply create a new class that inherits all the capabilities of the existing one but adds *help* feature. This ease with which existing software can be reused is a major benefit of OOP.

Exercise

[A] State whether the following statements are True or False:

(a) Object-oriented programming permits reusability of the existing code.

(b) Languages earlier than procedural programming languages made use of only global variables.

(c) It is easier to write, understand and maintain programs if they use Object-Oriented programming model as compared to Structured programming model.

(d) As compared to procedures, data is not given enough importance in Procedural programming.

(e) Structured programming model does not represent the real world problem as well as the Object-oriented programming model.

(f) A class permits us to build user-defined data types.

(g) Objects are to classes as variables are to built-in data types.

(h) Deriving a new class from an existing class promotes reusability of code.

(i) Encapsulation facilitates a single function name to be used for the same operation performed on related derived classes.

(j) In polymorphism even though the function names are same, their implementation may vary from class to class.

(k) Multiple objects can be created from the same class.

(l) Object-oriented Programming paradigm stresses on dividing the logic into smaller parts and writing procedures for each part.

(m) Classes and objects are cornerstones of structured programming paradigm.

(n) Object-oriented programming paradigm gives equal importance to data and the procedures that work on the data.

(o) Java is a structured programming language.

[B] Fill in the blanks:

(a) The two major components of an object are ____ and _____.

(b) The ability of a function or operator to act in different ways on different data types is called ________.

(c) The process of building new classes from existing ones is called ________.

(d) If a class A inherits its properties from class B, then A and B are known as _____ class and _____ class, respectively.

(e) Pascal and C are ______ languages, whereas, Java is _____ language.

[C] Answer the following:

(a) What is the basic difference between structured programming model and object-oriented programming model?

(b) Give at least 5 examples of classes and objects.

(c) What do you mean by encapsulation?

(d) What do you mean by inheritance?

(e) What do you mean by polymorphism?

(f) In structured programming data is given a step-motherly treatment and the whole emphasis is on doing things. What does this mean in programmer's language?

(g) What do you mean by abstraction?

(h) Is it necessary to create good abstractions?

(i) Why did people change over from structured programming to object-oriented programming?

(j) What is the difference between classes and objects in layman's terms?

(k) What is the difference between classes and objects in programmer's terms?

KanNotes

- Programming paradigm means way of organizing a program.
- Two major programming paradigms are :
  1) Structure programming paradigm - adopted by C, Pascal
  2) Object Oriented Programming (OOP) paradigm - adopted by C++, Java, C#, VB.NET
- Structured programming :
  1) Emphasis on breaking the given task into smaller sub-tasks
  2) For each sub-task functions are written
  3) These functions are called directly or indirectly from main()
  4) No importance given to data, it is just passed from one function to another as required
- Disadvantage of Structured programming - It is difficult to write programs involving complex tasks
- Object Oriented Programming (OOP) :
  1) Emphasis is on identifying objects in a given problem and then writing programs to facilitate interaction between objects
  2) Objects contain data and functions that can access/manipulate the data
  3) Equal importance to data as data and functions go together
- Example of classes and objects :

  Class – Human being   Objects – Amitabh, Sachin, Rahul
  Class – Birds   Objects – Sparrow, Crow, Parrot
- Class has Properties (data) and Methods (functions) :

  Ex. Vehicle has properties like wheels, engine, fuel
- Objects have specific values for properties :

  Car – 4 wheels, 4-stroke engine, Diesel
  Motorbike – 2 wheels, 2-stroke engine, Petrol

- Objects are always nameless and are created using new operator on heap

Classes and Objects

10

A good foundation is always important. Classes and Objects are to OOP, what functions were to structured programming ...

Let Us JAVA
3rd Edition

Chapter Contents

Having familiarized ourselves with the basic principles of object-oriented programming, it is time we start implementing these principles through Java programs. Let us begin with classes and objects.

In all programs that we created so far, we had just defined functions inside a class. Java permits us to combine data and functions together in a class. The functions defined within a class have a special relationship with the data elements present within the class. Placing data and functions (that work upon the data) together into a single entity is the central idea in object-oriented programming.

To begin with, let us look at a program that demonstrates the syntax and general features of classes in Java. In all programs that we did so far we had only one class. This class used to be created by the NetBeans wizard with the name same as the Project name. For the first time we are now going to see a program that uses two classes. While creating this project in NetBeans we would give the project name as **ClassesAndObjectsProject**. As a result, the wizard would create a package called **classesandobjectsproject** containing a class called **ClassesAndObjectsProject**. Additionally, we would create the **Rectangle** class in the same package. Here's the listing of the program.

```
// Demonstration of classes and objects
package classesandobjectsproject ;
import java.io.* ;

class Rectangle
{
    private int len, brd ;

    public void getData( ) throws Exception
    {
        BufferedReader br = new BufferedReader (
                                      new InputStreamReader ( System.in ) ) ;

        System.out.println ( "Enter length and breadth " ) ;
        len = Integer.parseInt ( br.readLine( ) ) ;
        brd = Integer.parseInt ( br.readLine( ) ) ;
    }

    public void setData ( int l, int b )
    {
```

```
        len = l ;
        brd = b ;
    }

    public void displayData( )
    {
        System.out.println ( "length = "+ len ) ;
        System.out.println ( "breadth = "+ brd ) ;
    }

    public void areaPeri( )
    {
        int a, p ;
        a = len * brd ;
        p = 2 * ( len + brd ) ;
        System.out.println ( "area = "+ a ) ;
        System.out.println ( "perimeter = "+ p ) ;
    }
}

public class ClassesAndObjectsProject
{
    public static void main ( String[ ] args ) throws Exception
    {
        Rectangle r1, r2, r3 ; // define three references

        r1 = new Rectangle( ) ;
        r2 = new Rectangle( ) ;
        r3 = new Rectangle( ) ;

        r1.setData ( 10, 20 ) ; // set data in elements of the object
        r1.displayData( ) ;     // display the data set by setData( )
        r1.areaPeri( ) ;        // calculate and print area and perimeter

        r2.setData ( 5, 8 ) ;
        r2.displayData( ) ;
        r2.areaPeri( ) ;

        r3.getData( ) ; // receive data from keyboard
        r3.displayData( ) ;
        r3.areaPeri( ) ;
```

```
    }
}
```

Look at the definition of **Rectangle** class in our program. The keyword **class** is followed by the name of the class, i.e., **Rectangle**. The body of a class is delimited by braces. The **Rectangle** class contains two data items **len** and **br** and four functions **setData( )**, **getData( )**, **displayData( )** and **areaPeri( )**. As their names suggest, the first function sets the data items (**len** and **brd**) to values passed to it, the second function receives the values of data items, the third displays these values, whereas the fourth calculates and prints the area and perimeter.

The data items defined in a class are often called data members, whereas the functions defined in it are called member functions or methods. The member functions provide controlled access to the data members of class. This controlled access is managed through two keywords—**private** and **public**.

Note that we have defined the data members as **private**. As a result, they cannot be accessed directly from outside the **Rectangle** class. Thus the data remains safe from accidental manipulation.

Only the member functions of **Rectangle** class can access the **private** data members. To permit access to these member functions from outside the **Rectangle** class, they have been defined as **public**. Thus, when we wish to access or manipulate the data members from outside the class we call the **public** member functions, which in turn access the **private** data members. This is what we mean by controlled access.

Usually the data members in a class are **private** and the member functions are **public**. This ensures that data remains safe from inadvertent manipulation. However, there is no rule that data must be **private** and functions **public**. In fact, in some situations you may be required to use **private** functions and **public** data.

Don't confuse data hiding with the security techniques used to protect computer data. Security techniques prevent illegal users from accessing data. Data hiding, on the other hand, is used to protect well-intentioned users from honest mistakes.

Let us now understand the meaning of the term **object** and how they are created. An object is an **instance** of a class, and the process of creating an object is called **instantiation**. In our program we have created three objects through the statements:

```
r1 = new Rectangle( ) ;
r2 = new Rectangle( ) ;
r3 = new Rectangle( ) ;
```

All the three objects are created in memory and each one of them would have data members **len** and **br** in them. None of these objects have names. The addresses at which these objects are created in memory are stored in variables **r1**, **r2** and **r3**. These variables are known as references to objects. Figure 10.1 illustrates this.

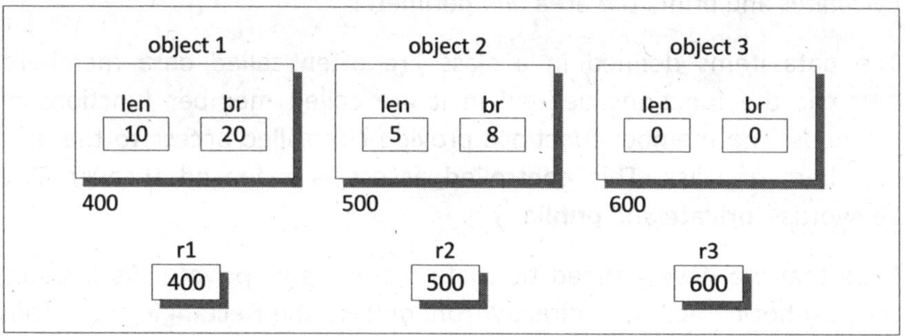

Figure 10.1

Once the objects are created, we can use them to call member functions of the class. For example, we can call the member function **setData( )** from **main( )** using the object whose address is stored in the reference **r1**, through the statement:

```
r1.setData ( 10, 20 ) ;
```

The 10 and 20 that are being passed to **setData( )** would be collected in **l** and **b** and would then be assigned to **len** and **br** of object whose address is present is reference **r1**.

Similarly, when we make the call to

```
r2.setData ( 5, 8 ) ;
```

5 and 8 get set up in **len** and **br** of object whose address is present in **r2**.

The dot operator (.) used to call **setData( )** through **r1** and **r2** is called 'class member access operator'. Calls to other functions like **displayData( ), areaPeri( )** are similar.

Note that the objects are created at a place in memory called heap, whereas, references to objects are created at a place in memory called stack.

Classes and Constructors

In the last section we had our first tryst with classes in Java. Just to reiterate, a class contains data and functions that operate upon this data. Both data and functions can be **private** or **public**, which essentially decides the access to the data and functions within the class. Let us now move one step further. Observe the following program carefully.

```
// Different types of constructors
package constructorsproject ;
import java.io.*  ;

class Number
{
    private int i ;

    public void setData ( int j )
    {
        i = j ;
    }

    public void getData( ) throws Exception
    {
        BufferedReader br = new BufferedReader (
                                    new InputStreamReader ( System.in ) ) ;
        System.out.println ( "Enter any integer" ) ;
        i = Integer.parseInt ( br.readLine( ) ) ;
    }

    public Number( ) // zero argument constructor
    {
    }

    public Number ( int j ) // one argument constructor
    {
        i = j;
    }
```

```
    public void displayData( )
    {
        System.out.println ( "value of i = "+ i ) ;
    }
}

public class ConstructorsProject
{
    public static void main ( String[ ] args ) throws Exception
    {
        Number  n1, n2, n3 ;

        n1 = new Number( ) ;
        n1.displayData( ) ;
        n1.setData ( 200 ) ;  // first method to set data in object
        n1.displayData( ) ;

        n2 = new Number( ) ;
        n2.displayData( ) ;
        n2.getData( ) ;   // second method to set data in object
        n2.displayData( ) ;

        n3 = new Number ( 100 ) ;   // third method to set data in object
        n3.displayData( ) ;
    }
}
```

This program shows three ways in which we can give values to data items in an object. One is through the member function **setData( )** to whom we pass the value to be set up. Another way is by receiving values through keyboard as shown in function **getData( )**. That brings us to the third method, which uses an entity called 'constructor' (or in short, Ctor). The constructor is a special member function that allows us to set up values while creating an object, without the need to make a separate call to a member function like **setData( )**. Thus, constructor is a member function that is called automatically whenever an object is created.

There are some unusual aspects to constructor functions. First, it is no accident that they have exactly the same name as the class of which they are members. In fact it's a rule that the class and the constructor function within it must have same names. This is how the compiler knows that the member function is a constructor.

Secondly, no return type is used for constructors. Why not? Since the constructor is called automatically when an object is created, returning a value would not make sense.

In our program the statements

```
n1 = new Number( ) ; // calls zero-argument constructor
n2 = new Number( ) ; // calls zero-argument constructor
n3 = new Number ( 100 ) ; // calls one-argument constructor
```

create three objects of the type **Number** and call the appropriate constructor function. Note the use of the **new** operator while creating objects. This operator allocates memory for the object and then calls that object's constructor function.

If you notice carefully, you would find that there are two constructors with the same name **Number( )**. Hence we call these constructors as **overloaded constructors**. Which of the two constructors gets called when an object is created, depends on how many arguments are used in the creation of the object.

Since we haven't done anything in the zero-argument constructor, the value of **i** is set to 0 for objects referred by **n1** and **n2**. This can be verified from the output of the program. The value of **i** for **n1** and **n2** can later be reset, as done here through calls to **setData( )** and **getData( )**.

If data can be set in an object through the constructor function as well as through the **setData( )** function, why should we define both in a class? This is because the constructor function can be called only during creation of an object, whereas the **setData( )** function can be called multiple times once an object is created. So initial data can be set in an object through the constructor and it can be changed later (if required) through the **setData( )** function.

What would happen if we declare an object of a particular class type and the class doesn't have a constructor? Nothing. Because when no constructor is present in a class, the compiler inserts a zero-argument constructor in it. Note that if we declare a one-argument constructor, it is necessary on our part to define the zero-argument constructor as well.

Object Destruction

When the object is created using the operator **new**, memory is allocated for it. Should we not free this memory when we are done with using this object? This is not necessary, as this is done for us by the JVM. It has a program called **Garbage Collector**, which it runs periodically. When it runs, it checks for objects that are no longer being used by an application. It then reclaims (frees) the memory used to store all such objects. So, as far as memory management for objects is concerned, we do not have to worry much about it, and can safely rely on garbage collector to do it for us. This is unlike traditional OO languages like C++ where programmers have to manage the memory explicitly.

However, in many Java programs, memory is not the only resource that is used. Other resources like files, network connections, database connections, are also used. When we no longer need the objects that use these resources the objects should release these resources in a disciplined manner. It this is not done resource leaks will happen. This is a waste of resources. At times, if the pool of resources gets exhausted then the program may even stop running. Java provides a mechanism called **finalize( )** function to give up the resources when the object is no longer needed. This function is defined inside the class and is called by the garbage collector just before reclaiming the object.

Thus the **finalize( )** function is opposite of a constructor. The constructor is called when an object is created. Similarly, when an object is destroyed by the garbage collector the **finalize( )** function is called. Note that we have no control over when the **finalize( )** function is called by the Garbage Collector.

The following program shows **finalize( )** at work:

```
/* Object destruction using finalize( ) */
package objectdestructionproject ;

class Example
{
    private int data ;

    public Example( ) // contstuctor (same name as class)
    {
        System.out.println ( "Inside the constructor" ) ;
    }
```

```
    protected void finalize( ) throws Throwable
    {
        super.finalize( ) ;
    }
}

public class ObjectDestructionProject
{
    public static void main ( String[ ] args )
    {
        Example e = new Example( ) ;
    }
}
```

When the object referred by **e** gets created, the constructor gets called. When control goes outside **main( )** this object is no longer used. When the garbage collector finds this, it calls the **finalize( )** function. **finalize( )** function does not receive any parameter, nor does it return any value. The **finalize( )** method cannot be called explicitly. Also, we should not declare it as **public**.

In the **finalize( )** method we have simply called the base class **finalize( )** method. Note that all classes in Java including the **Example** class are derived from a base class called **Object**. We would learn more about this derivation process in Chapter 13.

In this program we have done precious little inside the **finalize( )** function. In a program in which the object uses files, network and database connections the **finalize( )** method should perform operations like closing open files, terminating network connections, terminating database connections and other cleanup work.

Terminology

Consider the following code snippet:

```
Sample s1, s2 ;
s1 = new Sample ( 1.0f, 2.0f ) ;
s2 = new Sample( ) ;
s2.Function ( s1 ) ;
```

From the code it is obvious that we are creating two objects of the **Sample** class and calling its zero-argument and two-argument constructors. Can you guess what are we passing to **Function( )**? Simple, object **s1**. Well, actually speaking no. This is because, **s1** is not an object, but a reference to an object. The object as such doesn't have a name and we always access it using its address stored in the reference **s1**. But it is quite common to call the reference **s1** as object **s1**. Though this is slightly incorrect, it gives a lot of convenience and hence we too would be using this terminology in the rest of the chapter and the chapters to follow.

A Complex Class

As we know, a complex number consists of a real part and an imaginary part. The following program puts the concept of constructor to a practical stint by developing a class to implement complex numbers:

```
// Implementation of complex numbers
package complexnumbersproject ;
import java.io.* ;

class Complex
{
    private float real, imag ;

    public Complex( )
    {
    }

    public Complex ( float r, float i )
    {
        real = r ;
        imag = i ;
    }

    public void getData( ) throws Exception
    {
        float r, i ;

        BufferedReader br = new BufferedReader (
                                new InputStreamReader ( System.in ) ) ;
```

```
        System.out.println ( "Enter real and imaginary part" ) ;
        r = Float.parseFloat ( br.readLine( ) ) ;
        i = Float.parseFloat ( br.readLine( ) ) ;
        real = r ;
        imag = i ;
    }

    public void setData ( float r, float i )
    {
        real = r ;
        imag = i ;
    }

    public void displayData( )
    {
        System.out.println ( "real = "+ real ) ;
        System.out.println ( "imaginary = "+ imag ) ;
    }

    public Complex addComplex ( Complex y )
    {
        Complex t ;
        t = new Complex( ) ;
        t.real = real + y.real ;
        t.imag = imag + y.imag ;
        return t ;
    }

    public Complex mulComplex ( Complex y )
    {
        Complex t ;
        t = new Complex( ) ;
        t.real = real * y.real - imag * y.imag ;
        t.imag = real * y.imag + y.real * imag ;
        return t ;
    }
}

public class ComplexNumbersProject
{
    public static void main ( String[ ] args ) throws Exception
```

```
    {
        Complex c1, c2, c3 ;

        c1 = new Complex( ) ;
        c1.setData ( 2.0f, 2.0f ) ;
        c2 = new Complex( ) ;
        c3 = new Complex( ) ;
        c3 = c1.addComplex ( c2 ) ;
        System.out.println ( "Complex c3:" ) ;
        c3.displayData( ) ;

        Complex c4, c5, c6 ;

        c4 = new Complex( ) ;
        c4.getData( ) ;
        c5 = new Complex ( 2.5f, 3.0f ) ;
        c6 = new Complex( ) ;
        c6 = c4.mulComplex ( c5 ) ;
        System.out.println ( "Complex c6:" ) ;
        c6.displayData( ) ;

        Complex c7 ;
        c7 = new Complex( ) ;
        c7 = c1.addComplex ( c2.mulComplex ( c3 ) ) ;
        System.out.println ( "Complex c7:" ) ;
        c7.displayData( ) ;
    }
}
```

In this program we have once again used overloaded constructors and functions **getData( )** and **setData( )** to set up values of data items in different objects. To add two complex numbers we have called the member function **addComplex( )** through the statement,

```
c3 = c1.addComplex ( c2 ) ;
```

Here, the complex numbers **c1** and **c2** are being added and the result is being stored in **c3**. Out of **c1** and **c2**, **c2** is being passed explicitly, whereas **c1** becomes accessible to **addComplex( )** through a mechanism of **this** reference. This mechanism would be discussed in the next section. The syntax for arguments that are objects is the same as that for arguments that are simple data types like **ints** or **floats**. The complex object's reference returned by **addComplex( )** is collected in **c3**.

The call to **mulComplex( )** function works similarly:

```
c6 = c4.mulComplex ( c5 ) ;
```

There is another interesting call in this program:

```
c7 = c1.addComplex ( c2.mulComplex ( c3 ) ) ;
```

Here, result of multiplication of **c2** and **c3** gets added to **c1** and the result of addition gets stored in **c7**. What you must be wondering is, where does the result of multiplication of **c2** and **c3** gets stored when it is returned by **mulComplex( )**? Well, this result gets collected in a temporary object, and then this temporary object is passed to **addComplex( )**.

We could as well have implemented the addition and multiplication functions in the manner shown below.

```
void addComplex ( Complex x, Complex y )
{
    Complex t ;
    real = x.real + y.real ;
    imag = x.imag + y.imag ;
}
void mulComplex ( Complex x, Complex y )
{
    real = x.real * y.real - x.imag * y.imag ;
    imag = x.real * y.imag + y.real * x.imag ;
}
```

If we implement the functions in this fashion, the way they are called would also change. The calls would now look like this:

```
c3.addComplex ( c1, c2 ) ;
c6.mulComplex ( c4, c5 ) ;
```

Here, in the first call **c1** and **c2** are being passed explicitly, whereas, **c3** would be available to **addComplex( )** through the **this** reference mechanism. Similarly, in the second call, **c4** and **c5** are being passed explicitly, whereas, **c6** would be available through the **this** reference mechanism. Can we use both the forms of **addComplex( )** and **mulComplex( )** in the same class? Of course, you can. They would then be treated as overloaded functions. In such a case, you would have the flexibility of calling them in any of the two ways discussed above.

The *this* Reference

Whenever we call a member function of a class using an object, in addition to the parameters that are explicitly being passed to the function, address of the object is also passed to it implicitly. This address is implicitly collected by the member function in a reference with a special name—**this**. Thus, through the **this** reference every member function has access to address of the object through which it is called. The **this** reference ceases to exist when the control returns from the member function. The **this** reference can be treated like any other reference to an object. It can be used to access the data in the object it points to. The following program shows the working of the **this** reference:

```
// Working of this reference
package thisreferenceproject ;

class Example
{
    private int i ;

    public void setData ( int ii )
    {
        i = ii ; // one way to set data
        this.i = ii ; // another way to set data
    }

    public void showData( )
    {
        System.out.println ( i ) ; // one way to display data
        System.out.println ( this.i ) ; // another way to display data
    }
}

public class ThisReferenceProject
{
    public static void main ( String[ ] args )
```

```
    {
        Example e1 ;
        e1 = new Example( ) ;
        e1.setData ( 10 ) ;
        e1.showData( ) ;
    }
}
```

Here is the output of the program...

```
10
10
```

Since the **this** reference contains the address of the object, using it we can reach the data member of the **Example** object through statements like:

```
this.i = ii ; // another way to set data
System.out.println ( this.i ) ; // another way to display data
```

But if we can set the value in **i** and display it without using **this** reference, then why bother about it? There is one situation where we cannot get by without using **this** reference. Suppose that we had defined the **setData( )** function as shown below.

```
public void setData ( int i )
{
    this.i = i ;
}
```

Note that here we have collected the value passed to **setData( )** in the variable **i** and not in **ii**. This local **i** would now conflict with the **private int i** of the **Example** class. So we cannot expect the **private int i** to get set if we use the statement,

```
i = i ;
```

In this case the only way to refer the **private int i** of the **Example** object is to use the **this** reference through a statement,

```
this.i = i ;
```

Static Data and Functions

A class can contain instance data members and static data members. Multiple objects have their own instance data members, whereas, all of them would share the static data members. Static data members are useful when we wish to share some data between all objects. For example, if we wish to keep track of number of objects that have been created so far from a class, we can track it using a static data member, as shown below.

```
// Working of this reference
package sample ;

public class Sample
{
    public static void main ( String[ ] args )
    {
        Ex e1 = new Ex ( 10 ) ;
        Ex.showCount( ) ;
        Ex e2 = new Ex ( 20 ) ;
        Ex.showCount( ) ;
        Ex e3 = new Ex ( 30 ) ;
        Ex.showCount( ) ;
    }
}

class Ex
{
    private int i ;
    private static int count = 0 ;

    public Ex ( int val )
    {
        i = val ;
        count += 1 ;
    }
    public static void showCount( )
    {
        System.out.println ( count ) ;
    }
}
```

In class **Ex** we have an instance data member **i** and a static data member **count**. Each of the three **Ex** objects would have their own **i,** which would be set up with values 10, 20, 30 respectively. All the three objects would share a common **count** variable which would be incremented each time a new object is created. So the latest value of **count** can tell us how many **Ex** objects have been created so far. This value is printed through a static function **showCount( )**. Note the syntax of calling a **static** function—**classname.staticfunctionname( )**. Also note that a static function can access only static data.

Static Block

A **static** block is similar to **static** data members in the sense that it belongs to a class and not to a particular object. The **static** block is executed when the class is first loaded. It is typically used to initialize all the static data of the class at one place. In this block we can also use control instructions to validate the static data before initializing it. We cannot access non-static variables or methods in this block. Take a look at the following program:

```
// Usage of static block
package staticblockproject ;
import java.util.Calendar ;
public class StaticBlockProject
{
    public static void main ( String[ ] args )
    {
        Sample.showDate( ) ;
    }
}

class Sample
{
    private static int y ;
    private static int m ;
    private static int d ;

    // static block
    static
    {
        Calendar cal = Calendar.getInstance( ) ;
```

```
        y = cal.get ( Calendar.YEAR ) ;
        m = cal.get ( Calendar.MONTH ) ;
        d = cal.get ( Calendar.DAY_OF_MONTH ) ;
    }

    public static void showDate( )
    {
        System.out.println ( "Year: " + y ) ;
        System.out.println ( "Month: " + m ) ;
        System.out.println ( "Day: " + d ) ;
    }
}
```

In the static block we have called the **static** method **getInstance( )** of the **Calendar** class. This method creates a **Calendar** object and fills it up with current day, month and year data. We have then extracted this data by calling the **get( )** method of **Calendar** class.

Passing Objects to a Function

The way we can pass primitives to a function, we can also pass objects to a function. Since objects are nameless, while passing an object, we actually pass only its reference. The called function can collect this passed reference in another reference. Since only the address of the object has been passed, this reference in the function also points to the same object. So using it, if we change the values in the object, then we are actually changing the original object. The following program illustrates this fact.

```
package passingobjectsproject
public class PassingObjectsProject
{
    public static void main ( String[ ] args )
    {
        Ex e = new Ex( ) ;
        e.setData ( 1, 2.5f ) ;
        e.displayData( ) ;
        fun ( e ) ;
        e.displayData( ) ;
    }

    static void fun ( Ex  p )
```

```
    {
        p.setData ( 3, 8.5f ) ;
    }
}

class Ex
{
    private int i ;
    private float f ;

    public void setData ( int x, float y )
    {
        i = x ;
        f = y ;
    }

    public void displayData( )
    {
        System.out.println ( i + " " + f ) ;
    }
}
```

The second call to **displayData( )** prints the values 3 and 8.5, proving that through **fun( )** when we manipulate the object, the original object gets modified.

Exercise

[A] What will be the output of the following programs?

(a)
```
package sampleproject ;
class MyDate
{
    private int dd, mm, yy ;
    public MyDate( )
    {
        System.out.println ( "Reached here" ) ;
        System.out.println ( this ) ;
    }
}
public class SampleProject
{
    public static void main ( String[ ] args )
    {
        MyDate today = new MyDate( ) ;
        MyDate tomorrow = new MyDate( ) ;
    }
}
```

(b)
```
package sampleproject ;
class StudentRecord
{
    private int m1, m2, m3 ;
    private float percentage ;
    public StudentRecord( )
    {
        m1 = m2 = m3 = 0 ;
        percentage = 0.0f ;
    }
    public void calculatePercentage ( int x, int y, int z )
    {
        m1 = x ; m2 = y ; m3 = z ;
        percentage = ( m1 + m2 + m3 ) / 3.0f ;
    }
    public void displayPercentage( )
    {
        System.out.println ( "Percentage = " + percentage ) ;
    }
```

```
}
public class SampleProject
{
    public static void main ( String[ ] args )
    {
        StudentRecord s1 ;
        s1 = new StudentRecord( ) ;
        s1.displayPercentage( ) ;
        s1.calculatePercentage ( 35, 35, 35 ) ;
        s1.displayPercentage( ) ;
    }
}
```

(c)
```
package SampleProject ;
class Sample
{
    public static int d,m,y ;

    static
    {
        d = m = y = 10 ;
    }
    public Sample( )
    {
        y++ ; m++ ; d++ ;
    }
    public static void Show( )
    {
        System.out.println ( "y : " + y ) ;
        System.out.println ( "m: " + m ) ;
        System.out.println ( "d: " + d ) ;
    }
}
class SampleProject
{
    static void Main ( string[ ] args )
    {
        Sample s = new Sample( ) ;
        s.Show( ) ;
    }
}
```

[B] Answer the following:

(a) What are the two major components of an object?

(b) Where do objects get created in memory?

(c) Once objects are created in memory, are they accessed using their names or their references?

(d) Do member functions occupy space in objects?

(e) Can we create an object **s** of class **Sample** through a statement,

```
sample s ;
```

(f) How does a member function come to know on which object it has to work upon?

(g) What is the type of **this** reference?

(h) When does a **this** reference get created?

(i) Is it true that all objects in Java are created dynamically? If true why?

(j) Is it true that in a class data members are always private, whereas member functions are always public?

(k) Is it true that a class declaration creates space in memory for the members defined in it?

(l) Is it necessary that a constructor in a class should always be **public**?

(m) Is size of an object equal to sum of sizes of data members and member functions within the class?

(n) Define a class **Cartesian** which stores the Cartesian co-ordinates of a point. Define another class **Polar** which stores Polar co-ordinates of a point. Make a provision to convert co-ordinates from Cartesian to Polar and vice-versa.

```
// Polar to Cartesian conversion
x = radius * cos ( angle )
y = radius * sin ( angle )

// Cartesian to Polar conversion
angle = a tan ( x / y )
radius = sqrt ( x * x + y * y )
```

(o) Can we access non-static or instance member functions from the **static** block?

(p) If a method is called using two different objects, then would **this** reference contain same addresses during each call?

[C] Attempt the following:

(a) When the following code snippet is executed would contents of **s1** and **s2** be same or different?

```
// Sample is a user-defined class
Sample s1, s2 ;
s1 = new Sample( ) ;
s2 = new Sample( ) ;
```

(b) When the following code snippet is executed where would the object and the reference be created in memory?

```
Sample c ;
c = new Sample( ) ;
```

(c) Is it true that objects are always nameless and depending upon their size they either get created in the stack or on the heap?

(d) What is Garbage Collector? How is it important when working with classes and objects in Java?

(e) How many times can a constructor be called during lifetime of the object?

(f) Is it possible for you to prevent an object from being created by using zero-argument constructor? If yes, how?

(g) Constructor cannot return any value. If constructor fails, how do you let the caller know?

(h) Is it possible to call constructor for a class explicitly?

(i) What is a static constructor? When is it called?

(j) Is it possible to invoke Garbage Collector explicitly? If yes, how can it be done?

(k) Is it recommended that you provide **finalize( )** a method in all your classes?

(l) Can **static** procedures access instance data? If not, why not?

KanNotes

- Classes are user-defined data types
- Classes indicate how the objects created from them would look like
- Objects have specific data. Each object is a specific instance of a class
- Data values in objects are often called instance data or state of the object
- In a class data members are usually private, whereas member functions are usually public
- public members of a class are accessible from outside the class
- private members of a class are NOT accessible from outside class
- Within a class any member can access any other member
- By default class members are public
- Usually data in a class is kept private and the data is accessed / manipulated through public member functions of the class
- In principle every object has instance data and member functions
- In practice each object has instance data, whereas member functions are shared amongst objects
- Sharing is justified as from one object to another member functions are going to remain same
- Objects are nameless
- Objects are referred using references created on stack
- Objects are created on heap using new operator, which returns address (reference) of the object on its creation

- Usage of "this" reference is optional
- this is a constant reference - final
- this reference cannot be modified during execution of the method
- this reference dies once control returns from the method
- Three ways to initialize an object :

  Method 1 & 2 :

  Using member function like getData( ) / setData( )
  Benefit 1 - Data is protected from manipulation
  Benefit 2 - Better validation as it is done at one place
  Benefit 3 - Validation done by class designer

  Method 3 :

  Using special member function – Constructor
  Benefit 1 - Program is better organized
  Benefit 2 - Guaranteed initialization through constructor (Ctor)
- When an object is created, space is allocated in memory and Ctor is called
- Name of Ctor must be same as name of class
- Ctor is a function
- Ctor doesn't return any value
- Ctor gets called automatically when an object is created
- Ctor is called only once during entire lifetime of an object
- Ctor can be overloaded
- If we don't define a Ctor, compiler inserts a 0-arg Ctor
- A class may have Ctor as well as setData()

  Ctor – To initialize object
  setData() – To modify object

- finalize() method is called when an object is about to be destroyed
- finalize( ) method is called by Java Runtime just before garbage collection
- finalize() method is Not called when an object goes out of scope
- finalize() method is used to free non-Java resource like file handle of font
- A class can contain instance data and static data
- A class can contain instance functions and static functions
- Instance functions can access instance data and static data
- Static functions can access only static data
- Access from outside the class :
  Instance function : Object.function()
  Static function : Class.function()
  Object.function() - works, but is misleading
- An instance function can be called only after creating an object
- A static function can be called anytime
- this reference is never passed to a static function
- Static block gets executed exactly once when the class is loaded
- A static block can contain control instructions for validating data
- A static block is used to initialize all static data at one place
- Functions are called only by value. There is no call by reference. So when we pass an object to a function, we are actually passing its reference, by value

Arrays 11

Data abounds in nature and its problems. So when you have a lot of it to deal with, Arrays is a good answer...

Let Us JAVA 3rd Edition

Chapter Contents

The Java language provides a capability that enables the user to design a set of similar data types, called array. This chapter describes how arrays can be created and manipulated in Java. We would also discuss how and why arrays are implemented as objects.

What are Arrays

Suppose we wish to arrange the percentage marks obtained by 50 students in ascending order. To do this we must first be able to hold 50 students marks in memory. In such a case, we have two options to store these marks in memory:

(a) Construct 50 variables, each containing one student's marks.
(b) Construct one variable capable of storing all 50 values.

Obviously, the second alternative is better, as it would be much easier to handle one variable than handling 50 variables. Such a variable capable of storing multiple values is called an array.

An array is a collection of similar elements—all **int**s, or all **float**s, or all **char**s, etc. Usually, the array of characters is called a 'string', whereas an array of **int**s or **float**s is called simply an array. Remember that we cannot have an array of 10 numbers, of which 5 are **int**s and 5 are **float**s.

A Simple Program using Array

Let us try to write a program to find average marks obtained by a class of 30 students in a test. Here is the program...

```
// First array program
package firstarrayprogramproject ;
import java.io.* ;

public class FirstArrayProgramProject
{
    public static void main ( String[ ] args )
    {
        int  i, avg, sum = 0 ;

        int[ ] marks ;
        marks = new int[ 30 ] ;

        BufferedReader br = new BufferedReader (
                                    new InputStreamReader ( System.in )
) ;
```

```
        // store data in the array
        for ( i = 0 ; i <= 29 ; i++ )
        {
            System.out.println ( "Enter marks " ) ;
            marks[ i ] = Integer.parseInt ( br.readLine( ) ) ;
        }

        // read data from the array
        for ( i = 0 ; i <= 29 ; i++ )
            sum = sum + marks[ i ] ;

        avg = sum / 30 ;
        System.out.println ( "Average marks = "+ avg ) ;
    }
}
```

There is a lot of new material in this program, so let us understand it part-by-part.

Array Declaration

Like other variables, an array needs to be declared. In our program, we have done this with the statement:

```
int[ ] marks ;
```

This statement tells the compiler that **marks** is a reference to an array of integers.

Once the reference to the array is declared we have to allocate space for the array in memory. This is done using the statement,

```
marks = new int[ 30 ] ;
```

This statement allocates space for 30 integers in memory and returns the base address (starting address) of this memory chunk. This returned address gets stored in the reference **marks**. The array that gets created in heap it doesn't have any name. It is always referred to using **marks,** the reference to the array, which is stored in the stack.

Accessing Elements of an Array

Once an array is created, its individual elements can be accessed using the element's position in the array. All the array elements are counted, starting with 0. Thus, **marks[2]** is not the second element of the array, but the third. In our program, we are using the variable **i** to refer to various elements of the array. This variable can take different values and hence can refer to different elements in the array in turn. This ability to use variables to represent position of array elements makes arrays very useful.

Entering Data into an Array

Here is the section of code that places data into an array:

```
for ( i = 0 ; i <= 29 ; i++ )
{
     System.out.println ( "Enter marks " ) ;
     marks[ i ] = Integer.parseInt ( br.readLine( ) ) ;
}
```

First time through the loop, **i** has a value 0, so the first value read through **readLine( )** function will be stored in **marks[0]**. This process will be repeated 30 times till the last values gets stored at **marks[29]**.

Reading Data from an Array

The balance program reads the data back out of the array and uses it to calculate the average. The **for** loop is much the same, but now the body of the loop causes each student's marks to be added to a running total stored in a variable **sum**. When all the marks have been added up, the result is divided by 30, the number of students, to get the average.

More on Arrays

Array is a very popular data type with Java programmers. This is because of the convenience with which arrays lend themselves to programming. The features which make arrays so convenient to program would be discussed below, along with the possible pitfalls in using them.

Array Initialization

In the program in the previous section we have used and array that did not have any values in it to begin with. We managed to store values in it during program execution. Let us now see how to initialize an array while declaring it. Following are a few examples that demonstrate this:

```
int[ ] ages = new int[ ] { 32, 24, 31, 25, 26 } ;
float[ ] press = { 12.3f, 34.2f, -23.4f, -11.3f } ;
```

```
int[ ] num = { 2, 4, 1, 5, 6, 3 } ;
```

If the array is initialized where it is declared, there is no need to use the **new** operator for creating an array as shown in the second and the third examples above. Also, when we initialize the arrays in this manner, we are not allowed to mention the size of the array in [ ].

Note that both the following definitions are acceptable.

```
int[ ] num = { 2, 4, 1, 5, 6, 3 } ;
int num[ ] = { 2, 4, 1, 5, 6, 3 } ;
```

Array Access

In Java we can access array elements using any of the following three methods:

```
int[ ] marks = { 55, 65, 75, 56, 78, 78, 90 } ;
int i ;

// method 1
for ( i = 0 ; i <= 6 ; i++ )
    System.out.print ( marks[ i ] + "  " ) ;

// method 2
for ( i = 0 ; i <= marks.length - 1 ; i++ )
    System.out.print ( marks[ i ] + "  " ) ;

// method 3
for ( int j : marks )
    System.out.print ( j + "  " ) ;
```

The first method is as usual. In the second method we have obtained the number of elements in the array using its **length** property. In the third method, we don't have to worry about the number of elements in the array, as **j** takes different values present in **marks[ ]** array during each iteration through the loop.

Bounds Checking

In Java while accessing array elements if we exceed the bounds of the array an error would be reported during execution of the program. For example, if the following code snippet is executed an error would be reported as **num[6]** does not exist.

```
int [ ] num = { 2, 4, 12, 5, 45, 5 } ;
num[ 6 ] = 72 ;
```

Passing Array Elements to a Function

Like normal variables, we can also pass array elements to a function by calling the function. This is illustrated below.

```
// Demonstration of passing array elements
package passingarrayelementsproject ;
public class PassingArrayElementsProject
{
    public static void main ( String[ ] args )
    {
        int [ ] marks = { 55, 65, 75, 56, 78, 78, 90 } ;
        int i ;

        for ( i = 0 ; i <= 6 ; i++ )
            modify ( marks[ i ] ) ;

        for ( i = 0 ; i <= 6 ; i++ )
            System.out.println ( marks[ i ] ) ;
    }
    static void modify ( int  m )
    {
        m = m * 2 ;
    }
}
```

And here's the output...

```
55 65 75 56 78 78 90
```

Here, we are passing an individual array element at a time to the function **modify( ).** Since at a time only one element is being passed, this element is collected in an integer variable **m**. Even though we are doubling each element received in **m** in the **modify( )**, on return when we print all array elements we find that they have not been doubled at all. This is because we passed each array element by value.

Passing Array Reference to a Function

If we want that the modifications we make in the **modify( )** function should be reflected back in **main( )**, then we need to pass the reference to the array, instead of passing each individual element. This is shown in the following program:

```
// Passing array reference
package passarrayreferenceproject ;

public class PassArrayReferenceProject
{
    public static void main ( String[ ] args )
    {
        int[ ] marks = { 55, 65, 75, 56, 78, 78, 90 } ;
        int i ;

        modify ( marks ) ;

        for ( i = 0 ; i <= marks.length - 1 ; i++ )
            System.out.print ( marks[ i ] + " " ) ;
    }

    static void modify ( int[ ] m )
    {
        int i ;
        for ( i = 0 ; i <= m.length - 1 ; i++ )
            m[ i ] = m[ i ] * 2 ;
    }
}
```

The output of the program would be as under:

```
110 130 150 112 156 156 180
```

The array reference passed to **modify( )** is collected in another array reference **m**. **m** is a reference to the same array, as it contains the same address that is present in **marks**. Using this reference when we modify the array elements we are changing the array that we defined in **main( )**. So once control returns to **main( )**, using **marks** when we print this array we find that the array elements stand doubled.

Returning an Array

The way we can pass an array to a function, can we return an array from a function? Certainly. Even here what we would be returning would only be a reference to the array. The following program shows how this can be done:

```
package returningarrayproject ;

public class ReturningArrayProject
{
    public static void main ( String[ ] args )
    {
        int[ ] p ;
        p = func( ) ;
        for ( int i = 0 ; i <= p.length - 1 ; i++ )
            System.out.println ( p[ i ] + " " ) ;
    }

    static int[ ] func( )
    {
        int [ ] arr = { 10, 20, 30, 40, 50 } ;
        return arr ;
    }
}
```

Here the reference to the array **arr** is returned from **func( )** and collected in reference **p** in **main( )**. Using this reference when we iterate through the array in the **for** loop we are able to access all the elements of **arr**.

Common Array Operations

There are certain operations that are very commonly carried out on arrays. For example, rearranging array elements in ascending or descending order, or searching an element in an array, etc. To carry out these operations the Java Library provides a class called **Arrays**. The following program shows how to perform these operations using the **Arrays** class:

```
// Performing different array operations
package morearrayoperationsproject ;
import java.util.* ;
```

```
public class MoreArrayOperationsProject
{
    public static void main ( String[ ] args )
    {
        int [ ] arr = { 23, 45, 11, 54, 89, 32 } ;
        int i ;

        System.out.println ( "Original array" ) ;
        for ( i = 0 ; i < arr.length ; i++ )
            System.out.print ( arr[ i ] + " " ) ;

        Arrays.sort ( arr ) ;
        System.out.println ( "\nSorted array" ) ;
        for ( i = 0 ; i < arr.length ; i++ )
            System.out.print ( arr[ i ] + " " ) ;

        int index = Arrays.binarySearch ( arr, 54 ) ;
        System.out.println ( "\nElement 54 found at "+ index ) ;

        int[ ] newarr = new int[ 6 ] ;
        newarr = Arrays.copyOf ( arr, arr.length ) ;
        System.out.println ( "New array contents" ) ;
        for ( i = 0 ; i < newarr.length ; i++ )
            System.out.print ( newarr[ i ] + " " ) ;

        Arrays.fill ( arr, 0 ) ;
        System.out.println ( "\nCleared array" ) ;
        for ( i = 0; i < arr.length; i++ )
            System.out.print ( arr[ i ] + " " ) ;
        System.out.println( );
    }
}
```

Given below is the output of the program...

```
Original array
23 45 11 54 89 32
Sorted array
11 23 32 45 54 89
Element 54 found at 4
New array contents
```

11 23 32 45 54 89
Cleared array
0 0 0 0 0 0

The **sort( )** function arranges the elements of the array in ascending order, whereas, the **binarySearch( )** function searches for an element in the sorted array and reports its position in the array. The **copyOf( )** function copies the contents of one array into another, whereas **fill( )** function sets each array elements value to 0. You can watch these effects in the output of the program. All these functions are **static** functions, hence the syntax used to call them is **classname.functioname( )**. You can try your hand at other functions present in the **Arrays** class to get a hang of them.

You can also rely on context-sensitive help to get to know methods of the **Arrays** class. That is, as you type the word array and a '.' NetBeans pops up a list of methods available in this class. This list acts as a quick reference.

Array of Objects

So far we have constructed an array of pre-defined types like integers or floats. It is also possible to create an array of user-defined types as well. For example, we can create an array of 3 **Sample** objects as shown below.

```
// Creating and handling array of objects
package arrayofobjectsproject ;

class Sample
{
    private int i ;
    private float a ;

    public Sample ( int ii, float aa )
    {
        i = ii ;
        a = aa ;
    }

    public void display( )
    {
        System.out.println ( "i = " + i + " a = "+ a ) ;
```

```
    }
}

public class ArrayOfObjectsProject
{
    public static void main ( String[ ] args )
    {
        Sample[ ] arr = new Sample[ 3 ] ;
        arr[ 0 ] = new Sample ( 10, 3.14f ) ;
        arr[ 1 ] = new Sample ( 20, 6.28f ) ;
        arr[ 2 ] = new Sample ( 30, 3.55f ) ;
        for ( Sample s : arr )
            s.display( ) ;
    }
}
```

The output of the program would be as follows:

```
i = 10 a = 3.14
i = 20 a = 6.28
i = 30 a = 3.55
```

As objects get created in a heap, strictly speaking the array is not an array of objects, but an array of references to objects. This is shown in Figure 11.1.

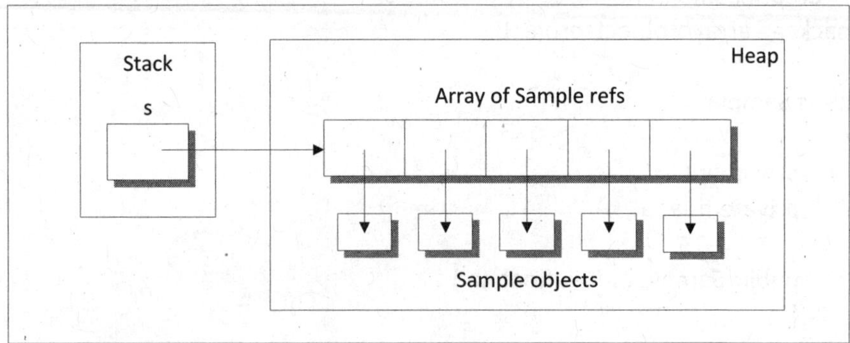

Figure 11.1

Once the array is created we can iterate through it using the **for** loop, calling **display( )** function for each object in turn. This is justified by the output of the program.

There is a more compact way in which we could have initialized the array of objects. This is shown below.

```
Sample[ ] arr = {
                    new Sample ( 10, 3.14f ),
                    new Sample ( 20, 6.28f ),
                    new Sample ( 30, 3.55f )
                };
```

Multi-Dimensional Arrays

So far, we have explored arrays with only one dimension. It is also possible for arrays to have two or more dimensions. The two-dimensional array is also called a matrix. Here is a simple program that stores numbers in a matrix and then reports the biggest number and its position in the matrix.

```
package twodarrayproject ;

public class Main
{
    public static void main ( String[ ] args )
    {
        int[ ][ ] a = { { 7, 2, 6, 1 }, { 3, 5, 4, 8 }, { 6, 2, 9, 50 } } ;
        int i, j, big ;
        int r, c ;

        big = a[ 0 ][ 0 ] ;
        r = 0 ;
        c = 0 ;

        for ( i = 0; i < a.length  ; i++ )
        {
            for ( j = 0 ; j < a[ i ].length ; j++ )
            {
                if ( a[ i ][ j ] > big )
                {
                    big = a[ i ][ j ] ;
                    r = i ;
                    c = j ;
                }
            }
```

```
            }
            System.out.println ( "Biggest number = "+ big ) ;
            System.out.println ( "Row = " + r + " Col = "+ c ) ;
        }
}
```

There are two parts to the program—in the first part, we define and initialize a 2-D array of 3 rows and 4 columns of integers, whereas, in the second part through a set of **for** loops, we find out the value of the biggest number in the 2-D array.

In **a[i][j]** the first subscript of the variable **a**, is row number. The second subscript tells which of the four columns we are talking about. Remember the counting of rows and columns begin with zero. Thus, 7 is stored in **a[0][0]**, 8 is stored in **a[1][3]** and so on.

Instead of initializing the 2-D array in-place we can also receive its values from the keyboard as shown below.

```
int [ ][ ] a = new int[ 3 ][ 4 ] ;
BufferedReader br = new BufferedReader (
                        new InputStreamReader ( System.in ) ) ;
for ( int i = 0; i < a.length ; i++ )
{
    for ( int j = 0 ; j < a[ i ].length ; j++ )
        a[ i ][ j ] = Integer.parseInt ( br.readLine( ) ) ;
}
```

On similar lines we can construct a 3-D array as a collection of several 2-D arrays.

Passing and Returning 2-D Array

We can pass a 2-D array to a function by passing its reference. Similarly, we can return a 2-D array from a function by returning its reference. This is illustrated in the following program:

```
package passingandreturning2darraysproject ;
public class PassingAndReturning2dArraysProject
{
    public static void main ( String[ ] args )
    {
        int[ ][ ] a = { { 1, 2, 3 }, { 4, 5, 6 } } ;
```

```
        int sum ;

        sum = getSum ( a ) ;
        System.out.println ( "Sum = "+ sum ) ;

        int[ ][ ] d ;
        d = getArray( ) ;
        int i, j, prod = 0 ;
        for ( i = 0 ; i < d.length ; i++ )
        {
            for ( j = 0 ; j < d[ i ].length ; j++ )
                prod = prod + d[ i ][ j ] ;
        }
        System.out.println ( "Product = "+ prod ) ;
    }

    public static int getSum ( int[ ][ ] b )
    {
        int i, j ;
        int s = 0 ;
        for ( i = 0 ; i < b.length ; i++ )
        {
            for ( j = 0 ; j < b[ i ].length; j++ )
                s = s + b[ i ][ j ] ;
        }
        return ( s ) ;
    }

    public static int[ ][ ] getArray( )
    {
        int[ ][ ] c = { { 1, 2, 3 }, { 4, 5, 6 }, { 7, 8, 9 } } ;
        return c ;
    }
}
```

And here is the output...

```
Sum = 21
Product = 45
```

Here in **main( )** we have defined a 2-D array and then passed it to the function **getSum( )**. The **getSum( )** function collects the reference to the

2-D array passed to it in **b**. Using this reference it then accesses all the array elements and adds them up. This sum is then returned to **main( )** which promptly prints it.

Next, **main( )** calls the function **getArray( )**. This function defines another 2-D array **c**, and returns its reference to **main( )**. When control returns from **getArray( )** even though the reference **c** dies, since the reference **d** points to the 2-D array, the array doesn't get collected by the Garbage Collector. Once in **main( )** it iterates through the 2-D array, this time calculating the product of all its elements. This product is then printed out.

From this program it is evident that whenever we have to pass or return an array all that we have to do is pass or return a reference to the array.

Jagged Arrays

It is not necessary that each row of a 2-D array would always have same number of columns. For example, the arrangement of seats in an auditorium is like a 2-D array, but number of seats in each row may not be equal. If we are to represent these seats in a 2-D array in Java we have to use jagged arrays. A jagged array permits unequal number of elements in each row of a 2-D array.

Let us now construct a 2-D jagged array containing 3 rows. The number of elements in these three rows is 4, 3 and 2, respectively. So the arrangement of this jagged array would be as shown in Figure 11.2.

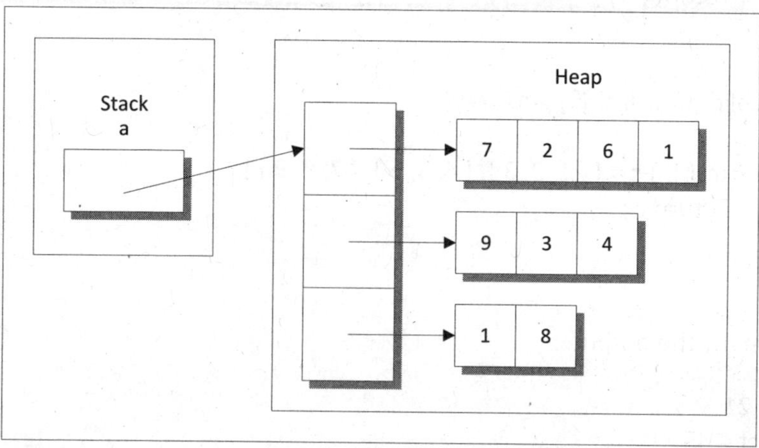

Figure 11.2

Here is a program that implements this jagged array.

```
// Implementation of a 2-D Jagged array
package twodjaggedarrayproject ;

public class Main
{
    public static void main ( String[ ] args )
    {
        int[ ][ ] a = new int[ 3 ][ ] ;
        a[ 0 ] = new int[ 4 ] ;
        a[ 1 ] = new int[ 3 ] ;
        a[ 2 ] = new int[ 2 ] ;

        a[ 0 ][ 0 ] = 7 ; a[ 0 ][ 1 ] = 2 ; a[ 0 ][ 2 ] = 6 ; a[ 0 ][ 3 ] = 1 ;
        a[ 1 ][ 0 ] = 9 ; a[ 1 ][ 1 ] = 3 ; a[ 1 ][ 2 ] = 4 ;
        a[ 2 ][ 0 ] = 1 ; a[ 2 ][ 1 ] = 8 ;

        for ( int i = 0 ; i < a.length ; i++ )
        {
            for ( int j = 0 ; j < a[ i ].length ; j++ )
                System.out.print ( a[ i ][ j ] + ", " ) ;

            System.out.println( ) ;
        }
    }
}
```

In this program **a** is a reference that refers to an array of references. Each reference in this array refers to a 1-D array of integers. Note how we have iterated through the jagged array. In the outer **for** loop we have used **a.length** to obtain number of 1-D integer arrays present in the jagged array, whereas in the inner for loop we have used **a[i].length** to obtain the number of integers in each 1-D array. I would leave it for you to figure out the output of this program.

There are two more ways in which we could have defined and initialized the jagged array. These are shown below.

```
// one more way to define the jagged array
int[ ][ ] a = { new int[ 4 ], new int[ 3 ], new int[ 2 ] } ;
a[ 0 ][ 0 ] = 7 ; a[ 0 ][ 1 ] = 2 ; a[ 0 ][ 2 ] = 6 ; a[ 0 ][ 3 ] = 1 ;
a[ 1 ][ 0 ] = 9 ; a[ 1 ][ 1 ] = 3 ; a[ 1 ][ 2 ] = 4 ;
a[ 2 ][ 0 ] = 1 ; a[ 2 ][ 1 ] = 8 ;
```

```
// yet another way to define the jagged array
int[ ] a1 = new int[ ] { 7, 2, 6, 1 } ;
int[ ] a2 = new int[ ] { 9, 3, 4 } ;
int[ ] a3 = new int[ ] { 1, 8 } ;
int[ ][ ] a = { a1, a2, a3 } ;
```

The way we can pass a normal 2-D array to a function, we can also pass or return a jagged 2-D array to/from a function

Resizing of Arrays

As we know, arrays are created on the heap dynamically during execution of the program. As a result, we can do two things with an array:

(a) We can decide the number of elements in the array at run-time and do not have to make any commitment about it while writing the program.

(b) Once the array is created we can increase or decrease its size during execution.

Let us now see how this can be done programmatically.

```
// Flexible arrays and resizing of arrays
package resizingarrayproject ;
import java.io.* ;

public class ResizingArrayProject
{
    public static void main ( String[ ] args )
    {
        int[ ] arr, newarr ;
        int i, num, newnum ;

        BufferedReader br = new BufferedReader (
                                new InputStreamReader ( System.in ) ) ;

        System.out.println ( "Enter number of students" ) ;
        num = Integer.parseInt ( br.readLine( ) ) ;
        arr = new int[ num ] ;

        System.out.println ( "Enter marks for "+ num + " students" ) ;
        for ( i = 0 ; i < arr.length ; i++ )
```

```
            arr[ i ] = Integer.parseInt ( br.readLine( ) ) ;

        System.out.println ( "Enter additional number of students" ) ;
        newnum = Integer.parseInt ( br.readLine( ) ) ;
        newarr = new int[ num + newnum ] ;

        // copy existing students marks to the new array
        for ( i = 0 ; i < arr.length ; i++ )
            newarr[ i ] = arr[ i ] ;

        System.out.println ( "Enter marks for "+ newnum +
                                            " new students" ) ;
        for ( i = arr.length ; i < newarr.length ; i++ )
            newarr[ i ] = Integer.parseInt ( br.readLine( ) ) ;

        System.out.println ( "The new array now contains" ) ;
        for ( i = 0 ; i < newarr.length ; i++ )
            System.out.print ( newarr[ i ] + " " ) ;
    }
}
```

Shown below is some sample interaction with the program.

```
Enter number of students
5
Enter marks for 5 students
55
43
65
78
66
Enter additional number of students
3
Enter marks for 3 new students
70
80
90
The new array now contains
55 43 65 78 66 70 80 90
```

Look at the way **arr** and **newarr** are defined in one statement:

```
int[ ] arr, newarr ;
```

The **int[ ]** applies to **arr** as well as **newarr**. Both are treated as references to an integer array.

Both these arrays are flexible in the sense that their size is decided by the user of this program during execution. The arrays are created based on the values of **num** and **newnum** supplied by the user during execution.

To increase the size of the array we have created a new array (**newarr**), copied elements of existing array (**arr**) into it and then filled additional values into it after the copied elements.

Once this is done, if we so desire, we can delete the old array by settings its reference to null. If we do so, the array would be reclaimed by the Garbage Collector.

The way this program lets you increase the size of an existing array during execution; if the need arises we can also shrink the size of an existing array during execution.

Exercise

[A] Answer the following:

(a) Which of the following array declarations is correct?

```
int a (25) ;
int size = 10, b[ size ] ;
int[ ] c = { 0, 1, 2 } ;
```

(b) What will happen if you assign a value to an element of an array whose subscript exceeds the size of the array?

(c) When you pass an array as an argument to a function, what actually gets passed?

(d) How will you initialize a three-dimensional array **threed[3][2][3]**? How will you refer the first and last element in this array?

(e) What will be output of the following code snippet?

```
int[ ][ ] a = new int[ 2 ][ ] ;
a[ 0 ] = new int[ ] { 6, 1, 4, 3 } ;
a[ 1 ] = new int[ ] { 9, 2, 7 } ;
System.out.println ( a[ 1 ].Length ) ;
```

(f) What will be the output of the following code snippet?

```
int[ ][ ][ ] a = new int[ 3 ][ 2 ][ 3 ] ;
System.out.println ( a.length ) ;
```

(g) What does a refer to in the following statement?

```
int[ ][ ][ ] a = new int[ 2 ][ ][ ] ;
```

(h) How will you obtain the number of elements present in the array given below?

```
int[ ] a = { 25, 30, 45, 15, 60 } ;
```

(i) How will you define and initialize an array of 5 integers? How will you increase its size to 10 elements?

(j) Which of the following statements are correct about the Java code snippet given below?

```
int[ ][ ] a = new int[ 2 ][ ] ;
a[ 0 ] = new int[ ] { 6, 1, 4, 3 } ;
a[ 1 ] = new int[ ] { 9, 2, 7 } ;
```

1. **a** is a reference to a 2-D jagged array.
2. **a[0]** refers to 0th 1-D array and a[1] refers to the 1st 1-D array.
3. **a** refers to a[0] and a[1].
4. **a** refers to a[1] and a[2].

[B] Attempt the following:

(a) Twenty-five numbers are entered from the keyboard into an array. The number to be searched is entered through the keyboard by the user. Write a program to find if the number to be searched is present in the array and if it is present, display the number of times it appears in the array.

(b) Twenty five numbers are entered from the keyboard into an array. Write a program to find out how many of them are positive, how many are negative, how many are even and how many odd.

(c) Write a program that interchanges the odd and even elements of an array.

(d) Write a program to copy the contents of one array into another in the reverse order.

(e) Write a program to obtain transpose of a 4 x 4 matrix. The transpose of a matrix is obtained by exchanging the elements of each row with the elements of the corresponding column.

(f) The **X** and **Y** coordinates of 10 different points are entered through the keyboard. Write a program to find the distance of last point from the first point (sum of distances between consecutive points).

(g) Create a jagged array of integers. This array should consist of two 2-D arrays. First 2-D array should contain 3 rows having length of 4, 3 and 2, respectively. Second 2-D array should contain 2 rows with length 3 and 4, respectively. Initialize array with suitable elements and display them without using **for** loops.

KanNotes

- Array is a variable capable of holding > 1 value at a time
- Two basic properties of an array :
  1) Similarity - All array elements are similar to one another
  2) Adjacency - All array elements are stored in adjacent memory locations
- 3 ways to declare an array if array elements are not known beforehand :

```
int per[ ] = new int[ 10 ] ;
int per[ ] ; per = new int[ 10 ] ;
int [ ] per ; per = new int[ 10 ] ;
```

- If all array elements are known before-hand array can be defined as

```
int a[ ] = { 7, 6, 11, -2, 26 } ; // Cannot mention the size in this case
```

- Array elements are always counted from 0 onwards. So arr[9] is 10th element
- Array elements can be calculated as in arr[5] = 3 + 7 % 2 ;
- Arithmetic on array elements is allowed as in arr[6] = arr[1] + arr[3] / 16 ;
- Java performs bounds checking on an array and warns if we exceed the bounds
- Three ways to process an array element by element :

```
int a[ ] = { 7, 9, 16, -2, 8 } ; int i ;
for ( i = 0 ; i <= 4 ; i++ )
    System.out.println ( a[ i ] ) ;

for ( i = 0 ; i < a.length ; i++ )  // length is property of an array
    System.out.println ( a[ i ] ) ;

for ( int item : a )  // special for loop for processing an array
    System.out.println ( item ) ;
```

- Array is implemented as an object, hence it is nameless. It is created on the heap and its reference is set in the stack. The reference contains the base address of the array object.

- It is possible to increase or decrease the array size during execution

- It is possible to free the array during execution for the garbage collector to collect it

- Passing an array to a function and returning an array from a function is similar as in both cases we are passing a reference or returning a reference

```
public static void int [] display ( int [] p ) // p - array reference
{
    int a[] = { 1, 4, 6, 2, 8 } ;
    return a ; // returns an array reference
}
```

- 2D array is a collection of several 1D arrays

```
int a[ ][ ] = { { 2, 3, 11, 4 }, { 4, 7, 8, 9 }, { 33, 2, 1, 1 } } ;
```

  Cannot mention dimensions as array is being initialized in place
  { } for each 1D array are compulsory
  , after each 1D array is compulsory
  a is a reference, it would be created on stack
  a would refer to an array of references (on heap). Each reference in this array would refer to a 1D array of integers

- a.length will give 3 as there are 3 1D arrays in the 2D array

- a[2].length will give 4 as there are 4 elements in the 2nd 1D array

- Passing and returning a 2D array is similar to passing and returning a 1D array

12

Strings and Enums

Strictly speaking, we can create Java programs without Strings and Enums. But, once you see the elegance that they add to your working, you would never give them up...

Let Us JAVA 3rd Edition

Chapter Contents

In the last chapter, you learnt how to define arrays of various sizes and dimensions, how to initialize them, how to pass them to a function, etc. With this knowledge under your belt, you should be ready to handle strings, which are, simply put, a special kind of array. And strings and the ways to manipulate them are going to be the topics of discussion in this chapter.

What are Strings?

The way a group of integers can be stored in an integer array, similarly a group of characters can be stored in a character array. Character arrays can be used to manipulate text, such as words and sentences. The nature of operations that can be carried out on a collection of characters are slightly different than the operations that can be carried out on a collection of numbers. For example, characters in an array can be converted to upper case or lower case. There is no such parallel operation on a numeric array. So common is the usage of character arrays, that to deal with them, Java library provides a special class called **String**. Java makes a further relaxation while creating objects of this class—even though it is a reference type, we don't have to use the **new** operator to create it. We can create it like an **int** or a **float**. This is shown below.

```
String s1 = "Lionel" ;
String s2 = "Messi" ;
```

Here **s1** and **s2** are references to two **String** objects. We can display these strings simply by saying:

```
System.out.println ( s1 ) ;
System.out.println ( s2 ) ;
```

The **String** class has an overloaded + operator using which we can append one string at the end of another. This is shown below.

```
String s1 = "Diego" ;
String s2 = "Maradona" ;
s1 = s1 + s2 ;
System.out.println ( s1 ) ;
```

This would produce the output LionelMessi. This code snippet makes it appear as if the string **s2** simply got attached at the end of **s1**, thereby changing **s1**. However, internally something different happened. This is because strings in Java are immutable. So when we attempted to do the append operation, a new string object containing "LinoelMessi" got created and **s1** was made to refer to this new string object instead of the old string object "Lionel".

Look at the following code:

```
String s1 = "Hoopster" ;
String s2 = "Hoopster";
if ( s1 == s2 )
    System.out.println ( "Equal" ) ;
else
    System.out.println ( "Unequal" ) ;
```

Here, when we create the second string, a new string object is not created. Instead **s2** is made to refer to the same string "Hoopster" to which **s1** is referring. Thus **s1** and **s2** both are referring to the same string. Therefore the condition in **if** is satisfied. As against this, in the following code **s3** and **s4** are referring to two different string objects, so the condition in **if** fails.

```
String s3 = new String ( "Hoopster" ) ;
String s4 = new String ( "Shuttler" ) ;
if ( s3 == s4 )
    System.out.println ( "Equal" ) ;
else
    System.out.println ( "Unequal" ) ;
```

In this case to check whether the contents of the two **String** objects are same we should use the following code:

```
if ( s3.equals ( s4 ) )
    System.out.println ( "Equal" ) ;
else
    System.out.println ( "Unequal" ) ;
```

More about Strings

Let us now try different operations on strings. For this we would take help of several methods defined in the **String** class. It is not possible to discuss every of these methods. Instead, I would show how to use the more commonly needed methods with the help of a program. Here is the program...

```
// Different string operations
package usingstringsproject ;

public class Main
{
    public static void main ( String[ ] args )
    {
        String s1 = "kicit" ;
        String s2 = "Nagpur" ;
        System.out.println ( "Char at 3rd pos: " + s1.charAt ( 2 ) ) ;

        String s3 ;
        s3 = s1.concat ( s2 ) ;
        System.out.println ( s3 ) ;

        System.out.println ( "Length of s3: " + s3.length( ) ) ;

        s3 = s3.replace ( "p", "P" ) ;
        System.out.println ( s3 ) ;

        s3 = String.copyValueOf ( s2.toCharArray( ) ) ;
        System.out.println ( s3 ) ;

        int c ;
        c = s2.compareTo ( s3 ) ;
        if ( c < 0 )
            System.out.println ( "s2 is less than s3" ) ;
        else if ( c == 0 )
            System.out.println ( "s2 is equal to s3" ) ;
        else
            System.out.println ( "s2 is greater than s3" ) ;

        if ( s1 == s3 )
            System.out.println ( "s1 is equal to s3" ) ;
        else
            System.out.println ( "s1 is not equal to s3" ) ;

        s3 = s1.toUpperCase( ) ;
        System.out.println ( s3 ) ;

        s3 = s2.concat ( "Mumbai" ) ;
```

```
        System.out.println ( s3 ) ;

        s3 = s2.replace ( s2.charAt ( 0 ), ' ' ) ;
        System.out.println ( s3 ) ;

        int fin, lin ;
        fin = s1.indexOf ( "i" ) ;
        System.out.println ( "First index of i in s1: " + fin ) ;
        lin = s1.lastIndexOf ( "i" ) ;
        System.out.println ( "Last index of i in s1: " + lin ) ;

        String s ;
        s = s1.substring ( fin, lin + 1 ) ;
        System.out.println ( "Substring: " + s ) ;

        int i = 10 ;
        float f = 9.8f ;
        s3 = String.format ( "Value of i = %d Value of f = %f" , i, f ) ;
        System.out.println ( s3 ) ;
    }
}
```

The output of the program is shown below:

```
Char at 3rd pos: c
kicitNagpur
Length of s3: 11
kicitNagPur
Nagpur
s2 is equal to s3
s1 is not equal to s3
KICIT
NagpurMumbai
 agpur
First index of i in s1: 1
Last index of i in s1: 3
Substring: ici
Value of i = 10 Value of f : 9.8
```

Let us now understand the operations that we have performed on strings in this program. To begin with, we have created two **String** variables **s1** and **s2** and initialized them to "kicit" and "Nagpur" respectively. To access individual characters of a **String,** we have to use the method **charAt( )**. Thus **s1.charAt (2)** fetches the character 'c' in the string **s1**. Unlike an array, we cannot access the 3rd character using **s1[2]**.

The **concat( )** method concatenates two strings, stores it in a new string object and returns its reference, which gets stored in **s3**. Thus the object referred to by **s3** would contain "kicitNagpur". The **length( )** method of a **String** class returns the number of characters in a string. The length of **s3** in our program is 11. The **replace( )** method replaces all the instances of a character (mentioned as the first parameter) with the character given as the second parameter. Here we have replaced 'p' with a 'P' in string referred to by **s3**. The **copyValueOf( )** method is a **static** method that returns a **String** that represents the character sequence in the character array passed to it.

The **compareTo( )** method compares two strings alphabetically. This means a string with a starting alphabet 'a' will always be lesser than a string with starting alphabet as 'b'. This method returns a negative integer if the **String** object that has called the **compareTo( )** method contains a string which is lesser than the string contained in the object whose reference is passed as the method's parameter. It returns a positive number if the string objects are interchanged. It returns zero when both strings are equal.

In the same way the == operator compares two strings and returns a **bool—true** if the strings are equal and **false** if they are not. To carry out string comparison in a case insensitive manner there is another method called **compareToIgnoreCase( )**.

The **toUpperCase( )** method creates a new object, stores in it the converted upper case string and returns the address of this object. This address is collected in **s3**. Note that **s1** is not affected here. Hence we can draw a conclusion that the object which we use to call the methods to manipulate the string, does not affect the object.

The **indexOf( )** method returns the index of first occurrence of a given character in the **string**. Similarly, **lastIndexOf( )** method returns the index of last occurrence of a given character in the **string.** In our program the first index of 'i' happens to be 1 whereas the last index is 3.

The **substring( )** method returns a new string which starts at an index passed as the first parameter and ends at an index passed as the second parameter to the method.

The **format( )** method is a **static** method which builds a new string object using strings and numbers. Here we have collected the address of the newly created string object in **s3**.

If we want, we can combine calls to **String** class functions as shown below.

```
String s1 = "Hello" ;
s1 = s1.toUpperCase( ).substring ( 2, 5 ) ;
System.out.println ( s1 ) ;
```

Here firstly, Hello is converted to HELLO using **toUpperCase( )** and from this string LLO is extracted using **substring( )**.

Function **isEmpty( )** is very commonly used when validating user input in many Java applications. This function allows us to check in one shot if the string is empty, i.e. its length is 0. In absence of this function we would have been required to write an equivalent **if** as shown below:

```
if ( s == "" )
```

Function **contains( )** returns true if input string is present anywhere in the current string object. It enables us to search substrings within a large string efficiently.

Splitting Strings

While processing strings in Java applications, it is required to split a string in parts based on certain *separator*, thereby getting an array of strings. The following program illustrates how this splitting of strings can be done:

```
// Split string operations
package splitandjoinproject ;
import java.io.* ;

public class SplitAndJoinProject
{
    public static void main ( String[ ] args ) throws Exception
    {
        File f =new File ( "." ) ;
        String d = f.getCanonicalPath( ) ;
        String[ ] parts = d.split ( "\\\\" ) ;
        System.out.println ( "Complete path: " + d ) ;
```

```
        System.out.println ( "Dir name: " + parts [ parts.length - 1 ] ) ;
    }
}
```

And here is the output for this program...

```
Complete path: D:\Books\J_LUJ\Programs\SplitAndJoinProject
Dir name: SplitAndJoinProject
```

In this program, firstly we have obtained the complete path of the current directory (represented by .) by calling the method **getCanonicalPath( )** of the **File** class.

Then we have used the **split( )** method to separate different elements of this path based on separator '\'. The last part of the array of string thus obtained gives us the directory from which program is being executed.

StringBuilder Class

As we noted in the previous section, when a string is manipulated it is not changed in-place. Instead, a new object containing the manipulated string is created and the reference which was pointing to the earlier string is now made to point to this new manipulated string.

Instead of this, if we want that the same string should get manipulated in-place, then Java library provides a **StringBuilder** class for this. When we create a string using this class we can modify it by appending, removing, replacing, or inserting characters. For carrying out these operations it has methods like **append( )**, **delete( )**, **replace( )** and **insert( )**.

Based on what operations that we wish to perform on the string created using **StringBuilder**, we can set the maximum number of characters that the object can store. This can be done by using the **EnsureCapacity( )** method.

Array of Strings

Very often we are required to deal with a set of strings rather than only one string. In such cases we should create an array of strings. The following program shows how to declare and process such an array. In this program we have stored names of persons in a string array called **masterList**. The program asks you to type your name. When you do so, it checks your name against the names in **masterList** to see if you are worthy of entry to the palace. Here's the program...

```
// Using array of strings
package arrayofstringsproject ;
import java.io.* ;

public class ArrayOfStringsProject
{
    public static void main ( String[ ] args ) throws Exception
    {
        String[ ] masterList = new String [ ] {
                                              "Akshay", "Parag",
                                              "Raman", "Srinivas",
                                              "Gopal", "Rajesh"
                                        } ;

        int i, a ;
        boolean flag ;
        String yourName ;

        BufferedReader br = new BufferedReader (
                            new InputStreamReader ( System.in ) ) ;

        System.out.println ( "Enter your name " ) ;
        yourName = br.readLine( ) ;

        flag = false ;
        for ( i = 0 ; i <= 5 ; i++ )
        {
            a = masterList[ i ].compareTo ( yourName ) ;
            if ( a == 0 )
            {
                System.out.println ( "You can enter the palace" ) ;
                flag = true ;
                break ;
            }
        }

        if ( flag == false )
            System.out.println ( "Sorry, you are a trespasser" ) ;
    }
}
```

And here is the output for two sample runs of this program...

```
Enter your name Dinesh
Sorry, you are a trespasser
Enter your name Raman
You can enter the palace
```

Notice how the array of strings **masterList** has been created. Actually speaking, it is an array of **String** references. That is, it contains base addresses of respective names. For example, address of **String** object representing "Akshay" is stored in **masterList[0]**, base address of **String** object representing "Parag" is stored in **masterList[1]** and so on. This is depicted in Figure 12.1.

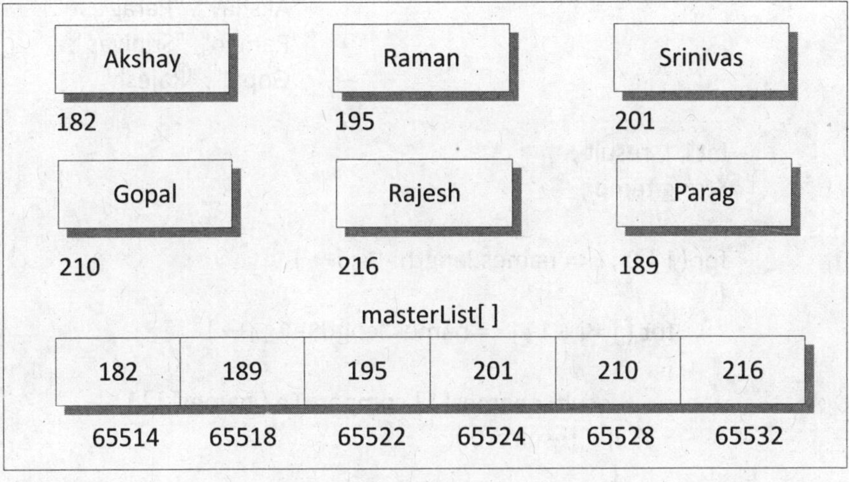

Figure 12.1

While comparing the strings using **compareTo( )**, true is returned if the strings match, otherwise false is returned. The variable **flag** is used to keep a record of whether the control reached inside the **if** or not. To begin with, we set **flag** to false. Later through the loop, if the names match, **flag** is set to true. When the control reaches beyond the **for** loop, if **flag** is still set to false, it means none of the names in the **masterList** matched with the one supplied from the keyboard.

Sorting Strings

Let us now create a program that stores names of persons in an array of strings, sorts these names in alphabetical order using the Bubble Sort logic and finally prints the sorted list of names. Here is the program...

```
// Sorting array of Strings
package sortingstringsproject ;

public class SortingStringsProject
{
    public static void main ( String[ ] args )
    {
        String[ ] names = new String[ ] {
                                        "Akshay", "Parag",
                                        "Raman", "Srinivas",
                                        "Gopal", "Rajesh"
                                    } ;
        int i, j, result ;
        String temp ;

        for ( i = 0 ; i <= names.length - 1 ; i++ )
        {
            for ( j = i + 1 ; j <= names.length - 1 ; j++ )
            {
                result = names[ i ].compareTo ( names[ j ] ) ;
                if  ( result > 0 )
                {
                    temp = names[ i ] ;
                    names[ i ] = names[ j ] ;
                    names[ j ] = temp ;
                }
            }
        }

        for ( String n : names )
            System.out.println ( n ) ;
    }
}
```

To sort the strings we have used the Selection Sort logic. To compare the alphabetical order of strings, we have used the function **compareTo( )**

which returns a value greater than 0 if the two strings being compared are not in alphabetical order. In such a case we swap the positions of the two strings in the array. Once the sorting of all strings is over, we have printed the sorted list using a **for** loop.

Enumerations

The enumerated data type gives you an opportunity to invent your own data type and define what values the variable of this data type can take. This can help in making the program listings more readable, which can be an advantage when a program gets complicated or when more than one programmer would be working on it. Using enumerated data type can also help you reduce programming errors.

As an example, one could invent a data type called **MaritalStatus** which can have four possible values—Single, Married, Divorced or Widowed. Here's how **MaritalStatus** data type can be implemented.

```
enum MaritalStatus
{
    single, married, divorced, widowed
}
MaritalStatus  person1, person2 ;
```

This declaration has two parts:

(a) The first part declares the data type and specifies its possible values. These values are called 'enumerators'.

(b) The second part defines variables of this data type.

Now we can give values to these variables:

```
person1 = MaritalStatus.married ;
person2 = MaritalStatus.divorced ;
```

Internally, the compiler treats the enumerators as integers. Each value on the list of permissible values corresponds to an integer, starting with 0. Thus, in our example, single is stored as 0, married is stored as 1, divorced as 2 and widowed as 3.

Lastly, the enumerators used in an **enum** should not contain white space in its name. Thus "elgible bachelor" would be an unacceptable enumerator for the **MaritalStatus**.

Use of Enumerated Data Type

Enumerated variables are usually used to clarify the operation of a program. For example, if we need to use employee departments in a payroll program, it makes the listing easier to read if we use values like assembly, manufacturing, accounts rather than the integer values 0, 1, 2, etc. The following program illustrates the point I am trying to make:

```
// Using Enumerations
package usingenumproject ;

enum Department
{
    assembly, manufacturing, accounts, stores
}

class Employee
{
    private String name ;
    private int age ;
    private float salary ;
    private Department dept ;

    public Employee ( String n, int a, float s, Department d )
    {
        name = n ;
        age = a ;
        salary = s ;
        dept = d ;
    }

    public void displayData( )
    {
        System.out.println ( name + " "+ age + " " +  salary+ " " + dept );
        if ( dept == Department.accounts )
            System.out.println ( name + " is an accountant\n" ) ;
        else
            System.out.println (name +  " is not an accountant\n" ) ;
    }
}

public class UsingEnumProject
```

```
{
    public static void main ( String[ ] args )
    {
        Employee e = new Employee ( "Sandeep Shah", 28, 15575.50f,
                                    Department.manufacturing ) ;
        e.displayData( ) ;
    }
}
```

And here is the output of the program...

```
Sandeep Shah 28 15575.5 manufacturing
Sandeep Shah is not an accountant
```

Let us now dissect the program. We first defined the data type **enum Department** and specified the four possible values, namely, assembly, manufacturing, accounts and stores. Then we declared a class **Employee** to manage employee data. It contains **name**, **age**, **salary** and **dept**. Of these, the last one is special—it is a variable of the type **Department**. The constructor of the **Employee** class is invoked from **main( )**. In this call to the constructor, the value of the department in which the employee is working is passed as **Department.manufacturing**. This is much more informative to anyone reading the program than simply passing a value 1 to represent the manufacturing department. In the constructor, the enum value passed to it is assigned to **private** variable of the class through the statement,

```
dept = d ;
```

In the next part of the program, the values assigned to **Employee e** are printed by calling the function **displayData( )**. Note that even though an integer value is assigned to **Dept**, while printing it, it prints **manufacturing** and not 1. Thus **enum** data type comes in very handy whenever we wish to use named constants in a Java program. Here are a few more **enum** declarations that would make programming quite convenient.

```
enum Days { Mon, Tue, Wed, Thu, Fri, Sat, Sun }
enum Color { Red, Green, Blue }
enum Months { January, February, March, April, May, June, July,
              August, September, October, November, December }
```

You must have noticed that in the previous program when we tried to print the department, it was printed as manufacturing though the underlying value was an integer. At times, we may want to access and print the integer value instead of the string. The following program shows how this can be done. This time however we are going to use an **enum CarTypes** instead of **Department**. Here is the program...

```
// Printing enumerators as String Value pairs
package enumstringvaluepairsproject ;

enum CarTypes
{
    suv, hatchBack, sedan, convertible
}

public class EnumStringValuePairsProject
{
    public static void main ( String[ ] args )
    {
        CarTypes car1 = CarTypes.sedan ;

        System.out.println ( "Value of car1 is " + car1 ) ;
        System.out.println ( "Value of car1 is " + car1.ordinal( ) ) ;

        System.out.println ( "Car names and their values:" ) ;
        for ( CarTypes c : CarTypes.values( ) )
            System.out.println ( c + " = " + c.ordinal( ) ) ;
    }
}
```

Given below is the output of the program:

```
Value of car1 is Sedan
Value of car1 is 2
Car names and their values:
suv = 0
hatchBack = 1
sedan = 2
convertible = 3
```

Here, to begin with we have declared an **enum** called **CarTypes** containing enumerators to represent different types of cars. Then we have created an enum variable **car1** and assigned the value **CarTypes.sedan** to it. Then we have printed the string “sedan” and the underlying value, i.e., 4 through two **println( )** calls. Note that to get the integer value we have called the **ordinal( )** method. This method returns the position of the enumeration constant in its enum declaration.

Exercise

[A] Answer the following:

(a) What will be the output of the Java code snippet given below?

```
String s1 = "Kicit" ;
System.out.println ( s1.indexOf ( 'c' ) ) ;
System.out.println ( s1.length( ) ) ;
```

(b) What will be the output of the Java code snippet given below?

```
String s1 = "Nagpur" ;
String s2 ;
s2 = s1.concat ( "Mumbai" ) ;
System.out.println ( s2 ) ;
```

(c) What will be the output of the Java code snippet given below?

```
String s1 = "Five Star" ;
String s2 = "FIVE STAR" ;
int c ;
c = s1.compareTo ( s2 ) ;
System.out.println ( c ) ;
```

(d) What will be the output of the Java code snippet given below?

```
String s1 = "ALL MEN ARE CREATED EQUAL" ;
String s2 ;
s2 = s1.substring ( 12, 3 ) ;
System.out.println ( s2 ) ;
```

(e) With reference to the following statements how will you copy the contents of **s1** into **s2**?

```
String s1 = "String" ;
String s2 ;
```

(f) How will you find out the index of the second 's' in the string "She sells sea shells on the sea-shore"?

[B] Attempt the following:

(a) Write a program that uses an array of strings **str**[ ]. Receive two strings **str1** and **str2** and check if **str1** is embedded in any of the strings in **str[ ]**. If **str1** is found, then replace it with **str2**.

```
String str[ ] = {
                    "We will teach you how to...",
```

```
                "Move a mountain",
                "Erase the past",
                "Make a million",
                "...all through Java!"
            };
```

For example if **str1** contains "mountain" and **str2** contains "car", then the second string in **str** should get changed to "Move a car".

(b) Write a program to reverse the strings stored in the following array of pointers to strings:

```
String s[ ] = {
                "To err is human...",
                "But to really mess things up...",
                "One needs to know Java!!"
            };
```

(c) Write a program to delete all vowels from a sentence.

(d) Write a program that will read a line and delete from it all occurrences of the word 'the'.

(e) Write a program that takes a set of names of individuals and abbreviates the first, middle and other names except the last name by their first letter.

(f) Write a program to count the number of occurrences of any two vowels in succession in a line of text. For example, in the sentence

"Please read this application and give me gratuity"

such occurrences are ea, ea, ui.

(g) Create a class called **Window** containing data members **height**, **width**, **cursortype** and **windowcolor**. Of these, the last two should be enumerations. Create two objects of type **Window** and set and print values of these objects. Make sure that the enum values are printed as strings.

KanNotes

- Strings are used to manage an array of characters
- Strings in Java are immutable
- The String class has an overloaded + to concatenate strings
- Different operations can be performed on string using functions of the String class
    - charAt( ) - obtain character at specified position
    - concat() - concatenate two strings
    - length() - obtain length of a string
    - replace() - a substring in a string with another
    - compareTo - compare two strings
    - toUpperCase() - convert string to uppercase
    - indexOf() - obtain first index of a substring in a string
    - lastIndexOf() - obtain last index of a substring in a string
    - substring() - extract substring from a string
- To manipulate a string in-place use StringBuilder class
- Use methods like append( ), delete( ), replace( ) and insert() to manipulate a string represented using StringBuilder class.
- To maintain several strings it is possible to create an array of strings
- Enumerations are user-defined types that are used to make programs more readable

13 Inheritance

Inheritance is all about genes... they better be good! So true in life, quite so in programming...

Let Us JAVA 3rd Edition

Chapter Contents

Now that we have familiarized ourselves with classes—the building blocks of object oriented programming—let us deal with another important Java concept called **Inheritance**. Inheritance is probably the most powerful feature of object-oriented programming after classes themselves. Inheritance is the process of creating new classes, called **derived classes**, from existing classes. These existing classes are often called **base classes**. The derived class inherits all the capabilities of the base class but can add new features and refinements of its own. By adding these refinements the base class remains unchanged.

Most important advantage of Inheritance is that it permits code reusability. Once a base class is written and debugged, it need not be touched again but at the same time it can be adapted to work in different situations. Reusing existing code saves time and effort and increases a program's reliability. Inheritance can also help in the original conceptualization of a programming problem, and in the overall design of the program.

The code reusability is of great help in the case of distributing class libraries. A programmer can use a class created by another person or company, and, without modifying it, derive other classes from it that are suited to particular programming situations. Let us now understand the concept of inheritance using a program.

Suppose we have designed a class called **Index** that serves as a counter. Suppose that the **Index** class can only increment the counter and not decrement it. To achieve this, we can insert a decrement function directly into the source code of the **Index** class. However, there are several reasons why we might not want to do this. Firstly, the **Index** class works well and has been thoroughly tested and debugged. This is an exaggeration in this case, but it would be true in a larger and more complex class. Now, if we start modifying the source code of the **Index** class, the testing process will have to be carried out again.

Sometimes, there might be another reason for not modifying the **Index** class—we might not have access to its source code, especially if it had been distributed as part of a class library.

To avoid these problems, we can use inheritance to create a new class based on **Index**, without modifying **Index** itself. Here's how this can be achieved.

```
// Demonstrating implementation and usage of Inheritance
package inheritanceusageproject ;
```

```
// base class
class Index
{
    protected int count ;

    public Index( )
    {
        count = 0 ;
    }
    public void display( )
    {
        System.out.println ( "count = " + count ) ;
    }
    public void increment( )
    {
        count += 1 ;
    }
}

// derived class
class Index1 extends Index
{
    public void decrement( )
    {
        count -= 1 ;
    }
}

public class InheritanceUsageProject
{
    public static void main ( String[ ] args )
    {
        Index1 i ;
        i = new Index1( ) ;
        i.increment( ) ;
        i.display( ) ;
        i.decrement( ) ;
        i.display( ) ;
    }
}
```

The first line of the **Index1** class,

class Index1 extends Index

specifies that the class **Index1** has been derived from the base class **Index**. By doing this, **Index1** inherits all the features of the base class **Index**. **Index1** doesn't need a constructor or the **increment( )** function, since they are already present in the base class. Figure 13.1 shows the relationship between the base class and the derived class. Note that the arrow in Figure 13.1 means "derived from". The direction of the arrow says that the derived class can refer to the functions and data in the base class, while the base class has no access to the derived class data or functions.

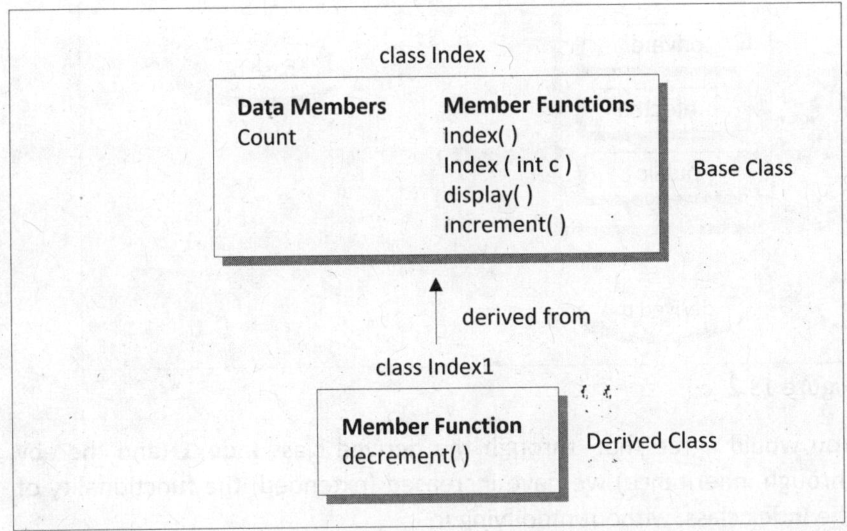

Figure 13.1

Since we have not declared any constructor in **Index1**, the compiler would insert an empty zero-argument constructor in it. When we create an object **i**, the constructor in the base class gets called followed by the empty zero-argument constructor in the derived class. When we call the function **increment( )** it is searched in the derived class. Since the derived class doesn't contain such a function, **increment( )** from base class is used to increment **count**.

Note that **count** has been marked as **protected**. Had it been **private** it would not have been available outside the **Index** class. By marking it as **protected**, it is now available in the **Index** class as well as in the inheritance chain, i.e. in functions of **Index1** class.

We don't want to make **count** as **public**, as that would allow it to be accessed from outside the class, and thereby eliminate the advantages of data hiding. Figure 13.2 clearly indicates who can access what, in a base class–derived class relationship.

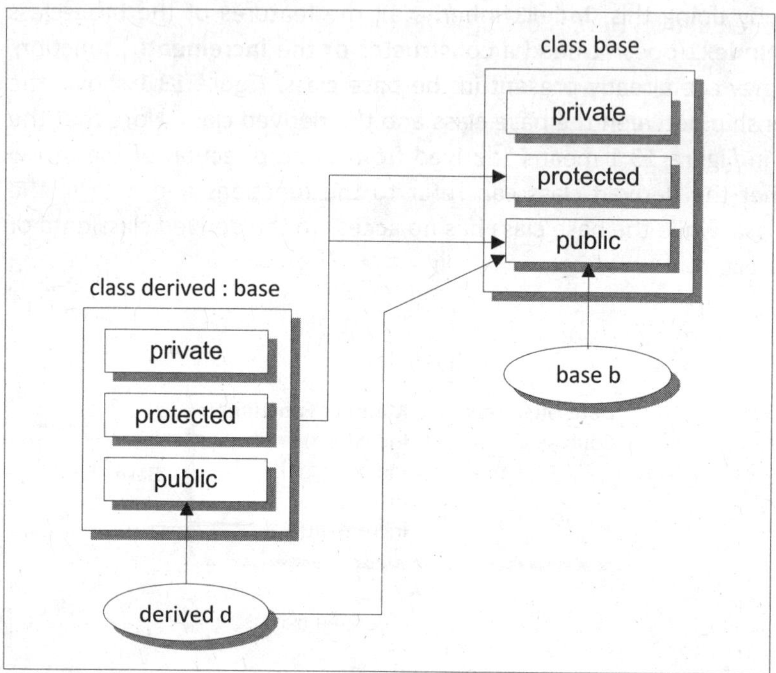

Figure 13.2

You would agree that, through the derived class **Index1** (and thereby through inheritance) we have increased (extended) the functionality of the **Index** class, without modifying it.

Note that inheritance doesn't work in reverse. That is, the base class and its objects have no knowledge about any classes derived from the base class. This means, in our program, had we built an object **j** from the class **Index**, then the **decrement( )** function would have remained inaccessible to this object.

Uses of Inheritance

Now that we have a basic idea about inheritance let us see in which scenarios is inheritance used in Java. The four common usages of inheritance are as follows:

Use existing functionality
Override existing functionality

Provide new functionality
Combination of existing and new functionality

Let us now look at a few examples of these usage patterns. We would begin with a scenario which demonstrates usage of all the four features mentioned above. Here is the program...

```
// Program demonstrating various Inheritance usage scenarios
package inheritancefeaturesusageproject ;

class Ex
{
    public void fun( )
    {
        System.out.println ( "Inside Ex - fun( )" ) ;
    }
    public void save( )
    {
        System.out.println ( "Inside Ex - save( )" ) ;
    }
    public void enc( )
    {
        System.out.println ( "Inside Ex - enc( )" ) ;
    }
    public void open( )
    {
        System.out.println ( "Inside Ex - open( )" ) ;
    }
}
class NewEx extends Ex
{
    public void save( )
    {
        System.out.println ( "Inside NewEx - save( )" ) ;
    }
    public void enc( )
    {
        System.out.println ( "Inside NewEx - enc( )" ) ;
    }
    public void autoUpdate( )
    {
        System.out.println ( "Inside NewEx - autoUpdate( )" ) ;
```

```
    }
    public void open( )
    {
        System.out.println ( "Inside NewEx - open( )" ) ;
        super.open( ) ;
    }
}
public class InheritanceFeaturesUsageProject
{
    public static void main ( String[ ] args )
    {
        NewEx e = new NewEx( ) ;
        e.fun( ) ;
        e.save( ) ;
        e.enc( ) ;
        e.autoUpdate( ) ;
        e.open( ) ;
    }
}
```

Given below is the output of the program...

```
Inside Ex - fun( )
Inside NewEx - save( )
Inside NewEx - enc( )
Inside NewEx - autoUpdate( )
Inside NewEx - open( )
Inside Ex - open( )
```

Here we have defined two classes—**Ex** as base class and **NewEx** as derived class. The **Ex** class contains member functions **fun( )**, **save( )**, **enc( )** and **open( )**, whereas **NewEx** class contains member functions **save( )**, **enc( )**, **open( )** and **autoUpdate( )**. In **main( )** we have created an object of **NewEx( )** class and then called different member functions. Now look at the output of the program to appreciate the different inheritance usage scenarios.

When we called the function **fun( )** it was first searched in the **NewEx** class. Since it was not found in **NewEx**, it was then searched in the base class. In the base class it was found. As a result, the base class function got called and the message "Inside Ex – Fun( )" got printed. This demonstrates that we have used one of the features of the base class, namely **fun( )**, as it is, through a derived class object.

When we called **save( )**, again the function was searched in derived class **NewEx**. Since the function was found in **NewEx**, this version of **save( )** (and not the one in **Ex** class) got called. This demonstrates that through inheritance we are able to override existing functionality. Same is the case with the function **enc( )**.

When we called the function **autoUpdate( )** the function was searched and found in **NewEx**. Since there was no **autoUpdate( )** function in base class this is the case where a totally new functionality is provided through inheritance.

Lastly, when we called **open( )** the function was searched and found in **NewEx**. This version of **open( )** got called and this function in turn called the base class version of **open( )** through the statement **super.open( )**. The resulting output was:

```
Inside NewEx - open( )
Inside Ex - open( )
```

This indicates the usage of inheritance to combine new functionality with old.

Note the following important points about Inheritance relationships:

(a) We can even derive a class from a class which itself has been derived from another class. Thus, multiple levels of inheritance can exist.

(b) A class cannot have multiple base classes. That is, a derived class cannot be derived from more than one class.

Constructors in Inheritance

As we know the base class member functions can be called from derived class member function using the syntax:

```
super.functionName( ) ;
```

Here **super** is a keyword and **functionName( )** is the name of the function in the base class. Unless explicitly called, the base class function doesn't get called from the body of the derived class function. Constructors in inheritance chain are given a different treatment.

Regarding constructors in inheritance chain we have to keep two things in mind:

(a) When a derived class object is created, the constructor of the base class followed by constructor of derived class gets called.

(b) While constructing a derived class object, if we do not call the base class constructor then, by default, the zero-argument constructor of base class gets called.

Let us illustrate these facts with the help of a program. Here is the program...

```
// Demonstrates calls to constructors in Inheritance chain
package constructorsininheritanceproject ;

class a
{
    public a( )
    {
        System.out.println ( "a's 0-arg Ctor" ) ;
    }
    public a ( int xx )
    {
        System.out.println ( "a's 1-arg Ctor" ) ;
    }
}
class b extends a
{
    public b( )
    {
        System.out.println ( "b's 0-arg Ctor" ) ;
    }
    public b ( int x )
    {
        super ( x ) ;
        System.out.println ( "b's 1-arg Ctor" ) ;
    }
}
public class ConstructorsIninheritanceProject
{
    public static void main ( String[ ] args )
```

```
    {
        b y = new b( ) ;
        b z = new b ( 10 ) ;
    }
}
```

Given below is the output of the program...

```
a's 0-arg Ctor
b's 0-arg Ctor
a's 1-arg Ctor
b's 1-arg Ctor
```

From the output we can see that when we construct the objects **y** and **z**, firstly the constructor of base class gets called followed by constructor of the derived class. While constructing the object **y** the zero-argument constructor of base class got called automatically. However, while constructing **z** the one-argument constructor had to be called explicitly through the syntax:

```
super ( x ) ;
```

Had we not used **super (x)**, then the zero-argument constructor of base class would have been called.

You must be wondering why it is necessary that the construction should proceed from base towards derived. This can be best understood with the help of the following program:

```
// Order of construction of object in Inheritance chain
package orderofconstructionproject ;

class base1
{
    protected int i ;

    public base1( )
    {
        i = 4 ;
    }
}
class der extends base1
{
```

```
        private int j ;

        public der( )
        {
            j = i * 4 ;
        }
}
public class OrderOfConstructionProject
{
        public static void main ( String[ ] args )
        {
            der d = new der( ) ;
        }
}
```

Here **i** is marked as a **protected** member, hence it is available to functions in the derived class **der**. For a moment, assume that the order of construction is not from base towards derived. In that case, firstly the constructor of **der** would get called. And since **i** is available in constructor and the base class constructor has not been called so far, it has not been set with a value so far. As a result, **j** would not be set properly. Thus, the value in the object **d** would not be set correctly. Unlike, this if the order of construction is from base towards derived then object **d** would be set initialized properly.

The *final* Keyword

By default, we can inherit a new class from any existing class. At times, we may want that inheritance should not be permitted on a class. This can be achieved by using a **final** keyword as shown in the following program:

```
// Demonstrates prevention of Inheritance
package preventinheritanceproject ;

final class base1
{
}
class derived extends base1
{
        public void fun( )
        {
            System.out.println ( "Too much noise, too little substance" ) ;
```

```
    }
}
public class PreventInheritanceProject
{
    public static void main ( String[ ] args )
    {
        derived d = new derived( ) ;
        d.fun( ) ;
    }
}
```

This program doesn't even cross the compilation hurdle. On compilation it reports an error—cannot derive from final 'preventinheritanceproject.base1'. This so happens, because we have marked the base class as non-inheritable by using the keyword **final**.

Though method overriding is one of the most important features of Java, at times you may want to prevent it from occurring. We can prevent a method from being overridden by declaring it as **final** in the base class. The following code snippet illustrates this:

```
// Demonstrates prevention of overriding
class base1
{
    final public void fun( )
    {
        System.out.println ( "In the final method" ) ;
    }
}
class derived extends base1
{
    public void fun( )
    {
        System.out.println ( "Illegal" ) ;
    }
}
```

Incremental Development

One of the advantages of inheritance is that it supports incremental development. It allows you to introduce new code without causing bugs in existing code. By inheriting from an existing, functional class and adding data members and member functions (and redefining existing member functions) you leave the existing code—that someone else may still be using—untouched and unbugged. If a bug happens, you know it's in your new code, which is much shorter and easier to read, than if you had modified the body of existing code.

It's rather amazing how cleanly the classes are separated. You don't even need the source code for the member functions to reuse the code. Just the byte-code containing the compiled member functions would do.

It's important to realize that program development is an incremental process. Nobody ever conceived the program in its entirety at the start of the project. The program should try to create and manipulate objects of various types to express a model in the terms given to you by the problem definition. Rather than constructing the program all at once it should grow out as an organic, evolutionary creature. Of course, at some point after things stabilize you need to take a fresh look at your class hierarchy with an aim to collapse it into a sensible structure. Inheritance fits this bill to perfection.

Other Code Reuse Mechanisms

Java facilitates code reuse at 2 levels—Source code level and Byte code level. In source code level reuse mechanism, the code cannot be reused to build new code, unless the source code is available. Source code level reuse is done in Java using Generic functions and Generic classes. Generics let us write generalized functions / classes and the compiler creates specific functions / classes from it. For creating specialized functions / classes source code has to be available. Chapter 18 discusses this reuse mechanism in detail.

Byte code level reuse is implemented in Java using Containership and Inheritance. Containership should be used when the two classes have a "has a" relationship between them. For example, a problem may have two classes Address and Employee. An Employee object may contain an Address object, apart from other data like name, age, salary etc.

Inheritance should be used when the two classes have a "like a" relationship. For example, if a problem has two classes Window and Button, then the Button class can be inherited from Window class since Button is like a Window.

Containership and Inheritance can be implemented even if source code is not available.

Exercise

[A] State whether the following statements are True or False:

(a) We can derive a class from a base class even if the base class's source code is not available.

(b) The way a derived class member function can access base class **protected** and **public** members, the base class member functions can access **protected** and public **member** functions of derived class.

(c) **private** members of base class cannot be accessed by derived class member functions or objects of derived class.

(d) The size of a derived class object is equal to the sum of sizes of data members in base class and the derived class.

(e) Creating a derived class from a base class requires fundamental changes to the base class.

(f) If a base class contains a member function **func( )**, and a derived class does not contain a function with this name, an object of the derived class cannot access **func( )**.

(g) If no constructors are specified for a derived class, objects of the derived class will use the constructors in the base class.

(h) If a base class and a derived class each include a member function with the same name, the member function of the derived class will be called by an object of the derived class.

(i) A class D can be derived from a class C, which is derived from a class B, which is derived from a class A.

(j) It is illegal to make objects of one class members of another class.

[B] Answer the following:

(a) Implement a **MyString** class containing the following functions:

- Function to display the length of a string.
- Function **toLower( )** to convert upper case letters to lower case.

- Function **toUpper( )** to convert lower case letters to upper case.

(b) Suppose there is a base class **B** and a derived class **D** derived from **B**. **B** has two **public** member functions **b1( )** and **b2( )**, whereas **D** has two member functions **d1( )** and **d2( )**. Write these classes for the following different situations:

- **b1( )** should be accessible in **main( )**, **b2( )** should not be.
- Neither **b1( )**, nor **b2( )** should be accessible in **main( )**.
- Both **b1( )** and **b2( )** should be accessible in **main( )**.

(c) If a class **D** that is derived from class **B**, then which of the following can an object of class **D** located in **main( )** access?

- **public** members of **D**
- **protected** members of **D**
- **private** members of **D**
- **public** members of **B**
- **protected** members of **B**
- **private** members of **B**

(d) In an inheritance chain which out of **static**, **protected**, **private** and **public** members of base class are accessible to the derived class members?

(e) Which of the following can be facilitated by the Inheritance mechanism?

1. Use the existing functionality of base class.
2. Override the existing functionality of base class.
3. Implement new functionality in the derived class.
4. Implement polymorphic behavior.
5. Implement containership.

(f) How can you prevent inheritance from a class in Java?

(g) If the base class has two versions of the overloaded function, and derived class contains one version of it, then using the derived class object can we call the other version of the base class?

(h) What will be the size of the derived class object if the base class contains two private integers, one static integer and the derived class contains two static integers and one private integer?

KanNotes

- Java facilitates code reuse at 2 levels : a) Sour code level b) Byte code level
- Source code level reuse is done using Generic functions and Generic classes
- Generics let us write generalized functions / classes and the compiler creates specific functions / classes from it
- For creating specialized functions / classes source code has to be available
- Byte code level reuse is done using Containership and Inheritance
- Containership should be used when the two classes have a "has a" relationship
- Inheritance should be used when the two classes have a "like a" relationship
- Containership and Inheritance can be implemented even if source code is not available
- Inheritance terminology : base - derived, parent - child, subclass, superclass
- Protected members are available in the inheritance chain
- Derived class object contains all base class data
- Derived class object may not be able to access all base class data
- In inheritance chain construction happens from base towards derived
- Inheritance facilitates :

  Inheritance of existing feature : To implement this just establish inheritance relationship

Suppressing an existing feature : Hide base class implementation by defining same function in derived class

Extending an existing feature : call base class function from derived class by using super.Baseclassfunction() ;

- Construction of an object always proceeds from base towards derived
- Base class constructor can be called using super()
- If a class is marked as final, then a new class cannot be derived from it
- If a function is marked as final, then the function cannot be overridden in the derived class

Polymorphism

14

More the caps one can wear, more versatile one becomes. Polymorphism is same...

Let Us JAVA
3rd Edition

Chapter Contents

After classes and inheritance, polymorphism is the third essential feature of an object-oriented programming language. Programmers who switch to Java after having learnt C seem to do so in two steps. In the first step they start using classes, objects, constructors, function overloading, etc. While doing this, they are using Java as a "object-based" programming language. This means that, at this stage, they start appreciating the benefits of grouping data together with the functions that act upon it, the value of constructors and perhaps some simple inheritance.

Many programmers carry a wrong impression that since they have started using classes, objects, function overloading and inheritance they have graduated to the object-oriented world. Though, on the face of it, everything may appear nice, neat and clean, don't get fooled. If you stop here, you're missing out on the greatest part of the language, which is the jump to true object-oriented programming. You can do this only when you have learnt polymorphism.

What is Polymorphism?

Overloading of functions is one kind of polymorphism—one thing existing in several distinct forms. We have already dealt with this type of polymorphism. The other type of polymorphism simplifies the syntax of performing the same operation with a hierarchy of classes. Thus, you can use polymorphism to keep the interface to the classes clean, because you do not have to define unique function names for similar operations on each derived class.

When polymorphism is used, a program that appears to be calling a function of one class may in reality be calling a function of a different class. But why on earth would we want this? Suppose we have three different classes called **Line**, **Circle** and **Rectangle**. Each class contains a **draw( )** function to draw the relevant shape on the screen. If we are to draw a picture containing numerous lines, circles and triangles we can create an array of references which would hold addresses of all the objects in the picture. The array definition may look like,

```
Shape[ ] arr ;
arr = new Shape[ 50 ] ;
```

When it is time to draw the picture we can simply run the loop,

```
for ( i = 0 ; i < 50 ; i++ )
```

```
arr[ i ].draw( ) ;
```

When **arr[i]** contains address of the **Line** object it would call the **Line** class's **draw( )** function. Similarly, when it contains the address of the **Circle** object it would call the **Circle** class's **draw( )** function. This is amazing for two reasons:

(a) Functions from different classes are executed through the same function call.

(b) The array **arr[ ]** has been defined to contain **Shape** references and not **Line** or **Circle** references.

This concept is called polymorphism. The functions have the same appearance, the **draw( )** function, but different actual functions are used. Which **draw( )** function would get used depends on the contents of **arr[i]**. However, for this polymorphic approach to work, several conditions must be met. These are

(a) The classes **Line**, **Circle** and **Rectangle** all must be derived from the same base class, **Shape**.

(b) The **Shape** base class must contain a **draw( )** function.

All this would be too much to digest at one shot. So let us break it into pieces and try to understand it part by part through simple programs. Here is the first one...

```
// Illustrates use of upcasted reference
package polymorphismproject ;

class One
{
    public void display( )
    {
        System.out.println ( "In base class" ) ;
    }
}
class OneOfOne extends One
{
    public void display( )
    {
        System.out.println ( "In OneOfOne class" ) ;
    }
```

```
}
class TwoOfOne extends One
{
    public void display( )
    {
        System.out.println ( "In TwoOfOne class" ) ;
    }
}
public class PolymorphismProject
{
    public static void main ( String[ ] args )
    {
        One ptr ;
        OneOfOne o1 = new OneOfOne( ) ;
        TwoOfOne o2 = new TwoOfOne( ) ;
        ptr = o1 ;
        ptr.display( ) ;
        ptr = o2 ;
        ptr.display( ) ;
    }
}
```

Here **OneOfOne** and **TwoOfOne** are classes derived from the base class **One**. Each of these three classes has a member function **display( )**.

Inside **main( )** having created the objects **o1**, **o2** (from the two derived classes) and a reference **ptr** to base class, we have assigned the address of a derived class object to the base class reference through the statement,

```
ptr = o1 ;
```

Should this not give us an error, since we are assigning an address of one type to a reference of another? No, since in this case the compiler relaxes the type checking. The rule is that references to objects of a derived class are type-compatible with references to objects of the base class. Assigning the address of a derived class object to a base class reference is called **upcasting**.

When we execute the statement,

```
ptr.display( ) ;
```

which function gets called—**display( )** of **OneOfOne** or **display( )** of **One**? Well, the function in the derived class gets called. On execution of the program we get the following output:

```
In OneOfOne class
In TwoOfOne class
```

As can be seen from the output, instead of the base class, the member functions of the derived classes got executed. Thus the same function call,

```
ptr.display( ) ;
```

executes different functions, depending on the contents of **ptr**. The rule here is that the compiler selects the function to be called based on the *contents* of the reference **ptr**, and not on the *type* of the reference.

Deciding which function to call in known as binding. As **ptr** may contain address of an object of the **OneOfOne** class or of the **TwoOfOne** class, the compiler is unable to bind the call to a specific version of **display( )**. Hence the decision is deferred until the program is executed. At runtime, when it is known what object is pointed to by **ptr**, the appropriate version of **display( )** gets called. This is called **Late Binding** or **Dynamic Binding**. Late binding requires some overhead but provides increased power and flexibility.

Thus this program is able to provide the feature mentioned at the beginning of this discussion—accessing functions of different classes using the same function call.

Abstract Classes and Functions

We can add another refinement to the function declared in the base class of the last program. Since the function **display( )** in the base class never gets executed we can easily do away with the body of this function and mark it using the keyword **abstract**, as shown below.

```
abstract class One
{
    public abstract void display( ) ;
}
```

The **abstract** function never has any statements in it. An abstract function must be contained in an **abstract** class. That is why we have marked **One** as abstract class as shown above. We can never create an object from an abstract class. So the following statement would report an error:

One o = new One ;

But when would a situation arise where we want to prevent creation of an object? Well, let us go back to our previous example. Suppose there is base class called **Shape** containing a **draw( )** function. From this **Shape** class three classes **Line**, **Circle** and **Rectangle** are derived. In this case we would never want to make an object of the **Shape** class; we would only make objects of the derived classes as they would help us draw specific shapes. In this case we would define **Shape** as an abstract class and **draw( )** as an abstract function in this class. We would then provide an implementation of **draw( )** function in each of the derived classes. These **draw( )** functions would let us draw specific line, circle or rectangle shapes.

Whenever an abstract function is placed in the base class, you must override it in all the derived classes from which you wish to create objects. If you don't implement the function in the derived class, then the derived class is treated as an abstract class.

Let us now reiterate a few facts that we have learnt in this section. A clear understanding of them is utmost necessary.

To help you fix your understanding of abstract classes and functions let us write one more program. Figure 14.1 shows the hierarchy of classes that we propose to implement in this program.

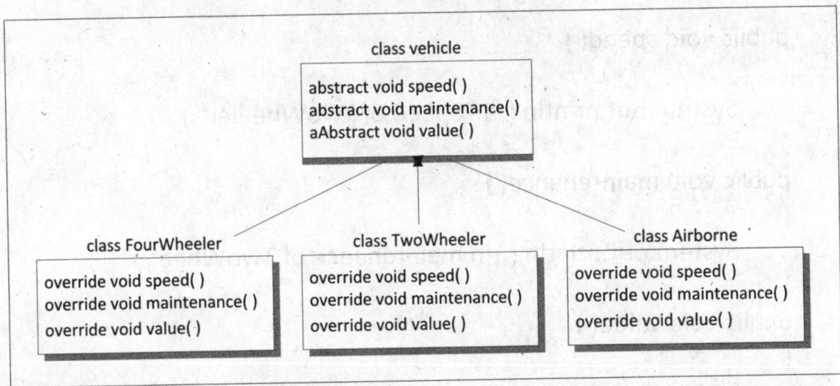

Figure 14.1

Given below is the code for the program that implements this class hierarchy.

```
// Program that illustrates working of abstract class & abstract functions
package abstractclassexampleproject ;

abstract class Vehicle
{
    public abstract void speed( ) ;
    public abstract void maintenance( ) ;
    public abstract void value( ) ;
}
class FourWheeler extends Vehicle
{
    public void speed( )
    {
        System.out.println ( "In speed of FourWheeler" ) ;
    }
    public void maintenance( )
    {
        System.out.println ( "In maintenance of FourWheeler" ) ;
    }
    public void value( )
    {
        System.out.println ( "In value of FourWheeler" ) ;
    }
}
class TwoWheeler extends Vehicle
{
    public void speed( )
    {
        System.out.println ( "In speed of TwoWheeler" ) ;
    }
    public void maintenance( )
    {
        System.out.println ( "In maintenance of TwoWheeler" ) ;
    }
    public void value( )
    {
        System.out.println ( "In value of TwoWheeler" ) ;
    }
}
```

```
class Airborne extends Vehicle
{
    public void speed( )
    {
        System.out.println ( "In speed of Airborne" ) ;
    }
    public void maintenance( )
    {
        System.out.println ( "In maintenance of Airborne" ) ;
    }
    public void value( )
    {
        System.out.println ( "In value of Airborne" ) ;
    }
}
public class AbstractClassExampleProject
{
    public static void main ( String[ ] args )
    {
        Vehicle maruti, bajaj, jumbo ;

        maruti = new FourWheeler( ) ;
        bajaj = new TwoWheeler( ) ;
        jumbo = new Airborne( ) ;

        maruti.speed( ) ;
        maruti.maintenance( ) ;
        maruti.value( ) ;

        bajaj.speed( ) ;
        bajaj.maintenance( ) ;
        bajaj.value( ) ;

        jumbo.speed( ) ;
        jumbo.maintenance( ) ;
        jumbo.value( ) ;
    }
}
```

Here is the output of the program...

```
In speed of FourWheeler
```

In maintenance of FourWheeler
In value of FourWheeler
In speed of TwoWheeler
In maintenance of TwoWheeler
In value of TwoWheeler
In speed of Airborne
In maintenance of Airborne
In value of Airborne

I would leave it to you to analyze the output of this program.

Abstract Functions – Practical Example

I hope that by now you have understood the mechanism of abstract functions. Let us now see where we can use them effectively. Suppose we wish to write an application which has to print a document to the printer. The application should be able to print to any printer. All that it has to know is the name of the printer. To do the printing, application should merely call the **pr`int( )** function. Note that every printer uses its own way to print. We can implement this scenario by creating classes as shown in Figure 14.2.

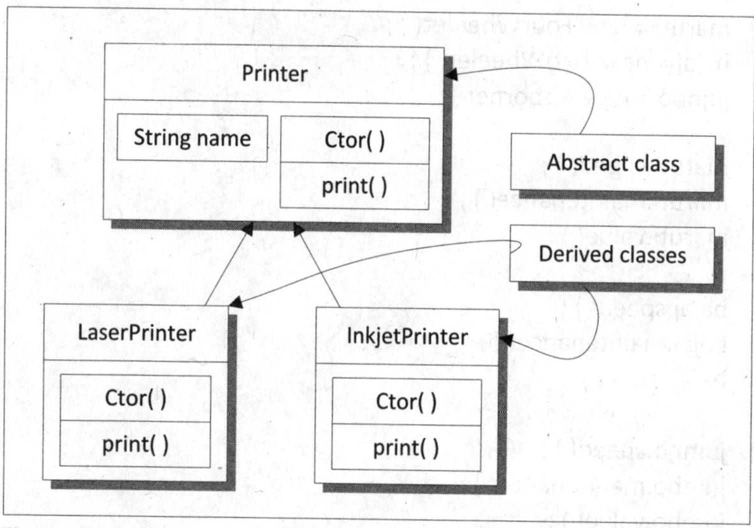

Figure 14.2

Given below is the implementation of the classes shown in Figure 14.2.

```
// Application that does printing using abstract class
package printingappproject ;
```

```
abstract class Printer
{
    protected String name ;

    public Printer ( String n )
    {
        name = n ;
    }
    public abstract void print ( String docName ) ;
}
class LaserPrinter extends Printer
{
    public LaserPrinter ( String n )
    {
        super ( n ) ;
    }
    public void print ( String docName )
    {
        System.out.println ( ">> LaserPrinter.print" ) ;
    }
}
class InkjetPrinter extends Printer
{
    public InkjetPrinter ( String n )
    {
        super ( n ) ;
    }
    public void print ( String docName )
    {
        System.out.println ( ">> InkjetPrinter.print" ) ;
    }
}
public class PrintingAppProject
{
    public static void main ( String[ ] args )
    {
        Printer p = new LaserPrinter ( "LaserJet 1100" ) ;
        p.print ( "hello1.pdf" ) ;
        p = new InkjetPrinter ( "IBM 2140" ) ;
        p.print("hello2.doc" ) ;
```

```
    }
}
```

Here is the output of the program...

```
>> LaserPrinter.print
>> InkjetPrinter.print
```

In this program we have first defined an abstract class called **Printer**. This class has a string that can store the name of the printer through the constructor. It also has an abstract function called **print( )**. This **print( )** function has been implemented in the two derived classes **LaserPrinter** and **InkjetPrinter**. Though in these implementations we have just displayed messages, in real-life it would contain the logic to actually do the printing on laser and inkjet printer, respectively. Based on whose address is present in the reference **p**, the **print( )** of the appropriate derived class would get called through the dynamic binding mechanism that we learnt earlier.

Given below is the summary of all that we learnt about abstract classes and functions.

(a) Object cannot be created from an abstract class.
(b) An abstract class can contain abstract as well as non-abstract functions.
(c) Abstract class may contain instance and static variables. These variables may be inherited.
(d) Abstract methods do not have a body.
(e) Abstract classes can participate in inheritance.
(f) If a class contains abstract methods, the class has to be abstract.
(g) Abstract functions cannot be private.

Interfaces

An interface contains only the signatures of methods (i.e., function declarations). The implementation of these methods is done in the class that implements the interface. For example, we can declare an interface called **Mouse**, and then implement this interface in a class **GeniusMouse** as shown below.

```
// Illustrates declaration and implementation of interface
package interfaceexampleproject ;

interface Mouse
```

```
{
    void lBtnDown ( int x, int y ) ;
    void rBtnDown ( int x, int y ) ;
}
class GeniusMouse implements Mouse
{
    @Override public void lBtnDown ( int x, int y )
    {
        System.out.println ( "Left Button: " + x + " " + y ) ;
    }
    @Override public void rBtnDown ( int x, int y )
    {
        System.out.println ( "Right Button: " + x + " " + y ) ;
    }
}
public class InterfaceExampleProject
{
    public static void main ( String[ ] args )
    {
        GeniusMouse m = new GeniusMouse( ) ;
        m.lBtnDown ( 10,20 ) ;
        m.rBtnDown ( 30,40 ) ;
    }
}
```

Here is the output of the program...

```
Left Button: 10 20
Right Button: 30 40
```

To declare an interface Java provides a keyword called **interface**. The syntax for defining the class that implements an interface is similar to the one used for inheritance, except the use of keyword **implements** instead of **extends**.

In **main( )** we have simply created an instance of **GeniusMouse** and called the implementations of interface methods **lBtnDown( )** and **rBtnDown( )**. The output of the program is simple to follow.

Note the use of an annotation **@Override** in the **GeniusMouse** class. Though not compulsory, we should use it every time we implement an interface method or override a base class method. This practice offers two benefits. By using **@Override** we can take advantage of the compiler checking to make sure we actually are overriding a method when we think we are. This way, if we make a common mistake of misspelling a method name or not correctly matching the parameters, we will be warned that your method does not actually override as we think it does. Secondly, it makes our code easier to understand.

It might occur to you is that the effect that we obtained in this program could have been achieved using an abstract class, instead of an interface. We could have defined an abstract class like this

```
abstract class Mouse
{
    public abstract void lBtnDown ( int x, int y ) ;
    public abstract void rBtnDown ( int x, int y ) ;
}
```

These abstract methods could have then been implemented in **GeniusMouse**. That leads to an important question—how is an abstract class different than an interface? Well, here are the differences...

(a) Abstract class functions may have a body, whereas interface functions never have a body.

(b) Abstract class may contain static, const or instance variables, whereas an interface cannot contain any variables.

(c) Abstract class can be inherited from only one base class, whereas an interface can be inherited from multiple interfaces.

One similarity that abstract classes and interfaces share is, we cannot create objects from either of them.

Now that we have created our first program that uses an interface, it is time for some small tips about interfaces. These are given below.

(a) Interfaces are not derived from **Object** class.
(b) Interfaces are not derived from any base interface.
(c) A class can implement multiple interfaces.
(d) Interfaces can be inherited.
(e) Multiple interface inheritance is allowed.
(f) Class cannot implement an interface partially.

Practical Uses of Interfaces

In my opinion, more than the syntax and the mechanism, it is more important to know the situations in which we should use interfaces. We would discuss three scenarios where interfaces are commonly used. These are as follows:

(a) Interfaces permit us have a focused view of a large implementation.
(b) Interfaces permit us to provide different implementation of same tasks.
(c) Interfaces let us inherit in a class desired qualities from unrelated sources.

Let us now understand each of these situations in detail, with the help of suitable programs.

Interfaces–Focused View

Often in professional software you would find a class that contains so many functions that a quick glance would possibly not give us an idea about their purpose. Instead, if we find that the class implements a particular interface then we would quickly get an idea about what the class is intending to do. For example, if we come to know that a class implements three interfaces—**IEncrypt**, **ICompress** and **IAuthenticate**, then we can guess that the class has something to do with encryption, compression and authentication. Following program defines and implements these interfaces:

```
// Illustrates how interfaces permit us to have a focused view of an
// implementation
package interfacesfocusedviewproject ;

interface IEncrypt
{
    void encrypt( ) ;
    void decrypt( ) ;
}
interface ICompress
{
    void compress( ) ;
    void decompress( ) ;
}
interface IAuthenticate
{
    void login( ) ;
    void logout( ) ;
}
class FocusedView implements IEncrypt, ICompress, IAuthenticate
{
```

```
    @Override public void encrypt( )
    {
        System.out.println ( ">> encrypt" ) ;
    }
    @Override public void decrypt( )
    {
        System.out.println ( ">> decrypt" ) ;
    }
    @Override public void compress( )
    {
        System.out.println ( ">> compress" ) ;
    }
    @Override public void decompress( )
    {
        System.out.println ( ">> decompress" ) ;
    }
    @Override public void login( )
    {
        System.out.println ( ">> login" ) ;
    }
    @Override public void logout( )
    {
        System.out.println ( ">> logout" ) ;
    }
}
public class InterfacesFocusedViewProject
{
    public static void main ( String[ ] args )
    {
        FocusedView o = new FocusedView( ) ;

        IEncrypt ie = o ;
        ie.encrypt( ) ;
        ie.decrypt( ) ;

        ICompress ic = o ;
        ic.compress( ) ;
        ic.decompress( ) ;

        IAuthenticate ia = o ;
        ia.login( ) ;
```

```
        ia.logout( ) ;
    }
}
```

Given below is the output of the program...

```
>> encrypt
>> decrypt
>> compress
>> decompress
>> login
>> logout
```

Few things that you can notice about the program are

(a) The class **FocusedView** implements three interfaces— **IEncrypt**, **ICompress** and **IAuthenticate**. The order in which the interfaces are mentioned in the list while defining the class does not matter.

(b) In **main( )** we have created a **FocusedView** object, assigned its address to an interface reference (say **ICompress**) and then called the methods (**Compress( )** and **Decompress( )**) that belongs to that interface (**ICompress**).

(c) If we call the method **Compress( )** using authentication interface reference **ia**, it would result into a compilation error. This means using an interface reference only methods belonging to that interface alone can be called.

(d) While typing the program when we type "**ia.**", the help shows only those methods that belong to **IAuthenticate** interface. This makes the development of the **FocusedView** class easy, as we get to concentrate only on that part of the class which we are developing right now.

(e) Though the **FocusedView** class implements only interfaces, we may as well derive **FocusedView** from another class. In that case, while defining the class the base class name should precede the interfaces as shown below.

```
class FocusedView extends BaseClass implements IEncrypt,
                                    ICompress, IAuthenticate
{
    // code
}
```

Interfaces–Different Implementations

There are different ways in which we can maintain data in memory. For example, we can store it in an array or a linked list. Each of these data structures would organize the same data in different manner. Hence the actual implementation of operations like counting number of elements, adding a new element, removing an existing element, etc. would be different for these two data structures. However, it would be nice if the way to use these operations remains same. Thus, no matter whether we are using an array or a linked list, we should be able to get the current number of elements in any of them by calling the method **count( )**. Likewise, it should be possible to add a new element to each of them by calling the method **add( )**. This is possible using an interface as shown in the following program:

```
// Same interface, different implemenations
package differentimplementationsproject ;

interface IListMethods
{
    int count( ) ;
    void add ( Object o ) ;
    void remove ( Object o ) ;
}
class MyArray implements IListMethods
{
    @Override public int count( )
    {
        System.out.println ( ">> MyArray.count" ) ;
        return 0 ;
    }
    @Override public void add ( Object o )
    {
        System.out.println ( ">> MyArray.add" ) ;
    }
    @Override public void remove ( Object o )
    {
        System.out.println ( ">> MyArray.remove" ) ;
    }
}
class MyLL implements IListMethods
{
    @Override public int count( )
```

```
    {
        System.out.println ( ">> MyLL.count" ) ;
        return 0 ;
    }
    @Override public void add ( Object o )
    {
        System.out.println ( ">> MyLL.add" ) ;
    }
    @Override public void remove ( Object o )
    {
        System.out.println ( ">> MyLL.remove" ) ;
    }
}
public class DifferentImplementationsProject
{
    public static void main ( String[ ] args )
    {
        IListMethods i ;

        i = new MyArray( ) ;
        i.add ( 1 ) ;
        i.remove ( 1 ) ;
        i.count( ) ;

        i = new MyLL( ) ;
        i.add ( 1 ) ;
        i.remove ( 1 ) ;
        i.count( ) ;
    }
}
```

The program produces the following output:

```
>> MyArray.add
>> MyArray.remove
>> MyArray.count
>> MyLL.add
>> MyLL.remove
>> MyLL.count
```

Here we have defined an interface **IListMethods** containing methods **count( )**, **add( )** and **remove( )**. All these methods have been implemented in the classes **MyArray** and **MyLL**. In **main( )** we have created objects of **MyArray** and **MyLL**, stored their references in the interface reference **i** and then called the three methods in turn. In each method we have just printed a message. In true implementation the methods would contain the logic for counting, addition or deletion.

Same interface, but different implementation is a very common theme followed in good object-oriented software development. Java permits us to use this feature through interfaces.

Interfaces–Unrelated Inheritance

We know that we cannot inherit a class from multiple base classes. However, it is possible to create a class which inherits from one base class and implements one or more interfaces. But when would such a need arise? The need arises when we wish to inherit desired qualities from unrelated sources. For example, a person may want to inherit looks of "John Abraham" and character of "Dr. Abdul Kalam". Looks of a person may include hairstyle, whereas character may include patriotism. These are unrelated qualities. Also, we cannot create a **Person** class and then inherit it from **Actor** class and **Character** class, as multiple inheritance is not permitted in Java. Moreover, you can appreciate that looks can be inherited, whereas character has to be implemented. So to represent this scenario we can create an **Actor** class and an **ICharacter** interface. Then we can create another class **Person** which is derived from **Actor** class and implements **ICharacter** interface. This is shown in the following program:

```
// Demonstrates inheritance from unrelated sources
package unrelatedinheritanceproject ;

interface ICharacter
{
    void patriotism( ) ;
}
class Actor
{
    protected String hairstyle = "Spikes" ;

    public void style( )
    {
        System.out.println ( ">> Actor.Style: " + hairstyle ) ;
    }
}
```

```
class Person extends Actor implements ICharacter
{
    public void doActing( )
    {
        System.out.println ( ">> Person.doActing" ) ;
    }
    public void style( )
    {
        super.style( ) ;
        System.out.println ( ">> Person.style" ) ;
    }
    public void patriotism( )
    {
        System.out.println ( ">> Character.patriotism" ) ;
    }
}
public class UnrelatedInheritanceProject
{
    public static void main ( String[ ] args )
    {
        Actor m ;
        Person p ;

        p = new Person( ) ;
        m = p ;
        m.style( ) ;

        ICharacter i ;
        i = p ;
        i.patriotism( ) ;
    }
}
```

Here, we have created a base class called **Actor** and an Interface called **ICharacter**. The base class has a method called **style( )** and the interface has a method called **patriotism( )**. Then we have created a class called **Person**. This class inherits from **Actor** class and implements **ICharacter** interface. In **main( )** we have created an object of **Person** class and stored its address in **Actor** reference **m** as well as **ICharacter** reference **i**. Then using **m** and **i** we have called the **style( )** and **patriotism( )** methods. The output of the program is given below.

```
>> Actor.Style: Spikes
>> Person.style
>> Character.patriotism
```

Exercise

[A] State whether the following statements are True or False:

(a) Java permits calling of derived class functions using a base class reference.

(b) Abstract functions can never have a body, whereas Abstract constructors can have a body.

(c) We can never build an object from an abstract class.

(d) While building an object it doesn't matter whether the base class constructor is called first or the derived class constructor is called first.

(e) Which of the following statements are correct about Interfaces used in Java?

1. All interfaces are derived from an **Object** class.
2. Interfaces can be inherited.
3. All interfaces are derived from an **Object** interface.
4. Interfaces can contain only method declarations.
5. Interfaces can contain static data and methods.
6. One class can implement only one interface.
7. In a program if one class implements an interface then no other class in the same program can implement this interface.
8. From two base interfaces a new interface cannot be inherited.
9. Interfaces cannot be inherited.
10. If a class implements an interface partially, then it becomes an abstract class.
11. A class cannot implement an interface partially.
12. A class that implements an interface can explicitly implement members of that interface.
13. The functions declared in an interface have a body.
14. Interfaces members are automatically public.

15. To implement an interface member, the corresponding member in the class must be **public** as well as **static**.

16. An explicitly implemented member can be accessed through an instance of the interface.

17. Interfaces can be overloaded.

18. A class can implement multiple interfaces.

19. An interface can implement multiple classes.

20. The static attribute can be used with a method that implements an interface declaration.

(f) How are interfaces different from classes?

(g) Does Java support partial implementation of interfaces?

KanNotes

- Upcasted reference - when a base class reference contains address of derived class object
- Binding means deciding which function to call
- If binding is done at the time of compilation it is called Early Binding
- If binding is done at the time of execution it is called Late Binding
- Java - Always uses Late Binding (Dynamic Dispatch)
- C++ - Does Early Binding when possible and Late Binding when Early Binding is not possible
- Early Binding is also known as Static Binding or Compile time Binding
- Late Binding is also known as Dynamic Binding or Runtime Binding
- For Late Binding the function being called must be present in base class as well as derived class
- To prevent an object from getting created from a class declare it as abstract class
- To prevent a base class method getting called through derived class object mark the method as abstract in the base class
- An abstract class can contain :

  Abstract & non-abstract functions
  Abstract methods do not have a body
  Instance & static variables
  Variables may be inherited
- Abstract classes can participate in inheritance
- If a class contains abstract methods, class has to be abstract

- Interface is an entity through which we interact with a system, person, organization, etc.
- Examples of Hardware Interfaces - RS232, USB, PCI, I2C, SATA
- Examples of Software Interfaces - Text, GUI
- Example of Programming Interface - Functions / Methods
- An interface is a collection of functions declarations
- Implementation (definition) of functions declared in an interface is done in classes that implement the interface
- Different classes may implement the same interface
- A class can implement any number of interfaces
- Interface indicates what a class must do
- Definition of interface functions indicate how to do it
- Difference between Interface and Abstract class :

  Functions :
  - Abstract class functions may have a body
  - Interface functions never have a body

  Instance variables :
  - Abstract class may contain variables. These variables may be inherited
  - Interface may contain variables. These variables are by default static and final
- Interfaces are useful in 3 situations :
  - When similar operation are to be performed on different collections
  - When a focused view is needed in a large implementation
  - When a class has to inherit desired qualities from unrelated sources

Exception Handling

15

Exceptions can't be eliminated completely. They are bound to occur in a Java program. You better know how to deal with them in an OO manner...

Let Us JAVA

3rd Edition

Chapter Contents

Programming is a difficult art. No matter how much confidence you have in your programming ability, several things may wrong during its development. This includes typing errors, compilation errors, linking errors runtime errors. The first three types of errors are comparatively easy to tackle. But when errors occur during execution, your program has to deal with the situation in an elegant fashion. This chapter discusses how to deal with such types of errors.

The errors that occur at runtime—i.e., during execution of the program—are called Exceptions. The reasons why exceptions occur are numerous. Some of the more common ones are as follows:

(a) Falling short of memory
(b) Inability to open a file
(c) Exceeding the bounds of an array
(d) Attempting to initialize an object to an impossible value
(e) Division by zero
(f) Stack overflow
(g) Arithmetic over flow or under flow
(h) Attempt to use an unassigned reference
(i) Unable to connect to Server

When such exceptions occur, the programmer has to decide a strategy according to which he would handle the exceptions. The strategies could be, displaying error messages on the screen, or displaying a dialog box in case of a GUI environment, or requesting the user to supply better data or simply terminating the program execution. Which of these strategies would be adopted depends on whether the exceptional condition can be anticipated or not. Figure 15.1 shows some examples of these exceptional conditions.

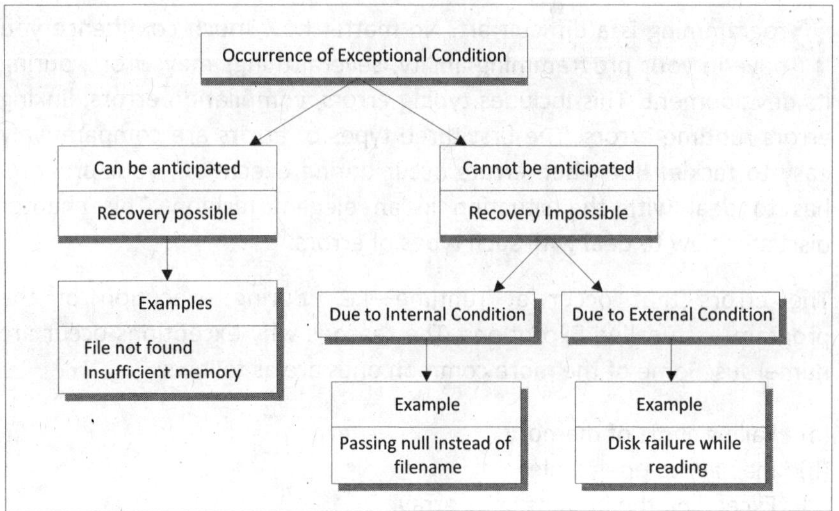

Figure 15.1

Exception Handling in Java

Java provides a systematic, object-oriented approach to handling runtime errors. The exception mechanism of Java uses three keywords—**throw**, **catch**, and **try**. Let us understand their purpose.

Suppose during the course of execution of a member function of a class an error occurs, then Java runtime informs the application that an error has occurred. This process of informing is called **throwing** an exception. This involves two steps:

(a) Creating an object called exception object and storing information about the exceptional condition in it.

(b) Throwing the exception object using the keyword **throw**.

Java runtime creates the exception object from ready-made exception classes provided in the Java Library. Each exception class represents a different exception situation. For example there is an exception class that represents a divide by zero situation, another which represents inability to open file, etc. All these classes are derived from a base class called **Exception**, which in turn is derived from an **Object** class.

If we anticipate an exception situation other than the ones represented through these exception classes, then we can define our own exception class, create an object from this class and then throw that object to report the error situation. To begin with, we would concentrate on exceptions reported by Java runtime and later move to user-defined exceptions. The essence of organization of exception classes is captured in Figure 15.2.

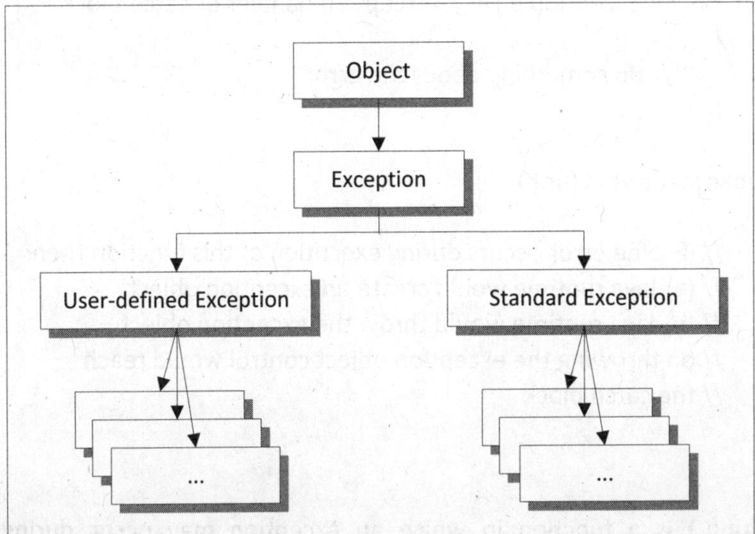

Figure 15.2

The code in the application that anticipates an exception to occur during its execution is enclosed in a **try block**. When the exception occurs and an exception object is thrown the control is transferred to another section of code in the application called **exception handler** or a **catch block**. Thus runtime errors generated in the **try** block are caught in the **catch** block. Code that doesn't expect an exception to occur need not be present within the **try** block.

The following code snippet shows the organization of **try** and **catch** blocks. It is not a working program, but it clearly shows how and where the various elements of the exception mechanism are placed.

```
package exceptionexampleproject ;

public class ExceptionExampleProject
{
    public static void main ( String[ ] args )
    {
        // normal code
        // try block – code where an exception condition is anticipated
        try
```

```
        {
            fun( ) ;
        }
        catch ( Exception e )    // exception handler or catch block
        {
            // do something about the error
        }
    }
    public static void fun( )
    {
        // if some error occurs during execution of this function then:
        // (a) Java runtime would create an exception object
        // (b) Java runtime would throw the exception object
        // on throwing the exception object control would reach
        // the catch block
    }
}
```

Here **fun( )** is a function in which an exception may occur during execution. Hence the call to **fun( )** has been placed in the **try** block. If an exception indeed occurs during execution of **fun( )** then the Java runtime creates an exception object and throws it. This thrown exception object is caught in **Exception** reference **e** in the **catch** block that immediately follows the **try** block.

There are three things that our code can do on receiving a thrown object. These are as follows:

(a) Do nothing and let the default exception handler handle the exceptional condition

(b) Rectify the situation that led to the exceptional condition and continue the execution

(c) Perform a graceful exit

These three possibilities are depicted in Figure 15.3.

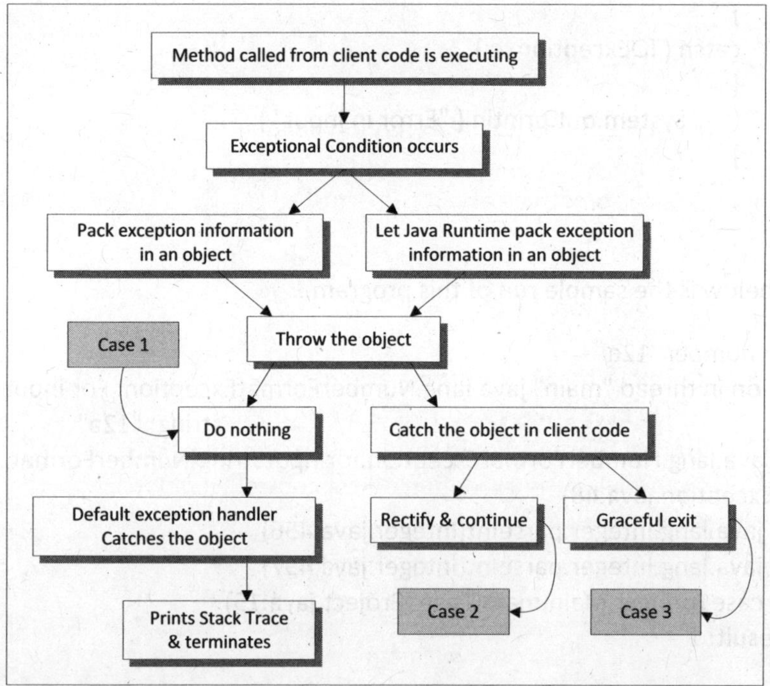

Figure 15.3

Let us now see programs for all these cases to get a real grasp of these situations. Here is the first one...

```
// Case 1 - Do nothing when an exception occurs
package case1project ;
import java.io.* ;

public class Case1Project
{
    public static void main ( String[ ] args ) throws
                                            NumberFormatException
    {
        int num ;
        try
        {
            BufferedReader br = new BufferedReader (
                                    new InputStreamReader ( System.in ) ) ;

            System.out.print ( "Enter a number: " ) ;
            num = Integer.parseInt ( br.readLine( ) ) ;
            System.out.println ( num ) ;
```

```
        }
        catch ( IOException e )
        {
            System.out.println ( "Error in input" ) ;
        }
    }
}
```

Given below is the sample run of this program...

```
Enter a number: 12a
Exception in thread "main" java.lang.NumberFormatException: For input
                                                            string: "12a"
    at java.lang.NumberFormatException.forInputString(NumberFormat
      Exception.java:48)
    at java.lang.Integer.parseInt(Integer.java:456)
    at java.lang.Integer.parseInt(Integer.java:497)
    at case1project.Main.main(Case1Project.java:15)
Java Result: 1
```

In our code there are two possible places where things may wrong:

(a) While reading using **readLine( )**
(b) While converting string into integer using **parseInt( )**

How do we know this? Well, these functions have advertised these exceptions through their prototypes, which read like this

```
public String readLine( ) throws IOException
public static int parseInt ( String s ) throws NumberFormatException
```

As you can see, these prototypes indicate that if something goes wrong with **readLine( )**, then it would throw **IOException** and if something goes wrong with **parseInt( )**, then it would throws **NumberFormatException**. This is known as advertising an exception.

For these advertised exceptions, we may adopt any of the following three approaches:

(a) Catch both the exceptions ourselves.
(b) Catch one and throw the other further, so that the default exception handler can deal with it.
(c) Throw both the exceptions further, so that the default exception handler can deal with them.

In our program we have followed approach (b)—we have caught **IOException** and thrown further the **NumberFormatException**.

From the output of the program you can see that when we enter the number as "12a" and attempt to convert it into a string through a call to **Integer.parseInt( )**, an exception occurs. Since we have thrown this exception further, the Java runtime prints a stack trace and then terminates the execution of the program. You should read the stack trace from bottom to top. If you do that, you can follow that the error occurred in the file "Case1Project" while executing line number 15. This line is present in **main( )** and contains a call to **Integer.parseInt( )**. And during execution of this function an exception occurred, as the input "12a" could not be converted into a number. Finally, it also reports the name of the exception—**NumberFormatException**.

Let us now look at the second case, where we would attempt to rectify the exception situation by prompting the user to provide correct input and then continue the execution of the program from the point where the exception occurred. Here is the program...

```
// Case 2 – Rectify and continue when an exception occurs
package case2project ;
import java.io.* ;

public class Case2Project
{
	public static void main ( String[ ] args )
	{
		int num ;
		while ( true )
		{
			try
			{
				BufferedReader br = new BufferedReader (
						new InputStreamReader ( System.in ) ) ;

				System.out.println ( "Enter a number: " ) ;
				num = Integer.parseInt ( br.readLine( ) ) ;
				break ;
			}
			catch ( IOException  e )
			{
```

```
                System.out.println ( "Error in input" ) ;
            }
            catch ( NumberFormatException  e )
            {
                System.out.println ( "Incorrect Input" ) ;
            }
        }

        System.out.println ( "You entered: " + num ) ;
    }
}
```

Shown below is a sample interaction with this program.

```
Enter a number:
12a
Incorrect Input
Enter a number:
12
You entered: 12
```

As you can see, when we provide the input as "12a" an exception occurs. But rather than terminating the execution, this time the program prompts the user to enter another number. When we supply "12", it gets converted into a number and then displayed Thus, we are now able to rectify the exceptional situation and continue with the execution of the program.

You can note three things about the **catch** block:

(a) **catch** block must immediately follow the **try** block.
(b) When an exception occurs, control goes to **catch** block.
(c) After **catch** block is executed, control goes to the next line after **catch** block unless there is a **return** or **throw** in the **catch** block.

Let us now turn our attention to case 3. It may not always be possible to recover from the exceptional situation. In such cases rather than printing the ugly and intimidating stack trace to the user, our program should report an error and gracefully terminate the execution. The program given below shows how this can be achieved.

```
// Case 3 – Exit gracefully when an exception occurs
package case3project ;
import java.io.*  ;
```

```
public class Case3Project
{
    public static void main ( String[ ] args )
    {
        int num ;
        try
        {
            BufferedReader br = new BufferedReader (
                                    new InputStreamReader ( System.in ) ) ;

            System.out.println ( "Enter a number: " ) ;
            num = Integer.parseInt ( br.readLine( ) ) ;
            System.out.println ( "You entered: " + num ) ;
        }
        catch ( IOException  e )
        {
            System.out.println ( "Error in input" ) ;
        }
        catch ( NumberFormatException e )
        {
            System.out.println ( "Incorrect Input" ) ;
        }
    }
}
```

From the interaction with the program shown below, you can see that when we supply the input as "12a" the program reports that the input is incorrect and then terminates the execution.

```
Enter a number:
12a
Incorrect Input
```

Catching Multiple Exceptions

If one thing can go wrong then multiple things may also go wrong. So true in real life, this is also true in programming. That is, while executing a piece of code there is a possibility of multiple exceptions. These can be tackled by providing multiple **catch** blocks for one **try** block. A program that illustrates how this can be done is given below.

```
// Multiple exceptions
package multipleexceptionsproject ;
import java.io.*  ;

public class MultipleExceptionsProject
{
    public static void main ( String[ ] args )
    {
        int i, j ;
        try
        {
            BufferedReader br = new BufferedReader (
                                    new InputStreamReader ( System.in ) ) ;

            System.out.println ( "Enter i: " ) ;
            i = Integer.parseInt ( br.readLine( ) ) ;

            System.out.println ( "Enter j: " ) ;
            j = Integer.parseInt ( br.readLine( ) ) ;

            System.out.println ( "You entered: " + i + " "+ j ) ;
            System.out.println ( "Result: "+ i / j ) ;
        }
        catch ( IOException  e )
        {
            System.out.println ( "Error in input" ) ;
        }
        catch ( NumberFormatException ne )
        {
            System.out.println ( "Incorrect Input" ) ;
        }
        catch ( ArithmeticException ae )
        {
            System.out.println ( "Arithmetic Exception, div by 0" ) ;
        }
        catch ( Exception e )
        {
            System.out.println ( "Unknown Error: " + e ) ;
        }
    }
}
```

Here we have accounted for three possibilities while executing the code in the **try** block. These are as follows:

(a) The input is incorrect, i.e., a value like "12a" is entered
(b) The denominator is equal to 0
(c) Some unknown error

To deal with each of these situations we have provided separate **catch** blocks. Based on which exception occurs, the Java runtime creates an appropriate exception object and throws it. That is why in each **catch** block the thrown object is collected in a different exception object. For example, if the input is incorrect then the exception object that is thrown is collected in an object of the type **NumberFormatException**. Unlike this, if the denominator is 0 then the exception object that is thrown is collected in an object of the type **ArithmeticException**.

There are two important things that you should note here:

(a) At a time only one **catch** block goes to work.
(b) Order of **catch** blocks is important. Their order should be derived to base as regards the exception object.

Let us elaborate the second point mentioned above. Since the **NumberFormatException** and **ArithmeticException** classes are derived from the **Exception** class, their **catch** blocks should occur before the one that catches an **Exception** object.

The *finally* Block

At times, we want that no matter whether an exception occurs or not, some statements must get executed. The **finally** block is the solution for these situations. The program given below illustrates its usage.

```
// Usage of finally block
package finallyblockproject ;
import java.io.*  ;

public class FinallyBlockProject
{
      public static void main ( String[ ] args )
      {
            FileWriter fw = null ;
```

```
        try
        {
            fw = new FileWriter ( "a.txt" ) ;
            fw.write ( "Hello World\n" ) ;
        }
        catch ( IOException ie )
        {
            System.out.println ( "Encountered IO Error" ) ;
        }
        finally
        {
            try
            {
                if ( fw != null )
                    fw.close( ) ;
            }
            catch ( IOException e )
            {
                System.out.println ( "Error in input" ) ;
            }
        }
    }
}
```

Though we intend to deal with File Input/Output in great detail in a later chapter, in this program we can have our first tryst with it. To write data into a disk file, we must first create a **FileWriter** object by passing to its constructor the name of the file into which we propose to write. The actual writing is done by calling the **write( )** function of the **FileWriter** class. If an exception occurs during construction of the **FileWriter** object or during writing, then the **catch** block would appropriately report it.

Now comes the crucial part—no matter whether writing is done successfully or not, before exiting the file that has been opened by the constructor, must be closed. The **finally** block serves this purpose. Statements in the **finally** block always get executed no matter whether an exception occurs or not. This is true even if a **return** statement is encountered beforehand. As you must have guessed, **finally** is a keyword, and is used following the **catch** block(s). In our **finally** block we have first checked whether the **FileWriter** object has been created successfully. If so, we have called the **close( )** method to close the file associated with the **FileWriter** object.

User-defined Exceptions

In all the programs in this chapter we have been using exception objects created from Java exception classes. It is time we explore the possibility of user-defined exception classes. Such classes are required when an exception condition that occurs cannot be represented using the standard exception classes. For example, a banking application may throw an exception when the amount being withdrawn makes the balance in an account go below the minimum prescribed limit. Another example could be when the amount of transaction in a credit card application is more than the credit limit of a credit card. In such cases we need to define our own exception class, and when an exception occurs, we need to create an object of this exception class and throw it. The following program illustrates this in a simple banking application:

```
// Usage of user-defined exception
package userdefinedexceptionproject ;

class Customer
{
    private String name ;
    private int accno ;
    private int balance ;

    public Customer ( String n, int a, int b )
    {
        name = n ;  accno = a ; balance = b ;
    }
    public void withdraw ( int amt ) throws BankException
    {
        if ( balance - amt <= 500 )
        {
            throw new BankException ( accno, balance ) ;
        }

        balance -= amt ;
    }
}
class BankException extends Exception
{
    private int acc ;
    private int bal ;
```

```
    public BankException ( int a , int b )
    {
        this.acc = a ;
        this.bal = b ;
    }
    public void inform( )
    {
        System.out.println ( "Acc. No.: "+ acc ) ;
        System.out.println ( "Balance: "+ bal ) ;
    }
}
public class UserDefinedExceptionProject
{
    public static void main ( String[ ] args )
    {
        try
        {
            Customer c = new Customer ( "Rahul", 2453, 900 ) ;
            c.withdraw ( 450 ) ;
        }
        catch ( BankException  ex )
        {
            System.out.println ( "Transaction failed" ) ;
            ex.inform( ) ;
        }
    }
}
```

Given below is the output of the program...

```
Transaction failed
Acc. No.: 2453
Balance: 900
```

In this program apart from the normal class that contains **main( )**, we have defined two new classes—**Customer** and **BankException**. From **main( )** we have constructed an object of **Customer** class to contain name, account number and balance amount. Then we have called the **withdraw( )** method from the **try** block to withdraw an amount of Rs. 450 from the customer's account. Since the amount being withdrawn makes the balance go below Rs. 500, an exception occurs. To represent this exceptional condition, an object of **BankException** (derived from **Exception** class) class is created. The account number and current balance values are stored in this **BankException** object. This object is then thrown using the keyword **throw**. This takes the control straightway to the **catch** block that matches the **try** block, from where **withdraw( )** method was called. In the **catch** block we have called the method **inform( )** which promptly displays the error message "Transaction failed" along with account number and the current balance.

A More Practical Example

Admittedly, the examples that we have used so far to understand exception handling were a bit amateurish. Let's now try to use exception handling in a more practical situation. We would try to implement a stack data structure. We would use exception handling to report errors in two situations:

(a) When the program attempts to store more objects in the stack than what it can accommodate.

(b) When the program tries to remove an object from the empty stack.

Here is the program that uses exceptions to handle these two errors.

```
// Use of exceptions to report errors while maintaining a stack
package stackswithexceptionsproject ;
class Stack
{
    private int capacity ;
    private int size ;
    private Object[ ] data ;

    public Stack ( int cap )
    {
        data = new Object[ cap ] ;
        capacity = cap ;
        size = 0 ;
    }
    public void push ( Object o ) throws StackException
    {
        if ( size == capacity )
            throw new StackException ( "Stack full" ) ;
```

```
        data[ size ] = o ;
        size++ ;
    }
    public Object pop( ) throws StackException
    {
        if ( size <= 0 )
            throw new StackException ( "Stack empty" ) ;

        size-- ;
        return data[ size ] ;
    }
    public int getSize( )
    {
        return size ;
    }
}
class StackException extends Exception
{
    private String errormsg ;

    public StackException ( String msg )
    {
        this.errormsg = msg ;
    }
    public void inform( )
    {
        System.out.println ( errormsg ) ;
    }
}
public class StacksWithExceptionsProject
{
    public static void main ( String[ ] args )
    {
        Stack s = new Stack ( 3 ) ;
        try
        {
            s.push ( "Vinod" ) ;
            s.push ( "Sanjay" ) ;
            s.push ( 25 ) ;
            s.push ( 3.14f ) ;
```

```
        }
        catch ( StackException ex )
        {
            System.out.println ( "Problem in stack" ) ;
            ex.inform( ) ;
        }

        try
        {
            while ( s.getSize( ) > 0 )
                System.out.println ( s.pop( ) ) ;
        }
        catch ( StackException ex )
        {
            System.out.println ( "Problem in stack" ) ;
            ex.inform( ) ;
        }
    }
}
```

Given below is the output that the program produces on execution:

```
Problem in stack
Stack full
25
Sanjay
Vinod
```

We have purposefully kept the capacity of the stack small so that it's easier to trigger an exception while adding objects to the stack. We would leave it for you to go through the program and figure out how it produces this output, as an exercise. Also, you can try to implement the Queue data structure on similar lines as stack.

From the above two programs—Banking and Stack—we can now generalize how to deal with user-defined exceptions. There are four parts involved in the exception handling mechanism. These are as under:

Define the Exception Class

We have defined such exception classes in our programs—**BankException** and **StackException**. Both classes were inherited from

Exception class and had a constructor using which an exception object can be created. Additionally these classes had a method called **inform( )** to report the error message.

Throw an Exception

When an exception situation occurs an exception object is created and thrown. In our first program an exception could occur in one situation—when the balance goes below 500, whereas, in the second program there were two exceptional situations—when the stack becomes full and we try to store another object in it, or when we try to remove an object from an empty stack. In the first program, we create and throw a **BankException** object, whereas in the second we create and throw a **StackException** object. On throwing an exception the control is transferred to the exception handler, i.e., the **catch** block.

The *try* Block

The statements that might cause the exceptions have been enclosed in a pair of braces and preceded by the **try** keyword. This code is the programs' normal code. We would have written it even if we weren't using exceptions. Note that all the code in the program need not be in a **try** block. Just the code that anticipates occurrence of exceptional condition during execution should be in **try** block..

The Exception Handler (*catch* Block)

The code that handles an exception is enclosed in braces, preceded by the **catch** keyword, with the exception object that it proposes to catch mentioned in parentheses.

How the Whole Thing Works?

Let's summarize the events that take place when an exception occurs:

(a) Code is executing normally outside a **try** block.
(b) Control enters the **try** block.
(c) A statement in the **try** block causes an error in a member function called from it.
(d) The member function creates and throws an exception object.
(e) Control transfers to the exception handler (**catch** block) following the **try** block.

You can appreciate how clean is this code. Just about any statement in the **try** block can cause an exception, but we don't need to worry which one. The **try-throw-catch** arrangement handles it all for us, automatically.

A Few Tips...

To round off all that we have learnt about exception handling, here are a few finer points about it that you must note:

(a) Don't catch and ignore. For example, it is a wrong practice to write a **catch** block like this:

```
catch ( Exception e )
{
}
```

Programmers are tempted to write this when runtime errors occur in their program and they wish to avoid displaying of an ugly and elaborate stack trace of the exception.

(b) Don't use exception handling for cosmetic purpose. It should serve the purpose of rectifying the exceptional situation or perform a graceful exit.

(c) Always try to distinguish between types of exceptions by writing multiple **catch** blocks wherever relevant.

(d) It is not necessary that the statement that causes an exception be located directly in the **try** block. It may as well be present in a function that is being called from the **try** block.

(e) A **try** block can be present inside another **try** block.

(f) If inner **try** block doesn't have a corresponding **catch block**, then the outer **try** block's **catch** handlers are inspected for a match when an exception occurs.

(g) If we are writing a class library for somebody else to use, we should anticipate what could cause problems to the program using it. At all such places we should throw exceptions.

(h) If we are writing a program that uses a class library, we should provide **try** and **catch** blocks for any exceptions that the library may throw.

(i) Exceptions impose an overhead in terms of program size and (when an exception occurs) in time. So we should not try to overuse it. Make it optimally elaborate—not too much, not too little.

Exercise

[A] State whether the following statements are True or False:

(a) The exception handling mechanism is supposed to handle compile time errors.

(b) It is necessary to declare the exception class within the class in which an exception is going to be thrown.

(c) Every thrown exception must be caught.

(d) For one **try** block there can be multiple **catch** blocks.

(e) When an exception is thrown an exception class's constructor gets called.

(f) **try** blocks cannot be nested.

(g) Proper destruction of an object is guaranteed by exception handling mechanism.

(h) All exceptions occur at runtime.

(i) Exceptions offer an object-oriented way of handling runtime errors.

(j) If an exception occurs, then the program terminates abruptly without getting any chance to recover from the exception.

(k) No matter whether an exception occurs or not, the statements in the **finally** clause (if present) will get executed.

(l) A program can contain multiple **finally** clauses.

(m) **finally** clause is used to perform cleanup operations like closing the network/database connections.

(n) While throwing a user-defined exception multiple values can be set in the exception object.

(o) In one function, there can be only one **try** block.

(p) An exception must be caught in the same function in which it is thrown.

(q) All values set up in the exception object are available in the **catch** block.

(r) If our program does not catch an exception then the Java Runtime catches it.

(s) It is possible to create user-defined exceptions.

(t) All types of exceptions can be caught using the **Exception** class.

(u) For every **try** block there must be a corresponding **finally** block.

[B] Answer the following:

(a) If we do not catch the exception thrown at runtime then who will catch it?

(b) Explain in short most compelling reasons for using exception handling over conventional error handling approaches.

(c) Is it necessary that all classes that can be used to represent exceptions be derived from base class **Exception**?

(d) What is the use of a **finally** block in Java exception handling sequence?

(e) How does nested exception handling work in Java?

KanNotes

- Three forms of decision control instruction :
- While creating and executing a Java program things may go wrong at 3 different stages :

  During Compilation : Reported by – Compiler, Action – Rectify program
  During Linking : Reported by – Linker, Action – Proper import statements
  During Execution (runtime) : Reported by – Java Runtime, Action – Tackle it on the fly
- Examples of Runtime errors :

  Memory Related - Stack / Heap overflow, Exceeding the bounds of an array
  Arithmetic Related - Divide by zero, Arithmetic over flow or under flow
  Others - Attempt to use an unassigned reference, File not found
- 2 Types of Exceptional conditions :

  (a) Checked Exceptions - Compiler checks whether they have been handled

      Ex. File not found, Insufficient memory

  (b) Unchecked exceptions - Up to us whether to handle them or not
- 2 Types of Unchecked Exceptions :

  (a) Due to Internal Condition - k/a Runtime Exceptions
      Ex. : Passing null instead of filename

  (b) Due to External Condition - k/a Errors
      Ex. : Disk failure while reading
- How to determine - Checked or Unchecked
  - Follow trail by clicking on exception
  - It is a Checked Exception, if you reach "Exception" class

- It is an Unchecked Exception, if you reach "RuntimeException" or "Error" class

- When a method called from client code is executing and an Exceptional Condition may occur. This condition can be tackled in 2 Ways :

  (a) Pack exception information in an object and throw it
  (b) Let Java Runtime pack exception information in an object and throw it

- Two things that can be done when the exception object is thrown :

  (a) Throw it further
  (b) Catch the object in client code

- If we throw the exception object further - Default exception handler Catches the object, Prints Stack Trace & terminates

- If we catch the exception object in client code we can either perform a Graceful exit or Rectify the exceptional situation & continue

- 2 Ways to create Exceptional Condition objects

  From Java API exception classes
  From User-defined exception classes

- Advantage of tackling exceptions in OO manner :

  - More info can be packed into Exception objects
  - Propagation of exception objects to caller is managed by Java Runtime

- How Java facilitates OO exception handling :

  - By providing keywords - try, catch, finally, throw, throws
  - By providing readymade exception classes - For Checked as well as Unchecked Exceptions
  - Advertise - Let methods advertise possibility of an exception
  - Force - Make users handle advertised exception

- How to use try - catch

  try block - Enclose in it the code that you anticipate would cause an exception catch block - Catch the thrown exception in it. It must immediately follow the try block

- When exception is thrown control goes to catch block. Once catch block is executed, control goes to the next line after catch block(s), unless there is a return or throw in the catch block

- When a method advertises that it will throw an exception, you have to either catch or rethrow it.

- try block :
  - Can be nested inside the another try block
  - If inner try doesn't have a catch, outer try's catch handlers are inspected for a match

- catch block :
  - Multiple catch blocks for one try block are OK
  - At a time only one catch block goes to work
  - Order of catch blocks is important - Derived to Base

- finally block :
  - finally clause is optional
  - Code in finally always runs, no matter what! Even if a return or break occurs first
  - it is placed after catch blocks (if they exist)
  - try block must have catch block and/or finally block

- Exception handling tips :
  - Don't catch & ignore an exception
  - Don't catch everything using "Exception", distinguish between types of exceptions
  - Make it optimally elaborate - Not too much, not too little

Effective Input / Output

16

No point in creating a program that tells secrets to itself. Input / Output is the way of life for a program...

Let Us JAVA

3rd Edition

Chapter Contents

- Expectations from an I/O System
- File, Directory and Drive Operations
- The Java Streams Solution
- Stream Classes
- Byte and Character Operations
- Reading Strings from a File
- Record I/O
- User-defined Streams
- File Encryption/Decryption
- Exercise
- KanNotes

Almost all programs have to perform Input/Output (I/O) in some form or the other. There is not much use of writing a program that spends all its time telling itself a secret. And since all languages have been dealing with input/output since the very first program came into existence, it is quite natural to expect that a modern object-oriented language like Java provides a *mature* input/output system. This chapter proposes to explore the ways provided by Java to effectively carry out I/O needs of a program.

Expectations from an I/O System

Since mankind has been creating software and writing programs for more than five decades now, a programmer has begun to expect some solid support from a language's I/O system to cater to his/her program's I/O needs. These expectations are as follows:

(a) **Communication with different sources and destination**: A Java program should be able to carry out reading operations from input devices like keyboard, port, disk, etc., and perform writing operations to disk, printer, port, etc.

(b) **Capability to I/O varied entities**: A Java program should be able to I/O byte, char, numbers of all kinds, strings, records and objects.

(c) **Multiple means of communication**: A Java program should be able to carry out I/O in different modes like sequential and random.

(d) **Communication with file system**: A Java program should be able to interact with file system entities like files and directories and be able to access and manipulate paths, times, dates, access permissions, etc.

Let us now see how Java meets these expectations.

File, Directory and Drive Operations

We are often required to programmatically perform operations on files, directories and drives. For example, we may wish to create, copy, delete, move, or open a file. Similarly, we may wish to create, move, and navigate through directories and subdirectories. To carry out such operations Java library provides a ready-made class called **File**. Based on the requirement, we can appropriately use the methods of this class to carry out the relevant file/directory operations.

Let us now create programs that use the **File** class. We would begin with one that receives name of a file as input and then checks whether such a file exists or not. If it does, then it reports the relevant information about this file. Here is the program...

```
// Obtain information about a file
package fileinfoproject ;

import java.io.* ;
import java.util.Date ;

public class FileInfoProject
{
    public static void main ( String[ ] args )
    {
        String str ;
        try
        {
            BufferedReader br = new BufferedReader ( new
                                    InputStreamReader ( System.in ) ) ;
            System.out.print ( "Enter filename: " ) ;
            str = br.readLine( ) ;

            File f ;
            f = new File ( str ) ;
            if ( f.exists() )
            {
                String dname = f.getParent( ) ;
                System.out.println ( "Directory name: " + dname ) ;
                String fname = f.getName( ) ;
                System.out.println ( "File name: " + fname ) ;
                String abspath = f.getAbsolutePath( ) ;
                System.out.println ( "Full Name: " + abspath ) ;

                long size = f.length( ) ;
                System.out.println ( "Size: " + size ) ;
                String ext ;
                int dot = str.lastIndexOf ( "." ) ;
                ext = str.substring ( dot ) ;
                System.out.println ( "Extension = " + ext ) ;
                System.out.println ( "Last Modified = " +
                                    new Date ( f.lastModified( ) ) ) ;
            }
        }
```

```
        catch ( IOException e )
        {
            System.out.println ( "Error in input" ) ;
        }
    }
}
```

And now a sample interaction with this program...

```
Enter filename: c:\a.txt
Directory name: c:\
File name: a.txt
Full Name: c:\a.txt
Size: 2748
Extension = .txt
Last Modified = Tue Feb 09 16:29:24 IST 2010
```

The program is pretty straight-forward. To begin with, it receives the name of the file—"C:\a.txt" (you may give any other file's path as input). Next, it creates a **File** object for this file and then extracts all the details of this file using different methods of the **File** class. To be able to use the **File** class and the **Date** class it is necessary to add the suitable **import** statements at the beginning of the program.

In addition to the methods used here, there are several other methods in the **File** class. You may explore them on your own.

Let us now create a program that gives a listing of all files in a directory. Here is the program...

```
// Recursive listing of files in directories
package directorylisterproject ;
import java.io.* ;

public class DirectoryListerProject
{
    public static void main ( String[ ] args )
    {
        File d ;
        d = new File ( "." ) ;
        ListFiles ( d, "" ) ;
    }
    static void ListFiles ( File d, String indent )
```

```
    {
        String str ;
        System.out.println ( indent + d.getName( ) + "/" ) ;
        for ( File fi : d.listFiles( ) )
        {
            str = indent + "  " + fi.getName( ) ;
            System.out.println ( str ) ;
        }

        // implement accept function of FileFilter interface
        FileFilter dirFilter = new FileFilter( )
        {
            public boolean accept ( File file )
            {
                return file.isDirectory( ) ;
            }
        } ;

        for ( File di : d.listFiles(dirFilter ) )
            ListFiles ( di, indent + "  " ) ;
    }
}
```

On executing the program on my machine it produced the following output:

```
./
 build
 build.xml
 manifest.mf
 nbproject
 src
 build/
  classes
  classes/
   .netbeans_automatic_build
   .netbeans_update_resources
   directorylisterproject
   directorylisterproject/
    DirectoryListerProject$1.class
    DirectoryListerProject.class
 nbproject/
```

```
    build-impl.xml
    genfiles.properties
    private
    project.properties
    project.xml
    private/
      private.properties
  src/
    directorylisterproject
    directorylisterproject/
      DirectoryListerProject.java
```

In the output every directory has been purposefully marked with a / to help identify an entry as a directory. Each nested directory is indented to the right to show the hierarchy clearly.

At the heart of the program is the function **ListFiles( )**. This function is first called from **main( )** with two arguments—"." and "". The first argument indicates from where to start the listing and second indicates the starting indentation level. "." means current directory. Thus, for our program **DirectoryListerProject** is the starting directory. In the **ListFiles( )** function we have first obtained and printed all files in this directory. In course of this, if we came across any directory then we have called **ListFiles( )** recursively to list files in this directory.

Let us now look at another interesting program. This one obtains and reports information about all the drives present in a machine. To obtain the list of drives, it uses the **listRoots( )** method of the **File** class. Then through a **for** loop it iterates through this list, gathering details of each drive using the methods of the **File** class. Rest of the program is pretty straight-forward. Here is the program...

```
// Obtain information about all drives
package driveinfoproject ;
import java.io.* ;

public class DriveInfoProject
{
    public static void main ( String[ ] args )
    {
        for ( File d : File.listRoots() )
        {
            System.out.println ( "Drive = " + d ) ;
```

```
                System.out.println ( "Total Space = "+ d.getTotalSpace( ) ) ;
                System.out.println ( "Free Space = "+ d.getFreeSpace( ) ) ;
                System.out.println ( " " ) ;
            }
        }
}
```

The machine on which I executed this program had 6 drives. Out of these 3 were hard disk drives whereas the other 3 were DVD reader, DVD read/write drive and a virtual drive. The output that I got on this machine is given below.

```
Drive = C:\
Total Space = 179583315968
Free Space = 18052345856

Drive = D:\
Total Space = 59624124416
Free Space = 20760801280

Drive = E:\
Total Space = 10737414144
Free Space = 6717689856

Drive = F:\
Total Space = 0
Free Space = 0

Drive = G:\
Total Space = 0
Free Space = 0

Drive = H:\
Total Space = 0
Free Space = 0
```

The Java Streams Solution

To meet the expectations of a mature I/O system Java designers decided that all I/O should be performed using I/O Streams. A stream is a sequence of bytes that travel from source to destination over a communication path. A program can read data from a stream or write data to a stream. The streams are linked to physical devices by Java I/O system. Most of the communication details are hidden from us by the I/O system and we are required to concentrate only on what we wish to read from where, and what we wish to write where. Figure 16.1 should help you understand this concept better.

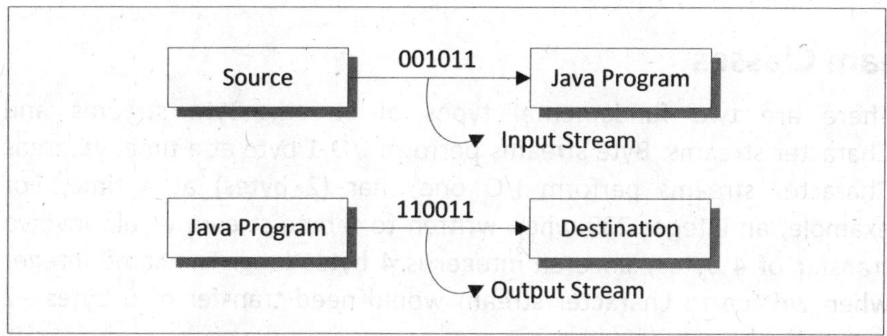

Figure 16.1

Streams are implemented using classes in **java.io** package. This abstraction of I/O operations using streams offers one important benefit—no matter from where we are reading or where we are writing, stream behaves similarly. For example, whether we are reading from a keyboard or a disk we call the same **readLine( )** method. The implementation of the **readLine( )** method is different for different devices. Thus because of stream-based I/O the programmer doesn't have to worry about the specific details of the operating system and underlying devices while performing I/O as shown in Figure 16.2. The differences in the devices and the OS are hidden away from us into different stream classes in the **java.io** package.

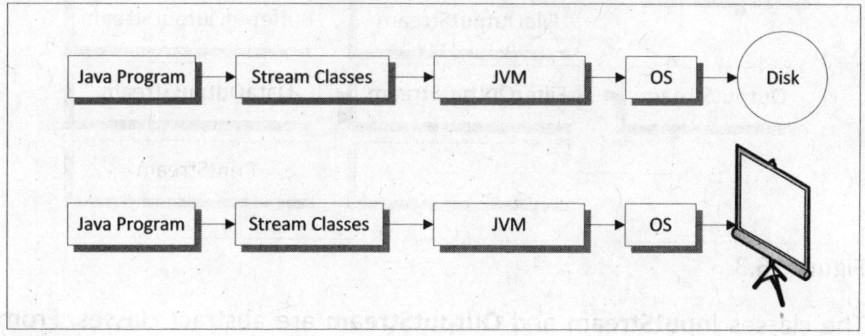

Figure 16.2

The two fundamental operations that can be performed on a stream are Reading and Writing. Reading involves transfer of data from a stream into a data structure, such as an array of bytes. Writing consists of transfer of data from a data source into a stream.

Every stream may not support reading and writing. Most stream classes contain methods called **canRead( )** and **canWrite( )** using which we can determine which operations that stream supports.

Stream Classes

There are two fundamental types of streams–Byte streams and Character streams. Byte streams perform I/O 1 byte at a time, whereas Character streams perform I/O one char (2 bytes) at a time. For example, an integer 235 when written to a byte stream would involve transfer of 4 bytes, since an integer is 4 bytes long. The same integer when written to character stream would need transfer of 6 bytes—2 bytes per character.

There are several classes available in the Java library to perform stream-based input/output of bytes/characters. Figure 16.3 and Figure 16.4 show the hierarchy of these classes.

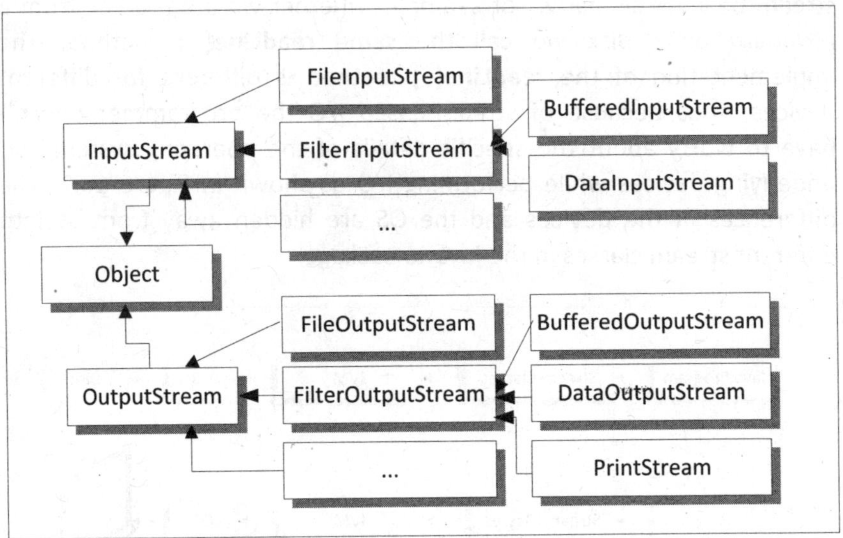

Figure 16.3

The classes **InputStream** and **OutputStream** are abstract classes. From these classes **FileInputStream** and **FileOutputStream** are derived. As their names suggest, these classes read/write streams of bytes from/to file. The **FilterInputStream** class uses some input stream as source of data and filters it based on some criterion. The **BufferedInputStream** class provides the buffering ability. Buffering is used to improve read/write performance of a stream. The **DataInputStream** class provides ability to read Java primitives.

Figure 16.4 shows the hierarchy of classes used for performing character based input/output.

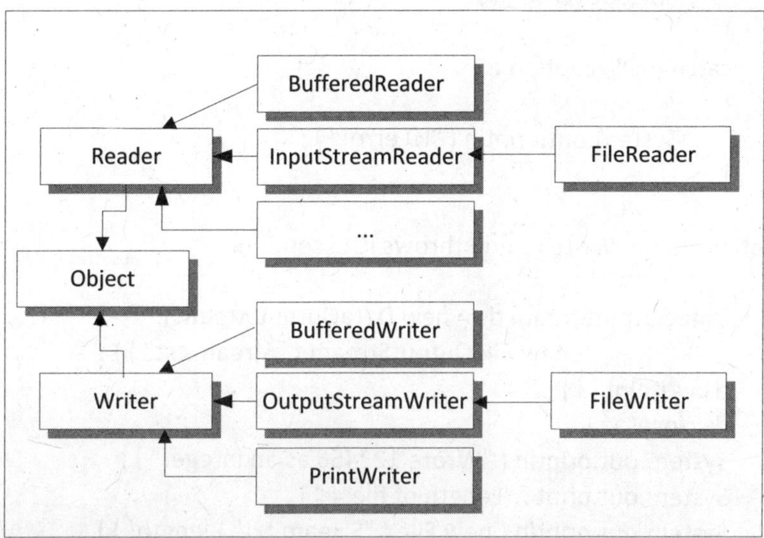

Figure 16.4

The classes **Reader** and **Writer** are abstract classes. The classes **InputStreamReader** and **OutputStreamWriter** are used to read/write character from/to stream. The **FileReader** and **FileWriter** classes are used to read/write from/to file. The **PrintWriter** class is used to carry out formatted writing in text representation.

Byte and Character Operations

Let us now create programs that use the different stream classes. We would begin with a program that writes an integer in multiple ways into a file. Here is the program...

```
package byteandcharacterstreams ;
import java.io.* ;

public class ByteAndCharacterStreams
{
    public static void main ( String[ ] args )
    {
        int i = 123456 ;
        try
        {
```

```
            rawWrite ( i ) ;
            charWrite ( i ) ;
            unicodeWrite ( i ) ;
        }
        catch ( IOException e )
        {
            System.out.println ( "IO error" ) ;
        }
    }
    static void rawWrite ( int i ) throws IOException
    {
        DataOutputStream ds = new DataOutputStream (
                        new FileOutputStream ( "Stream.txt" ) ) ;
        ds.writeInt ( i ) ;
        ds.close( ) ;
        System.out.println ( "Wrote 123456 as an integer" ) ;
        System.out.print ( "Length of file = " ) ;
        System.out.println ( new File ( "Stream.txt" ).length( ) ) ;
    }
    static void charWrite ( int i ) throws IOException
    {
        FileWriter fw = new FileWriter ( new File ( "Char.txt" ) ) ;
        fw.write ( ( ( Integer ) i ).toString( ) ) ;
        fw.close( ) ;
        System.out.println ( "Wrote 123456 as a string" ) ;
        System.out.print ( "Length of file = " ) ;
        System.out.println ( new File ( "Char.txt" ).length( ) ) ;
    }
    static void unicodeWrite ( int i ) throws IOException
    {
        OutputStreamWriter ow = new OutputStreamWriter (
            new FileOutputStream ( "CharU.txt" ), "UTF-16" ) ;
        ow.write ( ( ( Integer ) i ).toString( ) ) ;
        ow.close( ) ;
        System.out.println ( "Wrote 123456 as a Unicode string" ) ;
        System.out.print ( "Length of file = " ) ;
        System.out.println ( new File ( "CharU.txt" ).length( ) ) ;
    }
}
```

On executing this program, it produces the output shown below.

```
Wrote 123456 as an integer
Length of file = 4
Wrote 123456 as a string
Length of file = 6
Wrote 123456 as a Unicode string
Length of file = 14
```

The program writes the same integer into 3 files in different ways. For example, it is written as an **int** in the first file, as a **string** in the second and as a **Unicode string** in the third. These writing operations are done through three methods defined in the program—**rawWrite( )**, **charWrite( )** and **unicodeWrite( )**.

Note that after writing the same integer value (123456), the sizes of the three files "Raw.txt", "Char.txt" and "CharU.txt" are reported as 4, 6 and 14 bytes, respectively. This indicates that during raw write, each byte value of the 4-byte integer is written. Unlike this, during character writing, the integer was first converted into a string "123456" and then written to the file character-by-character. In Unicode writing, each character of the string was written as a 2-byte character.

Before writing to a file, the file is opened using either the **FileOutputStream** or **File** object. While writing the integer as an **int**, a **DataOutputStream** object is used, whereas, while writing it as a string or a Unicode string, a **FileWriter** and **OutputStreamWriter**, respectively are used. Objects of these writers are created before using them to call the **writeInt( )** and **write( )** methods. Instead of the statement,

```
DataOutputStream ds = new DataOutputStream (
                          new FileOutputStream ( "Stream.txt" ) ) ;
```

we can split it into two parts

```
fos = new FileOutputStream ( "Stream.txt" ) ;
DataOutputStream ds = new DataOutputStream ( fos ) ;
```

The **close( )** function is called at the end of writing operations to close the current stream and release any resources associated with the current stream.

Rest of the program is simple to understand. You can modify this program to write float values to a file.

Reading Strings from a File

Let us now create a program which can read a file's contents and display them on screen. For this we would read the file contents a line at a time, means as a string of characters. Here is the program...

```
package displayfilecontents ;
import java.io.* ;

public class DisplayFileContents
{
    public static void main ( String[ ] args ) throws IOException
    {
        File f ;
        f = new File ( "D:\\DisplayFileContents\\src\\
                    displayfilecontents\\DisplayFileContents.java" ) ;

        if ( f.exists( ) && f.canRead( ) )
        {
            BufferedReader br = null ;
            try
            {
                br = new BufferedReader ( new FileReader ( f ) ) ;
                String line ;
                while ( ( line = br.readLine( ) ) != null )
                    System.out.println ( line ) ;
            }
            catch ( FileNotFoundException ex )
            {
                System.out.println ( "Can't open " + f.getName( ) ) ;
            }
            finally
            {
                if ( br != null )
                    br.close( ) ;
            }
        }
    }
}
```

When we run this program it displays the contents of the file "DisplayFileContents.java". In the program, to begin with, we have created a **File** object, and then using it, we have checked whether the file exists, and whether we have a permission to read the file. If so, we have proceeded to read the file a line at a time using the **BufferedReader** object that has a **FileReader** object reference stored in it. Every line read is displayed on the screen using **println( )**.

Record I/O

Suppose we wish to write records of employees into a file and then read them back from the file and display them on the screen. Each record contains id, name and salary of an employee. Here is the program...

```
// receives employee records, writes them to file,
// reads them back and displays them on screen
package recordio ;
import java.io.* ;

public class RecordIO
{
    public static void main ( String[ ] args ) throws IOException
    {
        // prepare for writing records
        FileOutputStream  fos ;
        fos = new FileOutputStream ( "emp.dat" ) ;
        OutputStreamWriter osw ;
        osw = new OutputStreamWriter ( fos ) ;

        // prepare for console input
        InputStreamReader  isr1 ;
        isr1 = new InputStreamReader ( System.in ) ;
        BufferedReader  br1 = new BufferedReader ( isr1 ) ;

        // receive employee data, write it to file
        String  choice = "y", temp1, temp2, temp3 ;
        while ( choice.equals ( "y" ) )
        {
            System.out.println ( "Enter employee id: " ) ;
            temp1 = br1.readLine( ) ;

            System.out.println ( "Enter employee salary: " ) ;
            temp2 = br1.readLine( ) ;
```

```
            System.out.println ( "Enter employee name: " ) ;
            temp3 = br1.readLine( ) ;

            osw.write ( temp1 + "@" + temp2 + "@" + temp3 + "\n" ) ;
            System.out.println ( "Want another ( y/n ): " ) ;

            choice = br1.readLine( ) ;
        }
        osw.close( ) ;

        // prepare for reading records
        FileInputStream  fis ;
        fis = new FileInputStream ( "emp.dat" ) ;
        InputStreamReader isr2 ;
        isr2 = new InputStreamReader ( fis ) ;
        BufferedReader  br2 ;
        br2 = new BufferedReader ( isr2 ) ;

        String  rec, str[ ] ;

        // read employee data, display it on screen
        System.out.println ( "\nEmployees Info: " ) ;
        while ( true )
        {
            try
            {
                rec = br2.readLine( ) ;
                str = rec.split("@", 3) ;
                System.out.println ( "Id: " + str[ 0 ] ) ;
                System.out.println ( "Salary: " + str[ 1 ] ) ;
                System.out.println ( "Name: " + str[ 2 ] ) ;
            }
            catch ( Exception e )
            {
                if ( fis != null )
                    fis.close( ) ;
            }
        }
    }
}
```

To begin with we have created objects of **FileOutputStream**, and **OutputStreamWriter** classes. Of these, the **FileOutputStream** object is used to write employee data to a file. To carry out this writing we have used the function **write( )**. Once a set of records are written, we have closed the stream.

In the next part of the program, we have done the reverse—we have read the data from the same file "emp.dat" and displayed it on the screen. While reading, each record is read as a string. Hence to split it into id, salary and name we have used the **split( )** function. Here is the sample interaction with the program...

```
Enter employee id: 101
Enter employee salary: 12000
Enter employee name: Dinesh
Want another ( y/n ): y
Enter employee id: 201
Enter employee salary: 13500
Enter employee name: Shailesh
Want another ( y/n ): y
Enter employee id: 301
Enter employee salary: 13300
Enter employee name: Seema
Want another ( y/n ): n

Employees Info:
101
12000.0
Dinesh
201
13500.0
Shailesh
301
13300.0
Seema
```

User-defined Streams

Apart from using the standard streams Java permits us to define our own streams and their behavior. For example, we can define a filter stream called **UppercaseFilterStream** which would convert all characters passed through it into uppercase characters. Such a stream class should be derived from **FilterStream** class. The following program illustrates how this can be done:

```
// Converts all chars read from a file into uppercase using a filter stream
package filterstreamproject ;
import java.io.* ;

class UppercaseFilterReader extends FilterReader
{
    public UppercaseFilterReader ( Reader s )
    {
        super ( s ) ;
    }
    public int read ( char[ ] cbuf, int off, int count ) throws IOException
    {
        int nb = in.read ( cbuf, off, count ) ;

        for ( int i = off ; i < off + nb ; i++ )
            cbuf[ i ] = transform ( cbuf[ i ] ) ;

        return nb ;
    }
    private char transform ( char ch )
    {
        if ( Character.isLowerCase ( ch ) )
            return Character.toUpperCase ( ( char ) ch ) ;

        return ch ;
    }
}
public class FilterStreamProject
{
    public static void main ( String[ ] args ) throws
                        FileNotFoundException, IOException
    {
        File f = new File ( "C:\\a.txt" ) ;
        if ( f.exists( ) )
        {
            UppercaseFilterReader ufr ;
            BufferedReader br ;

            ufr = new UppercaseFilterReader (
```

```
                new FileReader ( "C:\\a.txt" ) ) ;
            br = new BufferedReader ( ufr ) ;

            String line ;
            while ( ( line = br.readLine( ) ) != null )
                System.out.println ( line ) ;

            br.close( ) ;
            ufr.close( ) ;
        }
    }
}
```

On executing this program it opens the file "a.txt" from C:\ and converts the text in it into uppercase. The uppercase characters are then displayed on the screen. In my case the "a.txt" file contained some interesting text. Once converted to uppercase it looked like this...

I CDNUOLT BLVEIEE TAHT I CLUOD AULACLTY UESDNATNRD WAHT I WAS RDANIEG. THE PHAONMNEAL PWEOR OF THE HMUAN MNID, AOCCDRNIG TO A RSCHEEARCH AT CMABRIGDE UINERVTISY, IT DSENO'T MTAETR IN WAHT OERDR THE LTTERES IN A WROD ARE, THE OLNY IPROAMTNT TIHNG is TAHT THE FRSIT AND LSAT LTTEER BE IN THE RGHIT PCLAE.. THE RSET CAN BE A TAOTL MSES AND YOU CAN SITLL RAED IT WHOTUIT A PBOERLM. TIHS IS BCUSEAE THE HUAMN MNID DEOS NOT RAED ERVEY LTETER BY ISTLEF, BUT THE WROD AS A WLOHE. AZANMIG HUH? YAEH AND I AWLYAS TGHUHOT SLPELING WAS IPMORANTT!

The **UppercaseFilterReader** class is derived from the abstract class **FilterReader.** We have added three methods to the **UppercaseFilterReader** class. These are constructor, **read( )** and **transform( )**. In the constructor, we simply pass the **FileReader** object passed to it, to the base class constructor. The **read( )** function reads the specified number of bytes from a given offset position in the stream and stores them in a buffer. It then calls the **transform( )** function to transform each character in the buffer into corresponding uppercase character.

In **main( )** we have first created a **FileReader** object. This object has then been passed to the constructor of **UppercaseFilterStream**, which passed it to the constructor of its base class—**FilterReader**. This class's constructor stores the object reference in a private variable. Next we have created a **BufferedReader** object and stored in it the **UppercaseFilterStream** object's reference. In both cases containership is being used as shown in Figure 16.5.

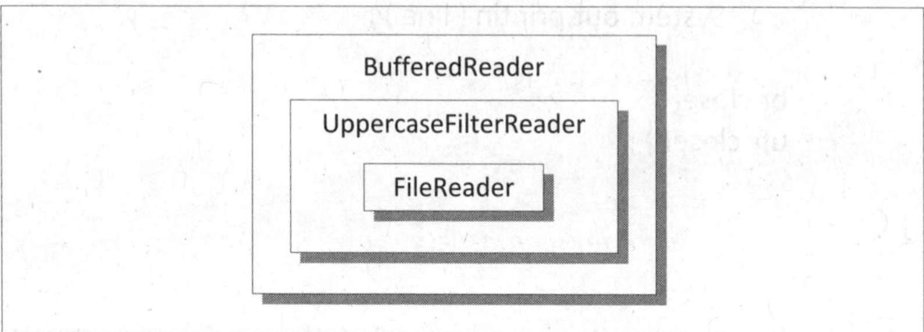

Figure 16.5

Once the construction of objects is over, we have called the **readLine( )** method of **BufferedReader** class. This method in turn calls the **read( )** method of the **UppercaseFilterStream** class. Here firstly the characters are read from the input stream by calling the **read( )** method of **FileReader** class. These characters are collected in the buffer **cbuf**. This buffer's contents are then converted to uppercase by calling the **transform( )** function for each character in the buffer. Thus we are able to change the behavior of a stream by implementing the desired behavior through a filter stream class.

File Encryption/Decryption

Security has gained paramount importance in the digital world. Often we wish to secure our data from others. There are various techniques through which this can be done. One of the most common techniques is to encrypt the data in such a fashion that even if the encrypted data falls into other people's hands they are unable to obtain the original data from it. At the same time we should be able to get back the original data by decrypting the encrypted data. Many Encryption/Decryption schemes are popularly used today to secure the data from misuse. Our intention here is not to discuss these schemes. Instead, we wish to evolve a very simple encryption/decryption scheme. In this scheme during encryption we would replace every lowercase alphabet in the source stream with another predetermined lowercase character. During decryption we would do the reverse. This type of encryption/decryption scheme is often called a Substitution Cipher. Given below is the program which implements the Substitution Cipher.

```
// Substitution Cipher implementation
package substitutioncipherproject ;
import java.io.* ;

interface ITransform
{
    public char transform ( char ch ) ;
}
class Encrypt implements ITransform
{
    String str = "xyfagchbimpourvnqsdewtkjzl" ;

    public char transform ( char ch )
    {
        if ( Character.isLowerCase ( ( char ) ch ) )
            ch = str.charAt ( ch - ( char ) 'a' ) ;

        return ch ;
    }
}
class Decrypt implements ITransform
{
    String str = "xyfagchbimpourvnqsdewtkjzl" ;

    public char transform ( char ch )
    {
        if ( Character.isLowerCase ( ( char ) ch ) )
            ch = ( char ) ( str.indexOf ( ( char ) ch ) + 'a' ) ;

        return ch ;
    }
}
class TransformWriter extends FilterWriter
{
    private ITransform trans ;

    public TransformWriter ( Writer s, ITransform t )
    {
        super ( s ) ;
        this.trans = t ;
    }
```

```
    public void write ( char[ ] buf, int off, int len )
    {
        for ( int i = off ; i < off + len ; i++ )
            buf [ i ] = trans.transform ( buf[ i ] ) ;

        try
        {
            out.write ( buf, off, len ) ;
        }
        catch ( IOException ex )
        {
            System.out.println ( "IO error" ) ;
        }
    }
}
public class SubstitutionCipherProject
{
    public static void main ( String[ ] args ) throws IOException
    {
        doEncDec ( "C:\\a.txt", "enc.txt", true ) ;
        doEncDec ( "enc.txt", "dec.txt", false ) ;
    }
    static void doEncDec ( String source, String target,
                            boolean IsEncrypt ) throws IOException
    {
        ITransform trans ;

        if ( IsEncrypt )
            trans = new Encrypt( ) ;
        else
            trans = new Decrypt( ) ;

        FileReader sstream ;
        BufferedReader sr ;

        sstream = new FileReader ( new File ( source ) ) ;
        sr = new BufferedReader ( sstream ) ;

        FileWriter tstream ;
        TransformWriter tw ;
        BufferedWriter sw ;
```

```
        tstream = new FileWriter ( new File ( target ) ) ;
        tw = new TransformWriter ( tstream, trans ) ;
        sw = new BufferedWriter ( tw ) ;

        String line ;
        while ( ( line = sr.readLine( ) ) != null )
            sw.write ( line + "\r\n" ) ;

        sw.close( ) ;
        sr.close( ) ;
    }
}
```

We have three classes in this program—**Encrypt**, **Decrypt** and **TrasformWriter**. Of these, the **Encrypt** and **Decrypt** classes implement an interface called **ITransform**. This interface contains a function **transform( )** which is implemented to do encryption in the **Encrypt** class and decryption in the **Decrypt** class.

Let us see how it does the encryption. It maintains an arbitrary string of lowercase characters. Once it receives a character to be encrypted it obtains an index value by doing the operation **ch – 'a'**, where **ch** is the character to be encrypted. It then uses this index value to pick a character from the arbitrary string. Thus this character is used as a *substitute* for the character to be encrypted. Decryption works in exactly the reverse way. The character to be decrypted is searched in the same arbitrary string (as the one used for encryption). Once this character is found, 'a' is added to its index value to obtain the original character. That forms the crux of our substitution cipher.

The **TransformWriter** class uses the substitution cipher by calling the **transform( )** function of either the **Encrypt** class or the **Decrypt** class depending on whether encryption or decryption is being carried out.

A helper function **doEncDec( )** is called from **main( )** twice—first time to carry out the encryption and second time to carry out the decryption. The files used in these calls are shown in Figure 16.6.

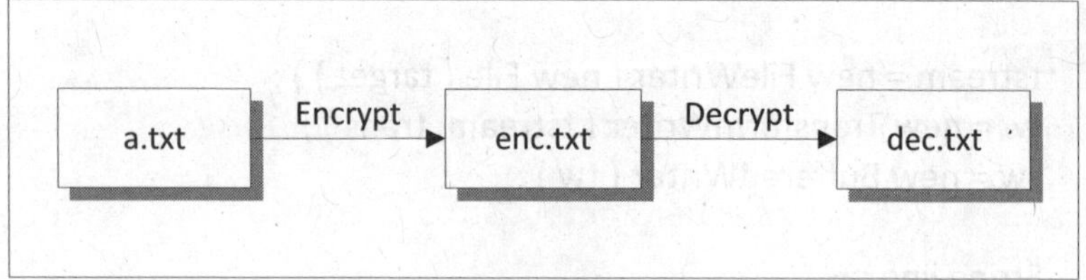

Figure 16.6

Rest of the program is similar to the uppercase filter stream program that we discussed in the last section. So I would not repeat the explanation here.

From this program and the one that we discussed in the last section we can make the following important observations:

(a) Stream is a very important abstraction for data modelling in a variety of applications. Being able to manipulate stream data effectively is immensely important in Java programming. The streams implementation in Java enables us to do that quite effectively. For example, the data that we are manipulating in our stream may come from a file stored on disk, a network socket or simply a buffer in memory.

(b) We too can create our customized stream classes. When we do so, we need to implement the abstract methods inherited from the base class.

Exercise

[A] State whether the following statements are True or False:

(a) **System.out** refers to standard output stream (console).

(b) **System.in** refers to standard input stream (keyboard).

(c) **System.err** refers to standard error stream (console).

(d) Standard output/input/error streams are already open and ready to supply/accept input/output data.

(e) The **File** class is used to perform file operations, whereas **Directory** class is used to carry out directory-related operations.

(f) All stream classes of Java library are derived from a base class **Object**.

(g) All stream classes of Java library are defined in the **java.io** package.

(h) **InputStreamReader** and **OutputStreamWriter** classes are used to perform character-oriented I/O.

(i) **FileInputStream** and **FileOutputStream** classes are used to perform byte-oriented I/O.

(j) If we wish to write characters to a file in Unicode, then we should use the enum **Encoding.Unicode** while creating the **OutputStreamWriter** object.

(k) It is possible to create user-defined filter streams by inheriting our stream class from **FilterReader / FilterWriter** class.

(l) The streams implementation in Java is such that the stream doesn't have to know source or destination of the data.

[B] Answer the following:

(a) What are the common expectations from a mature input/output system?

(b) Can we inherit new classes from **File** class available in the Java library?

(c) How would you check whether a given file exists or not?

(d) Is it possible to check the number of drives, the type of each drive and the drive format type through a Java program? If yes, how?

(e) What is a stream?

(f) What are the two fundamental types of I/O streams?

KanNotes

- Expectation from an IO System :
  - I should be able to communicate with sources & destinations
  - I should be able to I/O varied entities
  - I should be able to communicate in multiple ways
  - I should be able to deal with underlying file system
- Java solution - Perform all IO using Streams
- Stream is a sequence of bytes that travel from source to destination over a communication path
- Streams are implemented by classes in java.io package
- Linking of Streams to physical devices is done by Java IO system
- Java program performs IO by reading / writing from / to a stream
- Benefits of using Streams
  - Streams hide details of communication from programmer
  - Methods are same, implementation changes as per device
- Types of streams : 1) Byte Streams 2) Character streams
- Byte stream perform i/o one byte at a time. They are used to i/o binary data
- Character streams perform i/o one char (2 bytes) at a time. Used to i/o textual data
- To write 485000 to a file as sequence of bytes use byte stream
- To write "485000" as a sequence of Unicode characters to a file use character stream
- Byte Stream classes
  - FileInputStream, FileOutputStream - R/W streams of bytes from file

- FilterInputStream, FilteroutputStream - Filters data being read or written
- BufferedInputStream - Provides buffering ability
- DataInputStream - Provides ability to read Java primitives

- Character stream classes
  - InputStreamReader, OutputStreamWriter - R/W char from/to stream
  - FileReader, FileWriter - R/W characters from/to file
  - PrintWriter - Formatted writing in text representation

- System class contains 3 predefined public static variables - in, out, err which are accessible from any part of the program
  - out refers to standard output stream (screen)
  - in refers to standard input stream (keyboard)
  - err refers to standard error stream (screen)

- These streams are already open and are ready to receive/send input/output data

- In System.out.println ("Hello") ;
  - System - class
  - out - PrintStream object reference
  - out - public static member of System class
  - println(), print() – Members of PrintStream class

- How to decide which classes to use when :
  - What is your data format - text or binary
    Binary – InputStream, OutputStream
    Text – Reader, Writer
  - Do you want random access capability?
    Use RandomAccessFile class
  - Dealing with objects or non-objects?
    ObjectInputStream, ObjectOutputStream
  - What are your sources and sinks for data?
    Sockets, files, strings - All can be used by Byte and Character Streams
  - Do you need to use filtering?

Multithreading 17

Ability to do multiple things simultaneously is a great asset in life. So also in programming...

Let Us JAVA 3rd Edition

Chapter Contents

- Multitasking and Multithreading
- Multithreading in Java
- Launching Threads
- Launching Multiple Threads
- Another Way to Launch Threads
- A Practical Multithreading Example
- Synchronization
- The Synchronized Block
- Inter-thread Communication
- Thread Priorities
- Exercise
- KanNotes

Multithreading is the ability to perform several jobs simultaneously. Knowingly or unknowingly we make use of multithreading frequently in everyday life. For example, while driving a car we carry out several activities in parallel—we listen to music, we follow the traffic rules, and we talk to the co-passengers. All this, without losing the main focus, i.e. driving. There can be several such examples where we carry out several activities at the same time. Since programmers are people and programming is the art of solving people's problems, it is only natural that in programming in general, and in Java in particular, too, there is an effort to do several activities simultaneously.

Multitasking and Multithreading

Most modern OSs can execute several tasks in memory at a time. This ability to execute several tasks simultaneously is known as Multitasking. For example, while using Windows we can simultaneously print a document on the printer, receive e-mails, download files and compile programs. All these operations are carried out through different programs that are being executed in memory at the same time.

This ability of Windows to execute several tasks can be taken a step further, whereby we execute different parts of a program simultaneously. This can be experienced while working with many popular Windows software. Here are a few examples...

(a) While copying files one part of the 'Copy' program displays the copying progress through a green-colored progress bar, whereas, another part of the program carries out the actual copying.

(b) While working with MS-Word one part of the program lets us type the document, whereas two other parts perform the spelling check and grammar check.

(c) In anti-viral software one part of the program scans the disk files for viruses, whereas other part lets us interact with the user interface of the software.

This ability to execute different parts of the same program simultaneously is known as Multithreading.

If a multithreaded program is executing on a machine with a single microprocessor, though it may appear that several tasks are being performed by the processor simultaneously, in actuality it is not so. What happens is that the processor divides the execution time equally amongst all the running threads. Thus each thread gets the processor attention in a round robin manner. Once the time-slice allocated for a thread expires, the operation that it is currently being performed is put on hold and the processor now directs its attention to the next thread. Thus, at any given moment, if we take the snapshot of memory, only one thread is being executed by the processor. The switching of attention from one thread to another happens so fast that we get the effect as if the processor is executing several threads simultaneously.

In modern machines with multiple processors, the threads would actually be executed simultaneously, as each processor can execute a separate thread.

Multithreading has several advantages to offer. These are listed below.

(a) **Responsiveness:** Take MS-Word example again. Had the spell checker and the grammar checker not run as different threads, we would have been required to write documents and submit it to the checkers from time to time. This would have resulted in low responsiveness. Since the checkers run in different threads, our document gets checked as we type, thereby increasing the responsiveness of the application.

(b) **Organization:** Threading simplifies program organization. In the 'File Copy' example if both the operations—displaying the progress bar and the actual copying—run in the same thread, then after copying a few thousand bytes we would be required to advance the progress bar. If we run the copying code and the progress bar code in separate threads, we can avoid cluttering the copying code with progress bar code and vice versa.

(c) **Performance:** Many a times it happens that a program needs to wait for user input or has to give some output. The I/O devices are generally slower than the processor. So the application waits for the I/O operation to finish. Instead, if we use another thread for the I/O operation, the processor time can be allotted to other important tasks that can work independent of the I/O operation, thereby improving the performance.

Multithreading in Java

To help you appreciate the challenges of multithreading you can try a simple experiment. Make two phone calls to your friends and try to carry out conversation with both of them concurrently. This would involve major challenges—talking to one friend, putting him on hold, remembering where you left off, picking up the other receiver, talking to the other friend, putting him on hold, picking up the first receiver, carrying on the conversation from the point where you left off, and above all making the conversation sensible for everybody involved.

Java offers features that let you run multiple threads in a program. To create multiple threads the programmer has to specify which parts of the program he intends to execute concurrently. Although on the face of it this might appear simple, rest assured that often multithreaded programs are tricky and demand a substantial effort on your part to master all the issues involved in multithreading.

Any simple Java program has a single thread of execution. This running thread has a name called main, a priority and a group to which it belongs. If we wish we can change the name of the thread. This has been demonstrated in the program given below.

```
package mainthread ;
public class MainThread
{
    public static void main ( String args[ ] )
    {
        Thread  t = Thread.currentThread( ) ;
        System.out.println ( "Current thread: " + t ) ;
        t.setName ( "mythread" ) ;
        System.out.println ( "After name change: " + t ) ;
        String  s = t.getName( ) ;
        System.out.println ( "Thread name: " + s ) ;
    }
}
```

And here is the output of the program...

```
Current thread: main, 5, main
After name change: mythread, 5, main
Thread name: mythread
```

The object representing the running thread is obtained by calling the **static** method **currentThread( )** of the **Thread** class. If we print this object using **println( )** we get the name of the thread, its priority and its thread group. Note from the output that 5 is the default priority. 1 represents the lowest priority and 10 the highest, thus 5 is the average priority.

Once we have obtained the **Thread** object, we can set or get the name of the current thread using the methods **setName( )** and **getName( )** respectively.

It is possible to make multiple threads to belong to one group. If this is done, then it is possible to manipulate all those threads together, rather than individually. For example, we can start or suspend all the threads within a group with a single method call.

Launching Threads

There are two mechanisms to launch new threads in a Java program. These are:

(a) By extending the **Thread** class
(b) By implementing the **Runnable** interface

We wish to learn both these ways to launch a thread and assess the utility of each. Let us begin with a program that uses the first way.

```
package sample ;
public class Sample
{
    public static void main ( String args[ ] )
    {
        Ex t = new Ex( ) ;
        t.start( ) ;
        for ( int i = 0 ; i < 5 ; i ++ )
            System.out.println ( "Main thread" ) ;
    }
}
class Ex extends Thread
{
    public void run( )
    {
        for ( int i = 0 ; i < 5 ; i++ )
            System.out.println ( "New thread" ) ;
    }
}
```

Here we have derived the **Ex** class from the **Thread** class and defined a **run( )** method inside it. The method simply prints a message "New Thread" 5 times. In **main( )** we have created an object of **Ex** class, called the **start( )** method and then printed the message "Main Thread" 5 times.

The **start( )** method is defined in **Thread** class and by inheritance is available to **Ex** objects. Once we call the **start( )** method, the thread gets scheduled. This means we are informing the thread scheduler that the new thread is ready to run. When the thread scheduler deems fit, it would start executing this new thread by calling its **run( )** method.

The output of the program is shown below.

```
Main thread
Main thread
Main thread
Main thread
Main thread
New thread
New thread
New thread
New thread
New thread
```

Ideally the messages "Main thread" and "new Thread" should have been inter-mingled. But this did not happen because once the time slot got allotted to the main thread, in that time slot it printed all the messages, before the time slot could be snatched away and allotted to the new thread. Had each loop been executed 1000 times, then during each time-slot allocated to the two threads, each would not have been able to print all 1000 messages. This would have resulted in inter-mingling of messages.

Another way to get the inter-mingled messages is to put each thread to sleep for 1000 milliseconds when they get the time slot. This would ensure that in the first time-slot that they get, they don't finish the entire printing. This change is shown below.

```
package sample ;
public class  Sample
{
    public static void main ( String args[ ] )
    {
        Ex t = new Ex( ) ;
        t.start( ) ;
```

```
        try
        {
            for ( int  i = 0 ; i < 5 ; i ++ )
            {
                System.out.println ( "Main thread" ) ;
                Thread.sleep ( 1000 ) ;
            }
            catch ( Exception e )
            {
            }
        }
    }
}
class Ex extends Thread
{
    public void run( )
    {
        try
        {
            for ( int  i = 0 ; i < 5 ; i++ )
            {
                System.out.println ( "New thread" ) ;
                Thread.sleep ( 1000 ) ;
            }
        }
        catch ( Exception e )
        {
        }
    }
}
```

The static **sleep( )** method of the **Thread** class postpones the execution of next instruction by 1000 milliseconds. As a result, now the output is inter-mingled as shown below.

Main thread
Main thread
Main thread
New thread
New thread
Main thread
Main thread

New thread
New thread
New thread

Notice that the call to **sleep( )** method has to be present in the try block, as it is likely to throw an exception. Though, not the best of the ways, for the sake of simplicity we have used an empty **catch** block to catch the exception that **sleep( )** may throw.

Launching Multiple Threads

Do not be under the impression that we can create only one thread from the class derived from the **Thread** class. It is possible to create multiple threads from the same class. This is illustrated in the following program.

```
package sample ;
public class  Sample
{
	public static void main ( String args[ ] )
	{
		Ex  t1  = new  Ex( ) ;
		t1.start( ) ;
		t1.setname ( "First" ) ;
		Ex  t2  = new  Ex( ) ;
		t2.start( ) ;
		t2.setname ("Second" ) ;
		Ex  t3  = new  Ex( ) ;
		t3.start( ) ;
		t3.setname ( "Third" ) ;
		try
		{
			for ( int  i = 0 ; i < 10 ; i ++ )
			{
				System.out.println ( "Main thread" ) ;
				Thread.sleep ( 500 ) ;
			}
		}
		catch ( Exception e )
		{
		}
	}
```

```
}

class Ex extends Thread
{
    public void run( )
    {
        Thread t ;

        t = Thread.currentThread( ) ;
        String s = t.getName( ) ;

        for ( int i = 0 ; i < 10 ; i++ )
            System.out.println ( s ) ;
    }
}
```

Given below is the output of the program.

```
First
First
First
First
First
Third
Third
Third
Third
Third
Third
Main thread
Second
Second
Second
Second
Main thread
Main thread
Main thread
:::
```

Here, while launching the three threads we have given a name to each, which is displayed in a loop, when those threads get a time slot. In which situation we would want to launch multiple threads from the same class? Imagine if the thread is to display an animation from a GIF file. Then by launching different threads we can display different animations in different parts of the screen simultaneously.

When we launch several threads from the main thread there is a possibility that the main thread ends whereas the launched threads continue to execute. If we wish that main thread should be the last thread to finish execution, then we can employ the **join( )** method of the **Thread** class to ensure this, as shown below.

```
package sample ;
public class  Sample
{
    public static void main ( String args[ ] )
    {
        Ex t1 = new Ex( ) ;
        t1.start( ) ;
        t1.setname ( "First" ) ;
        Ex t2 = new Ex( ) ;
        t2.start( ) ;
        t2.setname ("Second" ) ;
        Ex t3 = new Ex( ) ;
        t3.start( ) ;
        t3.setname ( "Third" ) ;
        try
        {
            for ( int  i = 0 ; i < 10 ; i ++ )
            {
                System.out.println ( "Main thread" ) ;
                Thread.sleep ( 500 ) ;
            }
        }
        catch ( Exception e )
        {
        }

        System.out.println ( t1.isAlive( ) ) ;
        System.out.println ( t2.isAlive( ) ) ;
        System.out.println ( t3.isAlive( ) ) ;
        t1.join(  ) ;
        t2.join(  ) ;
        t3.join(  ) ;
```

```
        System.out.println ( t1.isAlive( ) ) ;
        System.out.println ( t2.isAlive( ) ) ;
        System.out.println ( t3.isAlive( ) ) ;
    }
}
```

On execution, out of the calls to **isAlive( )** some threads may return false if those threads have finished execution. By calling **join( )** the main thread would wait for the alive threads to finish their execution, before it terminates. Naturally, the second set of calls to **isAlive( )** would return false for each call.

Another Way to Launch Threads

So far we have been extending the **Thread** class and implementing the **run( )** method in it to launch new threads. This method has one important limitation. Once our class is derived from **Thread** class we cannot inherit it from any other class, as Java doesn't support multiple inheritance. If we wish to keep our class open for derivation from some other class and still be able to launch new threads, we should do so by implementing a **Runnable** interface in it. This method of launching new threads is given below.

```
package sample ;
public class Sample
{
    public static void main ( String args[ ] )
    {
        Ex t = new Ex ( "One" ) ;
        t.x.start( ) ;
        for ( int i = 0 ; i < 10 ; i ++ )
            System.out.println ( "Main thread" ) ;
    }
}
class Ex implements Runnable
{
    public Thread x ;

    Ex ( String n )
    {
        x = new Thread ( this, n ) ;
    }
```

```
    public void run( )
    {
        int i ;
        for ( i = 0 ; i < 10 ; i++ )
            System.out.println ( x.getName( ) ) ;
    }
}
```

Note that here we have not derived **Ex** from **Thread** class. Instead, we are implementing the **Runnable** interface in it. The **Runnable** interface has only one method in it—**run( )**.

While creating an object of the **Ex** class, in the constructor we have created an object of the **Thread** class and stored its address in a public reference called **x**. Then, from **main( )** we have used this **x** to call the **start( )** method of the **Thread** class. By doing this, we are informing JVM to schedule this thread. As a result, the **run( )** method gets called. In the **run( )** method we have simply printed the name of the thread.

Here is one more program that uses **Runnable** interface to launch threads. The difference is that this one launches multiple threads for each instance of the **Ex** class.

```
package sample ;
public class Sample
{
    public static void main ( String args[ ] )
    {
        Ex t1 = new Ex ( "First" ) ;
        t1.x.start( ) ;

        Ex t2 = new Ex ( "Second" ) ;
        t2.x.start( ) ;

        Ex t3 = new Ex ( "Third" ) ;
        t3.x.start( ) ;

        for ( int i = 0 ; i < 10 ; i ++ )
            System.out.println ( "Main thread" ) ;
    }
}
class Ex implements Runnable
```

```
{
    Thread x ;

    Ex ( String n )
    {
        x = new Thread ( this, n ) ;
    }

    public void run( )
    {
        String s = x.getName( ) ;
        int i ;
        for ( i = 0 ; i < 10 ; i++ )
            System.out.println ( s ) ;
    }
}
```

A Practical Multithreading Example

Suppose we wish to copy the contents of one folder into another. Naturally, if the source folder contains multiple files, each file has to be opened and its contents copied into a file in the target folder. If this operation is done in a loop in a single thread, then unless copying of the first file is over, the copying of second file cannot begin. Instead, a better approach would be to do the copying in multiple threads. Given below are two programs that follow the single thread and the multithread approach. To simplify things, instead of copying files, we simply open each source file, read it to the end and report the number of lines present in each file.

```
// Approach 1 : Read files in a single thread
package singlethread ;
import java.io.* ;

public class SingleThread
{
    static public void main ( String args[ ] ) throws Exception
    {
        System.out.println ( "Starting Time: " +
                                    System.currentTimeMillis( ));
        for ( int i = 0 ; i < args.length ; i++ )
        {
```

```
            FileReader  fr = new FileReader ( args[ i ] ) ;
            BufferedReader  br = new BufferedReader ( fr ) ;
            LineNumberReader  l = new LineNumberReader ( br ) ;

            while ( l.readLine( ) != null )
                Thread.sleep ( 10 ) ;

            System.out.println ( "Lines in " + args[ i ] + ":" +
                                        l.getLineNumber( ) ) ;
        }
        System.out.println ( "Ending Time: " +
                                        System.currentTimeMillis( ) ) ;
    }
}
```

The program reads three files **a.txt**, **b.txt** and **c.txt** that are provided to it as command-line arguments. To add these files to your project in NetBeans, right click on the project folder and select New | Empty File from the menu that pops up. Give the name of the file (say, **a.txt**) and type a few lines in it. Similarly add **b.txt** and **c.txt** to your project. Once this is done, add these filenames as command-line arguments through Right-click project name | Properties | Run | Arguments.

In the program, we print the current time in milliseconds before we start reading the files and after the reading is finished. This is done using the function **System.currentTimeMillis( )**. The actual reading of a file is done by using the **LineNumberReader** class. This class has a method **getLineNumber( )** which reports the number of lines present in the file that it has read.

When I executed this program I got the following output:

```
Starting Time: 1484131339431
Lines in a.txt:13
Lines in b.txt:25
Lines in c.txt:37
Ending Time: 1484131340184
```

Your output may vary as depending on the contents of the three files their reading times may vary. A quick calculation would show the difference in times to be 753 milliseconds.

Now let us look at the program that follows the multithreaded approach to achieve the same goal. Here it is...

```
// Approach 2 : Read files in multiple threads
package multithread ;
import  java.io.* ;
public class Multithread
{
    static public void main ( String args[ ] ) throws Exception
    {
        System.out.println ( "Starting time: " +
                                System.currentTimeMillis( ) ) ;
        linecounter  t[ ] = new linecounter [ args.length ] ;
        for ( int  i = 0 ; i < args.length ; i++ )
        {
            t[ i ] = new linecounter ( args[ i ] ) ;
            t[ i ].start( ) ;
        }
        for ( int  i = 0 ; i < args.length ; i++ )
            t[ i ].join( ) ;
        System.out.println ( "Ending Time: " +
            System.currentTimeMillis( ) ) ;
    }
}
class linecounter extends Thread
{
    String  fname ;
    linecounter ( String  str )
    {
        fname = str ;
    }
    public void run( )
    {
        try
        {
            FileReader  fr = new FileReader ( fname ) ;
            BufferedReader  br  = new BufferedReader ( fr ) ;
            LineNumberReader  l = new LineNumberReader ( br ) ;
            while ( l.readLine( ) != null )
                Thread.sleep ( 10 ) ;
            System.out.println ( "Lines :" + fname + " : " +
                                l.getLineNumber( ) ) ;
```

```
        }
        catch ( Exception  e )
        {
        }
    }
}
```

This time on execution the following times are reported:

Starting Time: 1484196850259
Lines: a.txt : 13
Lines: b.txt : 25
Lines: c.txt : 37
Ending Time: 1484196850646

This time the time difference is 387 milliseconds. Clearly the multithreaded approach is a better option than the single-threaded approach in such situations.

Synchronization

Software development is a team effort. Unless team members cooperate with one another and synchronize their work with the rest of the team, the team can't go far. Similarly, if in a program there are several threads running, unless their activities are synchronized with one another the disaster is not far away. For example, if a program instantiates two threads and if both the threads use the same resource and both of them change it simultaneously the situation would become unreliable and erratic.

Let me illustrate the need for synchronization of threads using a simple example. Consider the following method.

```
void display ( String msg )
{
    System.out.print ( "[" ) ;
    System.out.print ( msg ) ;
    Thread.sleep ( 1000 ) ;
    System.out.println ( "]" ) ;
}
```

Suppose three different threads decide to call this method to display a message. It is expected that this method would display the message passed to it within a pair of [ ]. However, in reality it produces the following output if the strings passed to it from three threads are KICIT, Nagpur and India respectively.

```
[India[Nagpur[KICIT]
]
]
```

To rectify this, we need to synchronize the activities of each thread. How this can be achieved is shown in the following program.

```
package sample ;
public class Sample
{
    static public void main ( String args[ ] ) throws Exception
    {
        output c = new Output( ) ;
        Ex t1 = new Ex ( c, "KICIT" ) ;
        t1.start( ) ;
        Ex t2 = new Ex ( c,"Nagpur" ) ;
        t2.start( ) ;
        Ex t3 = new Ex ( c,"India" ) ;
        t3.start( ) ;
        t1.join( ) ;
        t2.join( ) ;
        t3.join( ) ;
    }
}
class Ex extends Thread
{
    private Output o ;
    private String message ;

    public Ex ( Output c, String msg )
    {
        o = c ;
        message = msg ;
    }
    public void run( )
    {
        o.display ( message ) ;
    }
```

```
}
class Output
{
    synchronized void display ( String  msg )
    {
        System.out.print ( "[" + msg ) ;
        try
        {
            Thread.sleep ( 1000 ) ;
        }
        catch ( InterruptedException  e )
        {
        }
        System.out.println ( "]" ) ;
    }
}
```

On execution, this program produces the desired output shown below.

```
[KICIT]
[NAGPUR]
[INDIA]
```

In this program we have defined two classes—**Ex** and **Output**. In **main( )** we have created one object of **Output** class and three objects of **Ex** class. The **Ex** class is derived from the **Thread** class. When objects of **Ex** class are created, along with object of **Output** class, a message to be printed is passed to its constructor. It stores this message in a private string **message**. This **message** is passed to the **display( )** method of **Output** class, when **display( )** is called from **run( )**.

I want you to note a standard technique here. Since we do not explicitly call the **run( )** method, any objects that **run( )** needs should be passed to the constructor of the class to which **run( )** belongs, so that **run( )** can access them. In our case, we needed the **Output** object to call **display( )** from the **run( )** method. That is why we passed it to the constructor while creating the **Ex** objects.

Note that the **display( )** function in the **Output** class has been marked as **synchronized**. This ensures that once one thread makes a call to **display( )**, unless the execution of **display( )** in this thread is finished, the call by other threads to **display( )** would be put on hold. This results in producing the systematic output that we desire.

The Synchronized Block

At times it may so happen that a class has been developed with a view to use it in single thread situation. But later on a need arises to use it in a multithreaded situation. If we do not have an access to its source code, we cannot mark the methods in it as **synchronized**. In such situations, the solution is to use a syncronized block.

In the context of our program in the previous section, suppose we do not have an access to source code of **Output** class. So we cannot mark **display( )** as synchronized method. In this case we need to simply make the call to **display( )** in a **synchornized** block as shown below, to get the desired output.

```
public void run( )
{
    synchronized ( o )
    {
        o.display ( message ) ;
    }
}
```

Inter-thread Communication

The programs in the Synchronization section unconditionally blocked other threads from asynchronous access to certain methods. To improve the overall performance of the program there should be a mechanism to notify a waiting thread that it can start running. This means that one thread should be able to communicate with the other. To achieve this Java provides three methods—**wait( )**, **notify( )** and **notifyAll( )**. Given below is the purpose of each of these methods.

Method	Purpose
wait( )	Tell calling thread to go to sleep till notified
notify( )	Wakes up thread that called wait( ) on same object
notifyAll( )	Wakes up all threads that called wait( ) on same object

Figure 17.1

One of the places where usage of this method makes sense is in implementing a classical Computer Science algorithm called Producer - Consumer algorithm. This algorithm is described in the Exercise at the end of this chapter.

Thread Priorities

If we wish, we can assign priorities to each running thread. This helps the scheduler to determine the order in which these threads are executed. Threads with higher priority are more important to a program and are allocated processor time before lower-priority threads. A Java thread can have three standard Priorities—MIN_PRIORITY, MAX_PRIORITY, NORM_PRIORITY. These represent numbers 1, 10 and 5. Java provides following functions to set a new priority for a thread and to obtain a thread's current priority.

```
final void setPriority ( int level )
final int getPriority( )
```

Exercise

[A] State whether the following statements are True or False:

(a) Multithreading always improves the speed of execution of the program.

(b) A running task may have several threads running in it.

(c) Multitasking is same as multithreading.

(d) If we create a class that inherits from the **Thread** class, we can still inherit our class from some other class.

(e) Default thread priority is 10.

(f) A higher priority thread can preempt a lower priority thread.

(g) It is possible to change the name of the running thread.

(h) To launch a thread we must explicitly call the **run( )** method defined in a class that implements the **Runnable** interface.

(i) To launch a thread we must explicitly call the **run( )** method defined in a class that extends the **Thread** class.

(j) To synchronize a method defined in a class, we must have an access to the source code of the class.

[B] Answer the following:

(a) Which are the two methods available for launching threads in a Java program?

(b) What are the pros and cons of using two different methods of launching threads in a Java program?

(c) Which methods should be used to improve the performance of a multithreaded Java program that uses synchronization?

(d) If **Ex** class implements the **Runnable** interface, then can we launch multiple threads for objects of **Ex** class? If yes, how?

(e) Write a multithreaded program that copies contents of one folder into another. The source and target folder paths should be input through keyboard.

(f) Producer - Consumer algorithm is a popularly used algorithm in Computer Science. It is a technique for generating requests (by producer) and processing the generated requests (by consumer). Write a program to implement this algorithm to meet following specifications:

- The Producer produces numbers in sequence 0, 1, 2, ...
- Consumer consumes the produced numbers by printing them
- Both Producer and Consumer work as independent threads
- Consumer must wait while Producer is producing
- Once Producer has produced it would send a signal to Consumer
- Producer must wait while Consumer is consuming
- Once Consumer has consumed it should send a signal to Producer

KanNotes

- Multitasking - Ability to execute multiple tasks at a time

  Task = Process

- Multithreading - Ability to execute multiple parts of a program at a time

  Part = Thread = separate path of execution

- Examples of Multitasking :
  - Several Windows applications running in memory
  - Multiple instances of Paint or Notepad in memory
- Examples of Multitasking :
  - Scroll Web page as graphic continues to load
  - Printing one Word document while opening another
  - Replying an email while downloading another
- Advantages of Multithreading
  - Improves application's responsiveness
  - Simplifies program organization
  - Do other things while waiting for slow I/O operations
  - Exploitation of Multiple Processors
- Thread is a Java API class. It contains following useful methods :
  - currentThread() - returns current thread's object
  - setName - sets up name for a thread
  - getName() - returns name of the specified thread
  - sleep( ) - Postpone execution of next instruction by specified milliseconds
- Two methods to launch a thread :
  - By extending the Thread class
  - By implementing Runnable interface
- Extending Thread class
  - Easy to use
  - Thread related functions can be overridden

- Disadvantage : Cannot use in Multiple Inheritance situations

- Implementing Runnable Interface
  Can be used in Multiple Inheritance situations
  Disadvantage : Cannot override Thread class functions
- If multiple files are to be read then the reading time can be reduced by carrying out the reading in multiple concurrent threads
- When >= 2 threads access same shared resource if we wish to ensure that the resource is used by only 1 thread at a time, then it can be achieved using Synchronized methods
- If a method is declared as Synchronized then when it is called by multiple threads, when the first thread is executing it others are made to wait
- For older classes Synchronized blocks can be used to achieve the same results
- Often threads unconditionally block other threads from asynchronous access to certain methods - hampers performance
- To improve Performance - use wait(), notify(), notifyAll() methods
- wait() - Tells calling thread to go to sleep till notified
- notify() - Wakes up thread that called wait() on same object
- notifyAll() - Wakes up all threads that called wait() on same obj.
- Producer - Consumer algorithm is a technique for Generating requests and Processing the pending requests
- Producer produces requests, Consumer consumes generated requests
- Both work as independent threads
- Working :
  - Consumer must wait while Producer is producing

- Once Producer has produced it would send signal to Consumer
- Producer must wait while Consumer is consuming
- Once Consumer has consumed it would send signal to Producer

- Thread priorities are used to schedule thread execution
- Higher priority threads get more CPU time and may preempt lower priority threads
- Standard Priorities :
    - MIN_PRIORITY, MAX_PRIORITY, NORM_PRIORITY
    - These are constants with values 1, 10, 5
- Functions to set and get priorities :
    - final void setPriority (int level)
    - final int getPriority()

18

Generics in Java

Generalizations are good. Especially so, when the Compiler handles the specializations...

Let Us JAVA

3rd Edition

Chapter Contents

- Generic Functions
- Multiple Argument Types
- Generic Classes
- Bounded Generics
- Exercise
- KanNotes

Generics are a mechanism that make it possible to use one function or class to handle many different data types. By using generics, we can design a single function/class that operates on data of many types, instead of having to create a separate function/class for each type. In this chapter we would first look at using generics with functions and then move on to using generics with classes.

Generic Functions

Suppose you wish to print contents of an integer array. To achieve this we can write a function as shown below:

```
void printIntArr ( int [ ] arr )
{
    for ( int i : arr )
        System.out.println ( i ) ;
}
```

Here the function **printIntArr( )** is defined to receive an **int** array and then print all its elements through a **for** loop. What if we wish to print a **float** array—we would be required to write a completely new function **printFloatArr( )**. Similarly, to print a **char** array we would be required to write **printCharArr( )**—a separate version of the same function.

You would agree that this is a suitable case for overloaded functions, as all these functions have different names but essentially carry out the same activity—printing elements of an array passed to them. This way, at least the names of all these functions can be same. These overloaded functions are given below:

```
// printArr for ints
void printArr ( int [ ] arr )
{
    for ( int i : arr )
        System.out.println ( i ) ;
}

// printArr for floats
void printArr ( float [ ] arr )
{
    for ( float i : arr )
        System.out.println ( i ) ;
```

```
}

// printArr for chars
void printArr ( char [ ] arr )
{
    for ( char i : arr )
        System.out.println ( i ) ;
}

// etc...
```

Have we gained anything by writing these overloaded functions? Not much, because we still have to write a separate definition for each type. This results into three disadvantages:

(a) Rewriting the same function body over and over for different types is time consuming.

(b) The program consumes more disk space.

(c) If we decide to modify one such function, we need to remember to make the modification in other overloaded functions.

Won't it be nice if we could write such a function just once, and make it work for many different data types. This is exactly what function generics do for us.

The following program shows how to write the **printArr( )** function as a generic function, so that it will work with any standard type. We have invoked this function from **main( )** for different data types.

```
package genericfunction ;
public class GenericFunction
{
    public static <T> void printArray ( T[ ] arr )
    {
        for ( T i : arr )
            System.out.printf ( "%s ", i ) ;

        System.out.println( ) ;
    }
    public static void main ( String args[ ] )
    {
        Integer[ ] intarr = { 10, -2, 37, 42, 15 } ;
        Float[ ] floatarr = { 3.14f, 6.28f, -1.5f, -3.44f, 7.234f } ;
```

```
        Character[ ] chararr = { 'Q', 'U', 'E', 'S', 'T' } ;

        printArray ( intarr ) ;
        printArray ( floatarr ) ;
        printArray ( chararr ) ;
    }
}
```

Here's the output of the program:

```
10 -2 37 42 15
3.14 6.28 -1.5 -3.44 7.234
Q U E S T
```

As you can see, the **printArr( )** function now works with different data types that we use as arguments.

Isn't this code reuse? Yes, but of a different type. Inheritance provides a way to reuse object code. Generics provide a way to reuse the source code. Generics can significantly reduce source code size and increase code flexibility.

Let us now understand what grants the generic function the flexibility to work with different data types. Here is the definition of the **printArr( )** function...

```
public static <T> void printArray( T[ ] arr )
{
    for ( T i : arr )
        System.out.printf ( "%s ", i ) ;

    System.out.println( ) ;
}
```

In this generic function a data type has been represented by a name (**T** in our case) that can stand for any type. There's nothing special about the name **T**. We can use any other name like **type**, **mytype**, etc. Throughout the definition of the function, wherever a specific data type would ordinarily be written, we substitute it with type **T**.

Notice that while calling **printArr( )** function, we have passed to it an array of **Integer**s, **Float**s and **Character**s and not an array of **ints, floats** and **char**s. This is because a generic function can work only with reference types and not with primitives like **int, float, double, char**, etc.

To help you fix your ideas about generics, here is another program that uses a generic function. This one obtains the minimum of two quantities using a generic **minimum( )** function.

```
package minusinggenerics ;
public class MinUsingGenerics
{
    public static <T extends Comparable <T> > T minimum ( T a, T b )
    {
        if ( a.compareTo ( b ) < 0 )
            return a ;
        else
            return b ;
    }
    public static void main ( String[ ] args )
    {
        Float a = 3.14f, b = -6.28f, c ;
        c = minimum ( a, b ) ;
        System.out.println ( c ) ;

        Character ch = 'A', dh = 'Z', eh ;
        eh = minimum ( ch, dh ) ;
        System.out.println ( eh ) ;

        Double d = 1.1, e = 1.11, f ;
        f = minimum ( d, e ) ;
        System.out.println ( f ) ;
    }
}
```

Given below is the output that the program produces on execution.

```
-6.28
A
1.1
```

Note how we have defined the generic **minimum( )** function.

```
public static < T extends Comparable <T> > T minimum ( T a, T b )
{
    ...
}
```

The above definition means that this function would work with all those types which implement the **Comparable** interface. In our case the classes **Integer**, **Float** and **Character** classes implement this interface, so we can use the **minimum( )** function with these types.

Note that this function cannot compare two **Integer** or two **Float** objects using relational operators like >, <, etc. Hence to actually carry out the comparison we have used the **compareTo( )** function of **Integer** / **Float** / **Character** class.

We can extend the same comparison logic and write a program that sorts **Integer**s, **Float**s, **Character**s using a generic sorting function. Here it is...

```
package genericsorting ;
public class GenericSorting
{
    public static void main ( String[ ] args )
    {
        Float num[ ] = { 5.4f, 3.23f, 2.15f, 1.09f, 34.66f } ;
        Integer arr[ ] = { -12, 23, 14, 0, 245, 78 , 66, -9 } ;
        int i ;

        sort ( num, 5 ) ;
        for ( i = 0 ; i <= 4 ; i++ )
            System.out.print ( num[ i ] + " " ) ;
        System.out.println( ) ;
        sort ( arr, 8 ) ;
        for ( i = 0 ; i <= 7 ; i++ )
            System.out.print ( arr[ i ] + " " ) ;
    }
    public static <T extends Comparable <T> > void sort ( T[ ] n, int size )
    {
        int i, j ;
        T t ;

        for ( i = 0 ; i <= size - 2 ; i++ )
        {
            for ( j = i + 1 ; j <= size - 1 ; j++ )
            {
                if ( n[ i ].compareTo ( n[ j ] ) > 0 )
                {
```

```
                    t = n[ i ] ;
                    n[ i ] = n[ j ] ;
                    n[ j ] = t ;
                }
            }
        }
    }
}
```

The output of the program is given below:

```
1.09 2.15 3.23 5.4 34.66
-12 -9 0 14 23 66 78 245
```

I do not intend to explain the actual working of the sorting logic. This topic has been dealt with thoroughly in all the standard books on Data Structures. What you need to concentrate here is, how to write generic functions that can work for variety of data types.

Multiple Argument Types

In all the programs that we have seen so far in this chapter, the generic functions worked only with one type. But we can as well write a generic function that takes different types of arguments during a call. The following code shows such a generic function.

```
package mulitpletypesgenericfunction ;
public class MulitpleTypesGenericFunction
{
    public static void main ( String[ ] args )
    {
        Integer i = 10 ;
        Float j = 3.14f ;
        Character ch = 'A' ;
        printTypes ( i, j, ch ) ;
    }
    public static <T, S, Z> void printTypes ( T a, S b, Z c )
    {
        System.out.println ( "a = " + a ) ;
        System.out.println ( "b = " + b ) ;
        System.out.println ( "c = " + c ) ;
    }
}
```

The **printTypes( )** function can receive three different types of arguments represented by **T**, **S** and **Z**. It simply prints all the arguments that it receives. Would the function work, if we pass to it arguments of same types? Yes, it will. So the following call would be perfectly valid.

```
Integer i = 10, m = 20, n = 30 ;
printTypes ( i, m, n ) ;
```

Generic Classes

The concept of generics can be extended even to classes. Generic classes are often used for data storage. In fact Java provides a library of container classes that implement data structures like stack, queue, linked lists, binary tree, hash map, etc. These implementations are based on generic classes.

Let us try implementing a Stack class as a generic class. This class should be able to maintain a stack of **Integer**s, **Float**s, **Character**s etc. Here is a program with this generic stack class in action.

```
package genericstack ;
public class GenericStack
{
    public static void main ( String[ ] args )
    {
        Stack <Integer> s1 ;
        s1 = new Stack <Integer> ( 10 ) ;

        if ( ! s1.isFull( ) )
            s1.push ( 10 ) ;
        if ( ! s1.isFull( ) )
            s1.push ( 20 ) ;
        if ( ! s1.isFull( ) )
            s1.push ( 30 ) ;

        int data1 ;
        if ( ! s1.isEmpty( ) )
        {
            data1 = s1.pop( ) ;
            System.out.println ( data1 ) ;
        }
        if ( ! s1.isEmpty( ) )
```

```
    {
        data1 = s1.pop( ) ;
        System.out.println ( data1 ) ;
    }

    Stack <Float> s2 ;
    s2 = new Stack <Float> ( 10 ) ;

    if ( ! s2.isFull( ) )
        s2.push ( 10.5f ) ;
    if ( ! s2.isFull( ) )
        s2.push ( 20.5f ) ;
    if ( ! s2.isFull( ) )
        s2.push ( 18.5f ) ;

    float data2 ;

    if ( ! s2.isEmpty( ) )
    {
        data2 = s2.pop( ) ;
        System.out.println  ( data2 ) ;
    }
    if ( ! s2.isEmpty( ) )
    {
        data2 = s2.pop( ) ;
        System.out.println  ( data2 ) ;
    }

    Stack <Complex> s3 ;
    s3 = new Stack <Complex> ( 10 ) ;

    Complex c1 = new Complex ( 1.1f, 2.2f ) ;
    Complex c2 = new Complex ( 3.3f, 4.4f ) ;
    Complex c3 = new Complex ( 5.5f, 6.6f ) ;

    if ( ! s3.isFull( ) )
        s3.push ( c1 ) ;
    if ( ! s3.isFull( ) )
        s3.push ( c2 ) ;
    if ( ! s3.isFull( ) )
        s3.push ( c3 ) ;
```

```
        Complex c ;

        if ( ! s3.isEmpty( ) )
        {
            c = s3.pop( ) ;
            c.printData( ) ;
        }
        if ( ! s3.isEmpty( ) )
        {
            c = s3.pop( ) ;
            c.printData( ) ;
        }
    }
}

class  Stack <T>
{
    private T arr[ ] ;
    private int  top ;
    private int size ;

    Stack ( int sz )
    {
        size = sz ;
        top = -1 ;
        arr = ( T[  ] ) new Object[ sz ] ;
    }
    boolean isFull( )
    {
        if ( top == size )
            return true ;
        else
            return false ;
    }
    void push ( T  data )
    {
            top++ ;
            arr [ top ] = data ;
    }
    boolean isEmpty( )
```

```
    {
        if ( top == -1 )
            return true ;
        else
            return false ;
    }
    T pop( )
    {
        T val ;
        val = arr [ top ] ;
        top-- ;
        return val ;
    }
}

class Complex
{
    float r, i ;

    public Complex ( float rr, float ii )
    {
        r = rr ;
        i = ii ;
    }
    public void printData( )
    {
        System.out.println ( "Real = " + r + " Imag = " + i ) ;
    }
}
```

We have created three stacks here—**s1**, **s2** and **s3** and pushed three objects on each one. Then we have popped the values from the three stacks and displayed them on the screen. **s1** and **s2** maintain a stack of objects of ready-made classes **Integer** and **Float**. We have also declared a class called **Complex** and then pushed/ popped **Complex** objects to/from stack **s3**. Here's the output of the program...

```
30
20
18.5
20.5
```

```
Real = 5.5 Imag = 6.6
Real = 3.3 Imag = 4.4
```

You can observe that the order in which the elements are popped from the stack is exactly reverse of the order in which they were pushed on the stack.

The way to build a generic class is similar to the one used for building a generic function. The **<T>** signals that the class is going to be a generic class. This is precisely how we have defined the **Stack** class. Its skeleton is shown below.

```
class Stack <T>
{
    // code that uses the type T
}
```

It the **Stack** class, the type **T** is used at every place in the class where there is a reference to the type of the array **arr**. There are four such places—the definition of **arr**, the constructor, the argument type of the **push( )** function, and the return type of the **pop( )** function. Do take a look at these four functions in our program.

To create objects of this generic class we have used the statements like,

```
Stack <Integer> s1 ;
s1 = new Stack <Integer> ( 10 ) ;
```

While creating the object **s1** we are passing 10 to the constructor of generic stack class. The value 10 indicates the size of the array that is going to hold the values pushed into the stack. In the constructor we have created this array through the statement

```
arr = ( T[ ] ) new Object[ sz ] ;
```

Here, firstly an array of **Objects** is created and the address of this array is typecasted into an address of array of type **T**.

In the constructor, to indicate emptiness of stack we have initiated **top** to a value -1. This variable is going to act as an index into the array in which the values pushed into the stack are going to be stored. We have also preserved the value of array size in the variable **size**. Later, in functions **isEmpty( )** and **isFull( )** we have used these values to check whether stack is empty or full.

Note that it is also possible to inherit a new class from a generic class.

Bounded Generics

Let us now define and use a generic class called **Statistics**. This class obtains average of **Integer**s or **Float**s. This should be fairly simple. However, the twist here is, we should not be allowed to find average of types for whom average doesn't make any sense, strings for example. This means that the **Statistics** class should not work for strings. Such classes are known as Bounded Generics. It is very simple to accomplish this. While defining the **Statistics** class we should define it through the statement

```
class Statistics <T extends Number>
```

This ensures that **Statistics** class can work only with those types that are derived from **Number**. Incidentally, **Integer** and **Float** both are derived from **Number** class, so **Statistics** can work with objects of these classes. Here is the full-fledged program.

```
package statsdemo ;
public class StatsDemo
{
    public static void main ( String[ ] args )
    {
        Integer iarr[ ] = { 1, 2, 3, 4, 5 } ;
        Statistics <Integer> iobj ;
        double avg1 ;

        iobj = new Statistics <Integer> ( iarr ) ;
        avg1 = iobj.getAverage( ) ;
        System.out.println ( "avg1 = " + avg1 ) ;

        Float farr[ ] = { 1.1f, 2.1f, 1.0f } ;
        Statistics <Float> fobj ;
        double avg2 ;

        fobj = new Statistics <Float> ( farr ) ;
        avg2 = fobj.getAverage( ) ;
        System.out.println ( "avg2 = " + avg2 ) ;
    }
}
```

```
class Statistics <T extends Number>
{
      private T arr[ ] ;

      Statistics ( T[ ] obj )
      {
            arr =  obj ;
      }
      public double getAverage( )
      {
            double sum = 0.0 ;

            for ( int i = 0 ; i < arr.length ; i++ )
                  sum = sum + arr[ i ].doubleValue( ) ;

            return ( sum / arr.length ) ;
      }
}
```

The program is pretty straight-forward and I think you can understand it easily. The **doubleValue( )** method returns the value of the specified number as a **double**.

Exercise

[A] State True or False:

(a) Java supports generic classes but not generic functions.

(b) We can inherit a new class from a generic class.

(c) Using generic functions saves memory.

(d) Generic functions cannot work for primitives like **int**, **float**, **char**, etc.

(e) A generic function can receive multiple argument types.

(f) Bounded generics can work only with the objects of specified class.

(g) Generics are extensively used in Java collection classes.

(h) Generic function arguments can take default values.

(i) Generic classes describe the functionality without being bound to any type.

[B] Answer the following:

(a) Write a program that will implement a linked list through a generic class.

(b) Write a program that has a generic class that can sort dates and strings apart from integers and floats.

kn KanNotes

- Generics promote Source-code Level, whereas Inheritance promotes Byte-code Level
- It is possible to create generic functions as well as generic classes
- Once the generic function / class is ready we can use them with any reference type
- Primitives are often called value types, whereas classes are called reference types
- Syntax of defining and calling a generic function :

```
// call to generic function
Integer[ ] intarr = { 10, -2, 37, 42, 15 } ;
printArray ( intarr ) ;

// generic function definition
public static <T> void printArray ( T[ ] arr )
{
    ..
}
```

- Generic function that can work with types that implements a Comparable interface

```
public static <T extends Comparable <T> > T min ( T a, T b )
{
    ...
}
```

- Generic function that can receive multiple types

```
public static <T, S, Z> void printTypes ( T a, S b, Z c )
{
    System.out.println ( "a = " + a + " b = " + b + " c = " + c ) ;
}
```

- Syntax for using and defining a generic class :

```
// using generic class
stack <Integer> s1 ;
s1 = new stack <Integer> ( 10 );
s1.push ( 10 ) ;

// defining generic class
class stack <T>
{
    ..
}
```

- Bounded generic class restricts its usage only by those reference types which are derived from the specified type
- For example, the following class would work only for those types that are derived from the Java API Number class :

```
class Statistics <T extends Number>
{
    ..
}
```

Java Collections

19

There are many standard ways of storing and accessing data. Let Java collections handle that, so that you can concentrate on building something bigger using them...

Chapter Contents

As Java became a popular choice amongst programmers to implement solutions, a need was felt to have a standard way to handle the data in the program. So a set of classes were made available to handle the data. These included classes like **Vector**, **Stack**, **Dictionary**, etc. However, these classes lacked a unified approach in the sense, the usage of each class was not consistent with the usage of other. When Generics were introduced in Java a completely new set of classes and interfaces were created in Java API for handling data. These classes came to be known as Java Collections Framework. Let us now get to the root of it.

Why a New Approach?

Suppose in a program we wish to store, retrieve and manipulate numbers and strings. An easy and intuitive way to handle this situation would be to create arrays of numbers and strings. However, this approach has following limitations:

(a) We may not want fixed-size arrays. We may want arrays to grow in size dynamically as we keep adding new elements to it. This requirement cannot be met by normal arrays, at least not without an effort of allocating space for bigger-sized array, copying existing elements into this space, etc.

(b) There may be a need to maintain data in different ways like Dictionary (where order is important), Key-Value maps, like cell number (key) and name (value).

(c) There may be a need to access data in different ways—Last In First Out (as in a stack), First In First Out (as in a queue), or sorted order.

To handle all these dynamics a completely new Java library based on Generics, called Java Collections Framework was introduced. This collections framework contains Collection classes, Interfaces and Algorithms (set of static functions in the Collections class). Some of the highlighting features of this collection framework are:

(a) Since the collections framework is based on generics it lets you handle virtually any type of data.

(b) The collections framework provides a set of very efficient classes to carry out most data management functionality. Do not confuse this with database management, which involves management of data on disk. As against this, collections framework primarily manages data in memory.

(c) It contains readymade classes for most Data Structures like stack, queue, linked list, binary tree, hashmap, etc.

(d) There is a lot of consistency in usage of the collection classes. For example, the same **add( )** function is available for adding new data to different collections. So no matter how a queue or a linked list organizes the data internally, the call that the programmer has to make for adding a new element to them remains same.

(e) Rather than doing the entire implementation from scratch, it is easily possible to extend the collections framework using the usual inheritance rules, to suit our specific needs.

Given in Figure 19.1 is a very short list of classes and interfaces available in the collections framework. This list is by no means exhaustive or complete, but is given here just to give you an idea of how the collections framework is organized.

The classes and interfaces of the collections framework are defined in **java.util** package.

In summary, we can say that collections framework provides prepackaged data structures plus the algorithms to manipulate them.

Entity	**Examples**
Collection classes	ArrayList, LinkedList, LinkedHashSet, TreeSet, HashMap, PriorityQueue, etc.
Interfaces	Collection, List, Set, SortedSet, NavigableSet, Queue, DeQueue, etc.
Algorithms	fill( ), max( ), min( ), reverse( ), shuffle( ), sort( ), binarySearch( ), etc.

Figure 19.1

Array of Names and Numbers

Let us now see how to use the collections framework. We would begin with managing a set of names and a set of numbers. This can be done using the **ArrayList** collection class. Given below is a program that shows how this can be done.

```
package arraylistdemo ;
import java.util.* ;
public class ArrayListDemo
{
    public static void main ( String[ ] args )
    {
        ArrayList <String> alnames ;

        alnames = new ArrayList <> ( ) ;
        alnames.add ( "Shashank" ) ;
        alnames.add ( "Prasanna" ) ;
        alnames.add ( "Nimesh" ) ;
        alnames.add ( "Karun" ) ;
        alnames.add ( "Rajgopal" ) ;

        System.out.println ( "contents of al: " + alnames ) ;
        alnames.add ( 2, "Aditya" ) ;
        alnames.remove ( 3 ) ;
        alnames.remove ( "Karun" ) ;
        System.out.println ( "contents of al: " + alnames ) ;

        if ( alnames.contains ( "Aditya" ) )
            System.out.println ( "Aditya is present in the array list" ) ;

        ArrayList <Integer> alnums ;
        alnums = new ArrayList <> ( ) ;
        alnums.add ( 10 ) ;
        alnums.add ( 20 ) ;
        alnums.add ( 30 ) ;
        alnums.add ( 40 ) ;

        int sum = 0 ;
        for ( int i = 0 ; i < alnums.size( ) ; i++ )
            sum = sum + alnums.get ( i ) ;
```

```
        System.out.println ( "sum = " + sum ) ;

        Integer arr[ ] = new Integer [ alnums.size( ) ] ;
        arr = alnums.toArray ( arr ) ;

        sum = 0 ;
        for ( int n : arr )
            sum += n ;

        System.out.println ( "sum = " + sum ) ;
    }
}
```

Here is the output of the progam...

```
contents of alnames: [Shashank, Prasanna, Nimesh, Karun, Rajgopal]
contents of alnames: [Shashank, Prasanna, Aditya, Rajgopal]
Aditya is present in the array list
sum = 100
sum = 100
```

The program begins by creating an **ArrayList** object for storing strings and then adding a few names to it using **add( )** function. If we wish, we can also pass the initial size of the array list by passing the size to the constructor while creating the **ArrayList** object. After creating the object, we have added a new name at a specific position (using the overloaded **add( )** function) and removed name from a specific position (using the **remove( )** function). Thus addition, insertion and deletion operations are straight-forward.

There is a very simple way to print the entire **ArrayList** contents using **println( )**. Note that the **ArrayList** maintains the list in a dynamic fashion. Nowhere have we specified its size. It keeps growing as we keep adding new elements. The **contains( )** function helps us figure out whether a specific element is present in the array list or not.

What is important for you to notice is that the usage of **ArrayList** class doesn't change at all when it comes to maintaining an array of numbers instead of names.

We have obtained the sum of all integers by retrieving each integer using the **get( )** function. Note that **get( )** returns an **Integer**, not an **int**. The **size( )** function yields the current size of the array list.

The array maintained by array list can be converted into the normal Java array using the **toArray( )** function. This array can then be iterated over using the special **for** loop as shown in the program.

Maintaining a Stack

A Stack is a data structure in which addition of new element or deletion of an existing element always takes place at the same end. This end is often known as **top** of stack. This situation can be compared to a stack of plates in a cafeteria where every new plate added to the stack is added at the **top**. Similarly, every plate taken off the stack is also from the **top** of the stack. Thus stack is a last-in-first-out (LIFO) list. When an item is added to a stack, the operation is called **push**, and when an item is removed from the stack the operation is called **pop**.

Given below is a program that maintains a stack of city names using the collection class called **Stack**. Note that before calling the **pop( )** function we need to ascertain whether the stack has any element left in it. This is done by calling the **isEmpty( )** function.

```
package stackdemo ;
import java.util.* ;
public class StackDemo
{
    public static void main ( String args[ ] )
    {
        Stack < String > s ;
        s = new Stack <> ( ) ;
        s.push ( "Delhi" ) ;
        s.push ( "Nagpur" ) ;
        s.push ( "Indore" ) ;
        s.push ( "Raipur" ) ;
        s.push ( "Mysore" ) ;
        s.push ( "Mumbai" ) ;

        String str ;

        if ( ! s.isEmpty( ) )
        {
            str = s.pop( ) ;
            System.out.println ( str ) ;
        }
```

```
            if ( ! s.isEmpty( ) )
            {
                str = s.pop( ) ;
                System.out.println ( str ) ;
            }
        }
    }
```

Maintaining a Linked List

Linked list is a very common data structure often used to store similar data in memory. While the elements of an array occupy contiguous memory locations, those of a linked list are not constrained to be stored in adjacent locations. The individual elements are stored "somewhere" in memory, rather like a family dispersed, but still bound together. The order of the elements is maintained by explicit links between them. For instance, the marks obtained by different students can be stored in a linked list as shown in Figure 19.2.

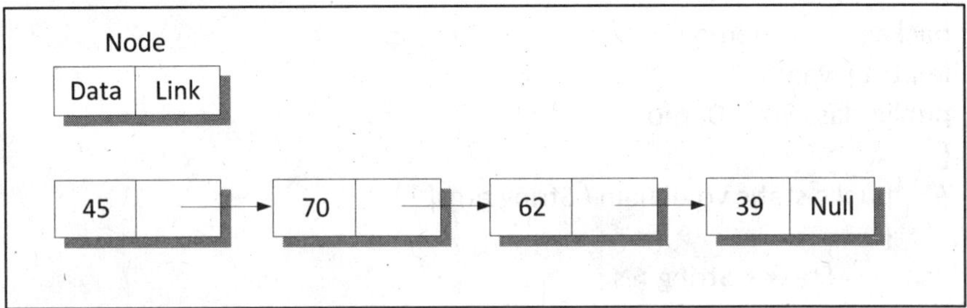

Figure 19.2

Observe that the linked list is a collection of elements called nodes, each of which stores two items of information—an element of the list and a link. A link is a reference or an address that indicates explicitly the location of the node containing the successor of the list element. In Figure 19.2, the arrows represent the links. The **data** part of each node consists of the marks obtained by a student, and the **link** part is a pointer to the next node. The **NULL** in the last node indicates that this is the last node in the list.

Instead of marks, we can maintain a linked list of names. If we want, we can maintain both in each node. The program given below uses the collection class **LinkedList** to maintain a linked list of names of students. Most of the operations in the program are self-explanatory. Go through the program carefully, a step at a time.

```
package linkedlistdemo ;
import java.util.* ;
public class LinkedListDemo
{
    public static void main ( String[ ] args )
    {
        LinkedList <String> ll ;
        ll = new LinkedList <> ( ) ;
        ll.add ( "Subhash" ) ;
        ll.add ( "Rahul" ) ;
        ll.add ( "Joe" ) ;
        ll.add ( "Vineeta" ) ;
        for ( String s : ll )
            System.out.println ( s ) ;

        ll.set ( 2, "Neha" ) ;
        System.out.println ( ll ) ;

        String name = ll.get ( 2 ) ;
        System.out.println ( "String at position 2 = " + name ) ;
        ll.add ( 3, "Sanjay" ) ;
        System.out.println ( ll ) ;
        ll.remove ( 1 ) ;
        System.out.println ( ll ) ;
    }
}
```

Here is the output of the program...

```
Subhash
Rahul
Joe
Vineeta
[Subhash, Rahul, Neha, Vineeta]
String at position 2 = Neha
[Subhash, Rahul, Neha, Sanjay, Vineeta]
[Subhash, Neha, Sanjay, Vineeta]
```

Maintaining a Tree

The data structures such as linked lists, stacks and queues are linear data structures. As against this, trees are non-linear data structures. In a linked list each node has a link which points to another node. In a tree structure, however, each node may point to several other nodes (which may then point to several other nodes, etc.). Thus a tree is a very flexible and powerful data structure that can be used for a wide variety of applications. For example, suppose we wish to use a data structure to represent a person and all of his or her descendants. Assume that the person's name is **Rahul** and that he has 3 children, **Sanjay**, **Sameer** and **Nisha**. Also suppose that **Sameer** has 3 children, **Abha**, **Ram** and **Madhu** and **Nisha** has one child **Neha**. We can represent **Rahul** and his descendants with the tree structure shown in Figure 19.3.

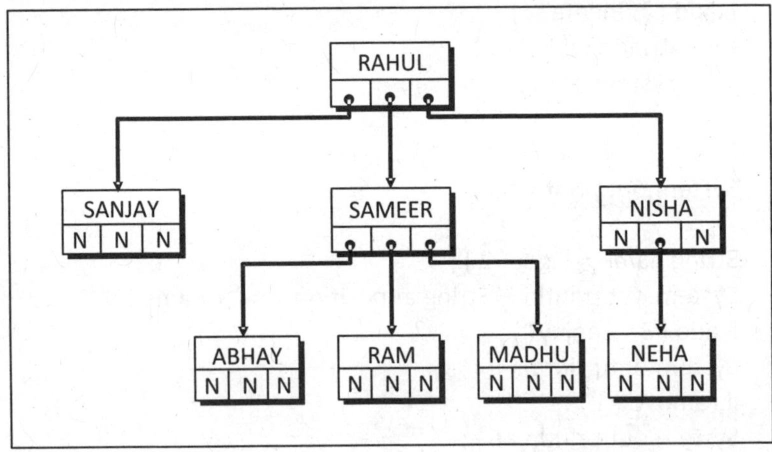

Figure 19.4

Notice that each tree node contains a name for data and one or more pointers to the other tree nodes.

Although the nodes in a general tree may contain any number of pointers to the other tree nodes, a large number of data structures have at the most two pointers to the other tree nodes. This type of a tree is called a **Binary Tree**.

Many algorithms that use binary trees proceed in two phases. The first phase builds a binary tree, and the second traverses the tree. Suppose we wish that while traversing the binary tree we should be able to access the elements in it in ascending order. To ensure this we need to arrange the elements properly during insertion. A simple logic to do so would be to compare the element to be inserted with the element in the root node and then take the left branch if the element is smaller than the element in the node, and a right branch if it is greater or equal to the element in the node. Thus if the input list is

20 17 6 8 10 7 18 13 12 5

then using this insertion method the binary tree shown in Figure 19.4 would be produced.

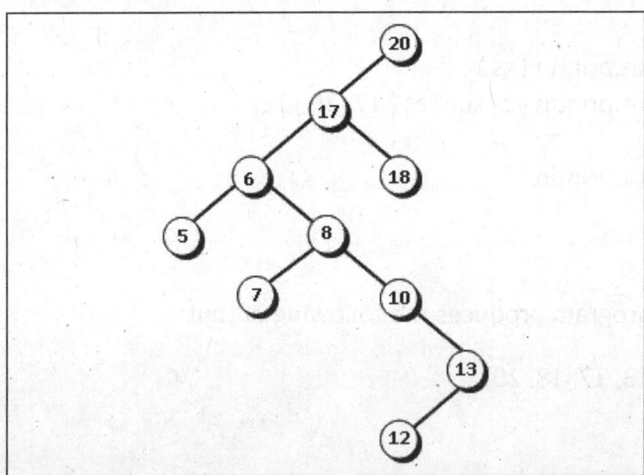

Figure 19.4

Such a binary tree has the property that all the elements in the left sub-tree of any node **n** are less than the contents of **n**. And all the elements in the right sub-tree of **n** are greater than or equal to the contents of **n**. A binary tree that has these properties is called a **Binary Search Tree**.

If a binary search tree is traversed in in-order, i.e., in the order left child, root, and right child and the contents of each node are printed as each node is visited, the numbers are printed in ascending order. This is demonstrated in the program given below.

```
package treesetdemo ;
import java.util.* ;
public class TreeSetDemo
{
    public static void main ( String args[ ] )
    {
        TreeSet <Integer> ts ;
        ts = new TreeSet <> ( ) ;
        ts.add ( 20 ) ;
        ts.add ( 17 ) ;
        ts.add ( 6 ) ;
        ts.add ( 8 ) ;
        ts.add ( 10 ) ;
```

```
        ts.add ( 7 ) ;
        ts.add ( 18 ) ;
        ts.add ( 13 ) ;
        ts.add ( 12 ) ;
        ts.add ( 5 ) ;

        System.out.println ( ts ) ;
        System.out.println ( ts.subSet ( 17, 35 ) ) ;
        ts.clear( ) ;
        System.out.println ( ts ) ;
    }
}
```

On execution the program produces the following output:

```
[5, 6, 7, 8, 10, 12, 13, 17, 18, 20]
[17, 18, 20]
[ ]
```

From the output you can see that the **subSet( )** function gives all those nodes that lie between the nodes passed to it. Also, to delete all the nodes in the tree at one shot, the **clear( )** function can be used.

Maintaining a HashMap

The **HashMap** class lets us maintain a set of key - value pairs. For example, we can maintain key - value pairs of cell numbers and names, or key - value pairs of day names in English and Hindi. Against each key multiple values may also be maintained. For example, against cell number we can store the name, address and photograph. The key - value pairs may not be stored in the same order as the order of insertion. We can get the order in which they are being maintained by printing out the hash map. This is shown in the following program.

```
package hashmapdemo ;
import java.util.* ;

public class HashMapDemo
{
    public static void main ( String args[ ] )
    {
        HashMap < String, String> hm ;
        hm = new HashMap < > ( ) ;
```

```
        hm.put ( "Sun", "Ravi" ) ;
        hm.put ( "Mon", "Som" ) ;
        hm.put ( "Tue", "Mangal" ) ;
        hm.put ( "Wed", "Budh" ) ;
        hm.put ( "Thu", "Guru" ) ;
        hm.put ( "Fri", "Shukra" ) ;
        hm.put ( "Sat", "Shani" ) ;

        System.out.println ( hm ) ;

        String str ;
        str = hm.get ( "Wed" ) ;
        System.out.println ( "Wed in hindi is " + str ) ;
    }
}
```

The output of the program is shown below. Note that the **get( )** function can be used to obtain the value stored against the key passed to it.

```
{Thu=Guru, Tue=Mangal, Wed=Budh, Sat=Shani, Fri=Shukra, Sun=Ravi,
Mon=Som}
Wed in hindi is Budh
```

Using the Algorithms

There are many operations that we wish to perform on collections. These include searching, sorting, finding minimum value, finding maximum value, etc. In terminology of collections framework these are called algorithms and are available for use in the form of **static** methods of the **Collections** class. A smaller version of the same is also available in the **Arrays** class. The program given below shows how to use these algorithms from the **Arrays** class.

```
package arraysdemo ;
import java.util.* ;
public class ArraysDemo
{
    public static void main ( String[ ] args )
    {
        int arr[ ] = new int[ 5 ] ;
        Random r = new Random( ) ;
```

```
        for ( int i = 0 ; i < arr.length ; i++ )
        {
            arr[ i ] =  r.nextInt ( 25 ) ;
            System.out.println ( arr[ i ] ) ;
        }
        Arrays.sort ( arr ) ;
        System.out.println ( "After sorting: " ) ;
        for ( int i = 0 ; i < arr.length ; i++ )
            System.out.println ( arr[ i ] ) ;

        Arrays.fill ( arr, 2, 4, -3 ) ;
        System.out.println ( "After filling: " ) ;
        for ( int i = 0 ; i < arr.length ; i++ )
             System.out.println ( arr[ i ] ) ;

        int pos ;
        pos = Arrays.binarySearch ( arr, -3 ) ;
        System.out.println ( "pos = " + pos ) ;
    }
}
```

Here is the output of the program.

```
15
13
13
2
18
After sorting:
2
13
13
15
18
After filling:
2
13
-3
-3
18
pos = 2
```

The program generates random numbers using **nextInt( )** function of **Random** class and then populates the array **arr** with these randomly generated integers. Next, it calls the **sort( )** function to sort these numbers.

The call to **fill( )** function fills the array with -3 starting from 2nd position up to and excluding the 4th position. Then the program uses the **binarySearch( )** function to search the position of first occurrence of -3 in the array.

I hope now you have got a fair idea of how to use the Java collections framework. You can explore the other collection classes, interfaces and algorithms of the framework on your own.

Exercise

[A] State True or False:

(a) Java collections framework provides common algorithms through **static** functions of **Collections** class.

(b) The Java collection framework is based on Generics.

(c) Key - value pairs can be maintained using **ArrayList** class.

(d) In a hashmap order of insertion and order of access are same.

(e) **ArrayList** class can grow and shrink an array dynamically.

(f) Elements of a linked list are stored in adjacent memory locations.

(g) Stack is a FIFO list.

(h) All binary trees are maintained by **TreeSet** class as binary search trees.

(i) It is possible to maintain elements of **ArrayList** in sorted order.

[B] Answer the following:

(a) Write a program that will implement a linked list where each node consists of name, age and salary of a person.

(b) Write a program that maintains a tree of city names in sorted order.

(c) Write a program that maintains a hash map of 10 cell numbers as keys and the name of the person and his email address as values.

KanNotes

- To store, retrieve and manipulate multiple numbers / strings arrays can be used
- Arrays suffer from 2 limitations :
  - They have no mechanism to maintain data in different ways like Key -Value maps, Dictionary, etc.
  - Arrays have no means to access data in FIFO, LIFO, Sorted order, etc.
- Instead of arrays we should use ready-made library called Java Collection Framework
- Advantages of using Java Collection f/w
  - Very efficient, time tested, written by experts
  - Readymade classes for most data structures, so we can concentrate on program rather than building data structures
  - It is possible to extend the collection classes to suit our needs
- Collection framework contains :
  - Collection classes - ArrayList, LinkedList, TreeSet, PriorityQueue, HashMap, etc.
  - Interfaces - Collection, List, Set, SortedSet, NavigableSet, Queue, DeQueue, etc
  - Algorithms – fill( ), max( ), min( ), reverse( ), shuffle( ), binarySearch(), sort(), etc.
- Algorithms are static methods of Arrays class
- All collection classes are implemented as Generics, hence can work only with reference types
- Vector class and ArrayList class both can maintain arrays that grow dynamically
- Vector is synchronized class, so slow. ArrayList is not synchronized, so fast

- For a Vector class :
  - capacity indicates how many elements can be stored in the vector
  - size indicates number of elements present in it
  - grow size indicates by how much would the capacity increase, when we store an element once the capacity is full
- Vector / ArrayList should be used if we are to store and process their elements sequentially
- LinkList should be used if frequent insertions / deletions of elements is required
- Rule for inserting elements in a Binary Search Tree (BST)- Greater to Right, Smaller to Left of Root
- The sequence of visiting nodes in BST in Inorder traversal – Left, Root, Right
- When elements are accessed using Inorder Traversal, they get accessed in ascending order
- The order in which we insert entries into a HashMap and the order in which they are stored may be different

User Interfaces

20

Text is gone! Graphics is the way to go. Learn how to build Graphical User Interfaces in Java...

Let Us JAVA

3rd Edition

Chapter Contents

- A Simple Swing Application
- Event Handling
- One More GUI Application
- Adapter Classes
- What Next?
- Exercise
- KanNotes

In today's GUI-centric world it is expected that Java programs would let a program interact with the user using GUI elements like text boxes, list boxes, combo boxes, push button, radio buttons, check boxes, scroll bars, etc. To facilitate this interaction Java provides three libraries—Active Window toolkit (AWT), Swing and JavaFX. Of these, AWT is the older library. Moreover, the world has now moved over to either Swing or JavaFX library. In fact Swing internally uses AWT. In that sense Swing is built on top of AWT. In this chapter we would see how to build simple GUI based applications using Swing library.

A Simple Swing Application

In this application the goal is to create and display a window shown in Figure 20.1. As you can see, this window has two labels, two text fields and a button. On entering the temperature in the text field for Centigrade degrees and clicking the Convert button, the program should do the conversion of temperature into Fahrenheit degrees and display this temperature in the second text field.

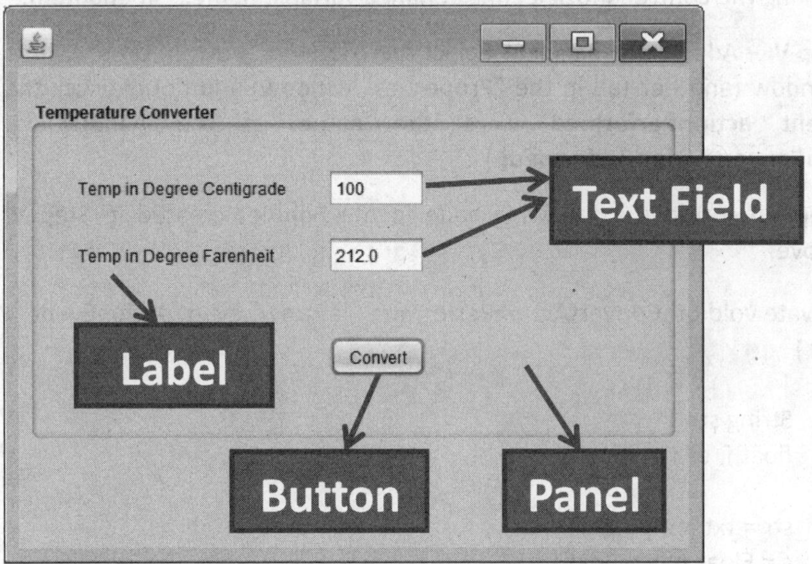

Figure 20.1

Given below are the steps that we should carry out to create this application using NetBeans.

Step I – Create a Java Application, give Project Name as **GUIApp**. Choose a suitable location on your disk for creating the files of this application. Uncheck the "Create Main Class" check box.

Step II – To create the window for the application, add new **JFrame** form to the application. For this right click on the **GUIApp** project in the project window and then select "New" followed by "JFrame Form". On doing so, it will ask you to supply the name of the class to represent the window. Type **ConvertTemp** as the class name and click on the "Finish" button.

Step III – At the end of step II a window would appear in NetBeans. Now we need to insert Container (Panel) and Controls (Labels, Text fields, Button) in this window. Drag and drop them from the Swing Containers and Controls window that appears besides the frame window.

Step IV – Change the values of "text" property of the two label controls and one button control. For the two labels give the values as "Temp in Degree Centigrade" and "Temp in Degree Fahrenheit". For the button give the value as "Convert". Note that the property values can be changed through the "Properties" window by typing the new values.

Step V – Change names of the two text fields and the button to **txtTempC**, **txtTempF** and **btnConvert** respectively. This can be done by right clicking the control and selecting "Change variable name..." menu item.

Step VI – Add Button handler - Select the "Convert" button, Go to Events Window (another tab in the "Properties" window) and double click the event **actionPerformed**. Give the name of the handler as **btnConvertActionPerformed( )**.

Step VII – Add the following code in the handler created in Step VI above.

```
private void btnConvertActionPerformed ( java.awt.event.ActionEvent
evt )
{
    String str ;
    float f, c ;

    str = txtTempC.getText( ) ;
    c = Float.parseFloat ( str ) ;
    f = c * 9 / 5 + 32 ;
    str = Float.toString ( f ) ;
    txtTempF.setText ( str ) ;
}
```

Step VIII – Compile and execute the program using F6. On execution the window with the container and controls we had inserted would appear.

On providing the temperature in Centigrade and clicking the Convert button the temperature in Fahrenheit would get displayed.

So much about creating our first GUI application using Swing library. Let us now understand what we did in this application. Given below is the source code that the wizard has created for us as we were creating the application.

```
package converttemp ;
public class ConvertTemp extends javax.swing.JFrame
{
    private javax.swing.JPanel jPanel1 ;
    private javax.swing.JLabel jLabel1 ;
    private javax.swing.JLabel jLabel2 ;
    private javax.swing.JTextField txtTempC ;
    private javax.swing.JTextField txtTempF ;
    private javax.swing.JButton btnConvert ;

    public ConvertTemp( )
    {
        initComponents( ) ;
    }

    public static void main ( String args[ ] )
    {
        /* code to create and display the form */
    }
}
```

When we added a JFrame form to our application and gave a name **ConvertTemp** to it, a class of this name, inherited from the Swing class **JFrame**, got inserted in our application. You can observe this inheritance from the code given above and also note that **main( )** is now present in this class.

For every container and control that we can drag and drop in the window there is a Swing class available. For example, for a panel there is a class called **JPanel**, for a button **JButton** and for a text field **JTextField**. These classes are defined in the package **javax.swing**. So when we dragged and dropped them into the window and gave names to them, **private** variables by these names got created in the **ConvertTemp** class.

But somewhere the objects of **JPanel**, **JButton**, **JTextField**, etc. also need to be created. Well, that is what is done in the **initComponents( )** function that has been called from the **ConvertTemp**'s constructor. In fact if you take a look at this function you would see apart from creation of these objects, properties of these objects being setup. These include position, size, color, etc. You can also observe statements to add all these controls to the window. You are best advised not to edit the code in **initComponents( )** directly.

The wizard would add the code to create and display the window in **main( )**. When the window is created, an object of **ConvertTemp** would be created. This would result into call to its constructor and in turn to **initComponents( )**.

One question that must be troubling you—what is the difference between a container and a control? A control is something that the user interacts with, like a push button, a check box or a combo box. As the name suggests, a container is something that would hold these visual controls.

Now that we have understood the code to create the window, container and controls, let us now turn our attention to a phenomenon called event handling.

Event Handling

In simplest words an event is a thing that takes place. Programmatically it means change in the state of an object. Events occur all the time when we are interacting with a GUI application. For example, when we enter a character from keyboard, or move the mouse, or click the left mouse button, events occur. These events are generated as a consequence of interaction with the graphical components in the GUI. Such events are known as Foreground events.

Apart from these, events also occur without any user interaction. For example, expiry of a timer, completion of some ongoing task, occurrence of an interrupt, etc. Such events are known as Background Events.

When an event occurs, the program is supposed to react to that event. That reaction is known as event handling. Programmatically, a function known as event handler gets executed when an event occurs. To ensure that all events are handled in a standard manner, Java uses a mechanism called Event Delegation Model to handle the events. This model involves two key players:

(a) Source – The source is an object on which the event occurs. For example objects of **JButton**, **JTextField**, **JComboBox** are all sources. These sources provide information of the occurred event to their respective handlers.

(b) Listener – The listener listens to (i.e. it waits for) an event to occur. When an event occurs, the listener processes the event. Programmatically, listener is an interface containing prototypes of functions. For example, the **MouseListener** interface contains prototypes of functions like **mouseClicked()**, **mousePressed( )**, **mouseReleased( )**, etc.

The events themselves are represented using readymade classes like **MouseEvent**, **KeyEvent**, **ActionEvent**, etc. When an event occurs, event objects are created and passed to the listener functions (defined in a class that implements the listener interface) to tackle the event.

Different applications would react to occurrence of same event differently. For example, on clicking a mouse one application may print a page on the printer, whereas, another application may draw a circle in the window. Hence, in both applications, different functions would have to be written for the same mouse event. These functions are nothing but the implementations of the functions declared in the **MouseListener** interface.

Let us understand this inter-play of multiple classes, objects and interfaces with reference to our temperature converter application. We did two specific things in this application. These are as follows:

(a) We dragged and dropped the button in our window and gave it a name **btnConvert**.

(b) For the Convert button, for the **actionPerformed** event, we added an event handler function. We called this function **btnConvertActionPerformed( )**.

As a result of step (a) above, a **private** variable **btnConvert** of the type **JButton** got declared in the **ConvertTemp** class. An object of **JButton** class got created in **initComponents( )** and its address got stored in **btnConvert**.

When we performed step (b) above, a call to the function **addActionListener( )** got added in **initComponents( )**. This call is made using **btnConvert**. This call ties the **ActionListener** interface with the Convert button. **ActionListener** interface has the following method declaration in it:

```
void actionPerformed ( ActionEvent  e ) ;
```

In **initComponents( )** this method is implemented in a class (often called anonymous class). Object of this class is passed to the **addActionListener( )** method.

When we click the Convert button, an **actionPerformed** event occurs. Information about this event is packed in an **ActionEvent** object. This object is then passed to the **actionPerformed( )** method of the anonymous class. From this method our event handler—the function **btnConvertActionPerformed( )** gets called. In this method we do the temperature conversion and display the result in the text field.

It is said that for event handling Java uses Event Delegation model. This means that the responsibility of event handling is delegated (assigned) to listeners. As a result, the logic that displays the controls and generates the events remains completely separated from the logic that reacts to these events.

In this model, the listener needs to be registered with the source object (button in our example), so that the listener can receive the event notification. This way the event notifications are sent only to those listeners who wish to receive them.

One More GUI Application

Now that we are familiar with creation of a GUI application and its working, let us now create one more application to help you fix your ideas. The window and the controls for this application are shown in Figure 20.2.

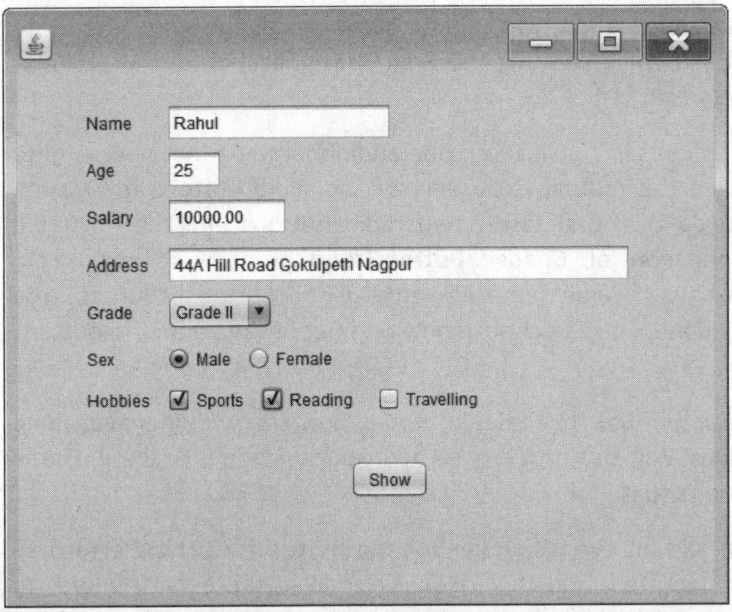

Figure 20.2

As you can see in Figure 20.2, there are several labels, 4 text fields (for Name, Age, Salary and Address), 1 list box (for Grade of employee), 2 radio buttons (for Sex of employee), 3 check boxes (for Hobbies of employee) and 1 button (Show button) in the window. The user would interact with different controls and either type or select the data values for an employee. Once the Show button is clicked the typed or selected values should be displayed in a message box as shown in Figure 20.3.

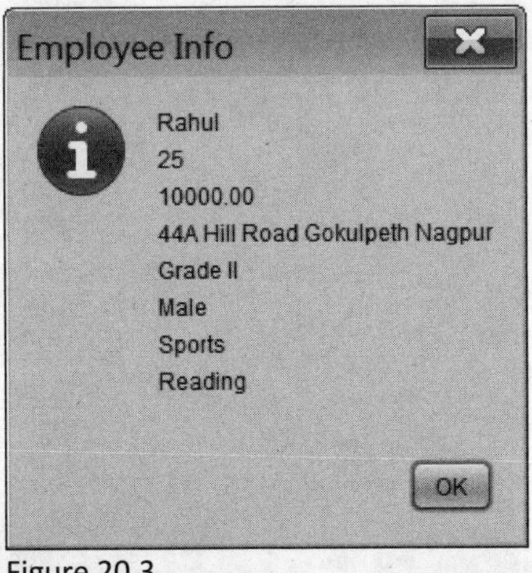

Figure 20.3

To create this application, you should follow exactly the same steps that were discussed while creating the first GUI application in the previous section.

Regarding GUI in this application, one additional thing that you need to do is manage the mutual exclusivity of the radio buttons for Male / Female. To do this, first insert two radio buttons and then insert a Button Group control. Change **ButtonGroup** property of both radio buttons to have a value same as name of the Button Group control. Once this is done, you can choose only one out of the two radio buttons at a time.

Also, for Combo Box by default **model** property would have some default values. Edit this property to add values Grade I, Grade II, Grade III and Grade IV to it.

Once again add an event handler for the button for **actionPerformed** event. Once created, add the following code in the event handler to display the typed / selected values in a message box.

```
private void btnShowActionPerformed (java.awt.event.ActionEvent evt )
{
    String str,str1,str2 ;
    String strName ;
    String strAge ;
    String strGrade ;
    String strSalary ;
    String strAddress ;
    String strSex = "" ;
    String strReading = "" ;
    String strTravelling = "" ;
    String strSports = "" ;

    strName = txtName.getText ( ) ;
    strAge = txtAge.getText( ) ;
    strSalary = txtSalary.getText( ) ;
    strAddress = txtAddress.getText( ) ;
    strGrade = cbGrade.getName( ) ;

    if ( rbMale.isSelected( ) )
        strSex = rbMale.getText( ) ;

    if ( rbFemale.isSelected( ) )
```

```
            strSex = rbFemale.getText( ) ;

        if ( ckbxSports.isSelected( ) )
            strSports = ckbxSports.getText( ) ;

        if ( ckbxReading.isSelected( ) )
          strReading = ckbxReading.getText( ) ;

        if ( ckbxTravelling.isSelected( ) )
          strTravelling = ckbxTravelling.getText( ) ;


       str1 = strName + "\n" + strAge + "\n" + strSalary + "\n" +
            strAddress + "\n" + strGrade + "\n" ;
       str2 = strSex + "\n" + strSports + "\n" + strReading + "\n"+
                strTravelling + "\n" ;
       str = str1+str2 ;
      JOptionPane.showMessageDialog ( null, str,"Employee Info",
            JOptionPane.INFORMATION_MESSAGE ) ;
}
```

In this event handler we have extracted the values from the text fields using calls to the **getText( )** function. Which of the radio buttons and check boxes have been selected is checked using the **isSelected( )** function. The actual selections are again obtained using the **getText( )** function. The grade selected from Combobox is collected using the function **getName( )**.

All the strings extracted from these functions are concatenated, with "\n"s added to separate values into multiple lines. Lastly, the final string **str** is displayed using the static method **ShowMessage( )** of the **JOptionPane** class. The information icon is displayed using the enum value INFORMATION_MESSAGE.

Adapter Classes

Suppose we wish to interact with mouse in our GUI application. For this we need to add the **MouseListener** interace. If we do this then all the methods in the **MouseListener** interface need to be implemented in our class. Problem is that **MouseListener** has five methods in it. These are as follows:

```
public void mouseClicked ( MouseEvent  e ) ;
```

```
public void mousePressed ( MouseEvent  e ) ;
public void mouseReleased ( MouseEvent  e ) ;
public void mouseEntered ( MouseEvent  e ) ;
public void mouseExited ( MouseEvent  e ) ;
```

Suppose we wish to react only to the **MouseClicked** event; we still have to implement all the methods of the interface. So only the **mouseClicked( )** function would have some meaningful code, whereas the rest of them would have empty body. Two such functions are shown below.

```
public void mousePressed ( MouseEvent e )
{
}

public void mouseReleased ( MouseEvent e )
{
}
```

Providing such empty-bodied function becomes tedious when the interface has a large number of functions. To avoid this unnecessary work Java provides Adapter Classes, one per interface. Thus, for **MouseListener** interface there would be an equivalent adapter class known as **MouseAdapter**. This class would contain five empty-bodied functions. Now all that we need to do is, inherit our class from this adapter class and override only the **mouseClicked( )** function. Smart work, you would agree!

What Next?

There are many controls and interfaces in Java swing API. The intention of this chapter was to introduce you to some of them and discuss the basic philosophy behind creating modern GUI and handling events. The Swing library is very exhaustive and covering all classes in it would need a separate book. Nevertheless, through this chapter you got introduced to the Swing API and its working. Rest you are free to explore on your own.

Exercise

[A] State True or False:

(a) There is no difference between a container and a control.

(b) A control has to be in a container for it to become visible and usable.

(c) For every control that can be inserted in a window there is a readymade class available in Swing API.

(d) All Swing classes are defined in **javax.gui** package.

(e) We can modify Adapter classes by adding new methods to them.

(f) For every event related interface available in Swing library there is one equivalent adapter class.

(g) Methods in adapter classes are empty-bodied.

(h) We can avoid using Adapter classes by implementing all the methods of an interface in our class.

(i) The Even Delegation model ensures that the code that creates controls and events remains separate from the code that reacts to events.

[B] Answer the following:

(a) Write a program that creates a window and displays a message "Hello" in it at a position where you click with left mouse button in it.

(b) Modify the above program to display "Hello" for a left click and "Bye" for the right click.

(c) Write a program that draws a line, rectangle and ellipse of suitable size and color in a window.

KanNotes

- Three ways to provide input to a Java program :
  - Console IO - Input from keyboard, Output to screen
  - Command Line Arguments
  - GUI elements like Text Fields, Buttons, Combo Boxes, Menu, etc.
- GUI Libraries : AWT - Older way, Swing - Newer way
- For every window and control there are Swing classes available
- Event is a thing that takes place
- Java uses Event Delegation model - Responsibility of event handling is delegated (assigned) to Listeners
- Programmatic elements involved in GUI - Sources, Events, Listeners, Adapters
- Sources are classes for controls. All classes are subclasses of java.awt.Component
- To represent an event that a control may generate, many event classes exist
  - Ex. : Button, Menu - ActionEvent
  - Ex. : Frame - WindowEvent
- Event Listeners are Interfaces. Different listeners exist for different controls
  - Ex. : Button, TextField - ActionListener
  - Ex. : Mouse - MouseListener, MouseMotionListener
- Adapters – Abstract classes. There is 1 abstract class per listener
- Adapters contain empty body of all interface methods
- Idea behind Adapters - Inherit and override only desired functions

JDBC

21

World is full of data. You are in a commanding position if you know how to deal with it in a professional manner...

Let Us JAVA

3rd Edition

Chapter Contents

- Data Organization
- Common Database Operations
- Database Operations through Java
- JDBC Architecture
- JDBC Driver Types
- MySQL Database Installation
- Common JDBC API Components
- Putting it to Work
- Exercise
- KanNotes

Data is the King! In today's digital world enormous amount of data is being generated and exchanged. All this data finally gets stored in a database. As a Java programmer one must know how to handle this data programmatically. To help us do this Java provides an API called JDBC. It stands for Java Database Connectivity. This API lets us write Java programs that can interact with a wide range of databases. How this can be done is discussed in this chapter.

Data Organization

Modern way of organizing data is storing it in a Relational Database Management System or RDBMS. Different vendors provide this RDBMS software. These include Oracle, Microsoft, IBM, etc. There are several open source implementations available as well, the most popular amongst which is MySQL. All these RDBMSs are accessible through the JDBC API.

Each of these RDBMS organizes the data in the form of different tables. One database may contain multiple tables. Each table contains data organized in the form of records (rows). Each record may contain multiple fields (columns).

For example, a company may have a database containing Employees table containing records about employees working in an organization. Each record may contain fields like Name, Age, Salary, etc.

Likewise a University database may consist of tables for students, professors, courses, examinations, payments, etc. It is also possible to establish relationships between tables. For example, if a student pays fees, then the record of fees paid can be linked to his record in the student table. This would be a one-to-one relationship. If the same student pays fees multiple times then it would become a one-to-many relationship.

Common Database Operations

There is a set of typical operations that one needs to carry out on database of any kind. These are as follows:

(a) Create Table - Create a table by specifying its name and the fields that it would contain along with the type of each field.

(b) Modify Table - Modify the specifications of different fields, or add / delete certain fields.

(c) Drop Table - Delete the table from the database including all the records present in it.

To carry out these operations a simple language has been created. It is called SQL, standing for Structured Query Language. This language provides simple English like statements to perform database operations. SQL is supported by almost every RDBMS and it allows you to work with a database independently of the underlying RDBMS.

Given below are some sample SQL statements for carrying out database operations. The comments before each SQL statement would help you understand the operation being performed by the SQL statement.

```
// Create a table called Persons containing two fields EmpID of the type
// int and Name of the type variable length string of 255 characters
CREATE TABLE Persons ( EmpID int, Name varchar ( 255 ) )

// Modify Persons table by adding a field DateOfBirth of the type date
ALTER TABLE Persons ADD DateOfBirth date

// Modify the Persons table by deleting the column DateOfBirth
ALTER TABLE Persons DROP COLUMN DateOfBirth

// Delete the Customers table
DROP TABLE Customers
```

SQL also provides statements that let you work with the records of each table. Common operations on a table include **C**reate new record(s), **R**ead existing record(s), **U**pdate existing record(s), **D**elete existing record(s). In short these are known as CRUD operations. The SQL statements that carry out these operations are often known as SQL queries. Given below are some sample SQL statements for carrying out CRUD operations.

```
// Insert a new record in Persons table, with values 101 and Sunil in the
// EmpID and Name respectively
INSERT INTO Persons ( EmpID, Name) VALUES ( 1001, 'Sunil' )

// Read all records from Employees table
SELECT * FROM Employees

// Modify record whose Employee ID is 1001 by changing its Name field
// to hold a value Satish
```

UPDATE Persons SET Name = 'Satish' WHERE EmpID = 1001

// Delete that record from the Persons table whose Employee ID is 1244
DELETE FROM Persons WHERE EmpID = 1244

Database Operations through Java

The operations mentioned in the previous section were performed using SQL. Let us now see how these operations can be carried out through Java. Creation, Modification and Deletion of a table are infrequent operations. By this what I mean is Customers or Students table is not going to get created, altered or deleted every other day. In fact once you have set up all the fields in a table to your satisfaction, you would rarely change it. More common operations would be the CRUD operations.

Hence usually the operation of creation of tables is done manually using the tools that come with each RDBMS. For example, in this chapter we propose to use MySQL RDBMS and perform these operations using the MySQL WorkBench that comes with MySQL.

The CRUD operations can be performed using the JDBC objects called **Connection**, **Statement** and **ResultSet**. The purpose of each of these objects is mentioned below.

(a) Connection – To establish connection with database
(b) Statement – To execute SQL statements
(c) Resultset – To process results of a SQL query

Before we can use these objects in our Java program we need to understand the JDBC architecture and install a RDBMS. Our choice of database would be MySQL, primarily because it is free of cost and quite popular amongst open source community. The JDBC architecture and MySQL installation are discussed in the following sections.

JDBC Architecture

To help programmers communicate with the database, vendors provide vendor-specific JDBC driver software. For example, Oracle provides a JDBC driver to help programmers communicate with databases maintained by it. Likewise, Microsoft provides a JDBC driver to help programmers communicate with databases maintained by MS SQL.

Java programmers must have a standard and uniform way to communicate with any third-party JDBC driver. To facilitate this, an interface called **Driver** is declared in the **java.sql** package. The third-party database vendors implement this interface in their driver.

To manage different JDBC drivers there is a component called Driver Manager. For example, through a Java program when we attempt to connect to a database, the Driver Manager would load the suitable JDBC driver. Thus, JDBC Manager ensures correct driver usage to access each database.

Once the driver is loaded we have to use the different classes present in JDBC API to interact with the database.

The various layers of JDBC Architectures are shown in Figure 21.1.

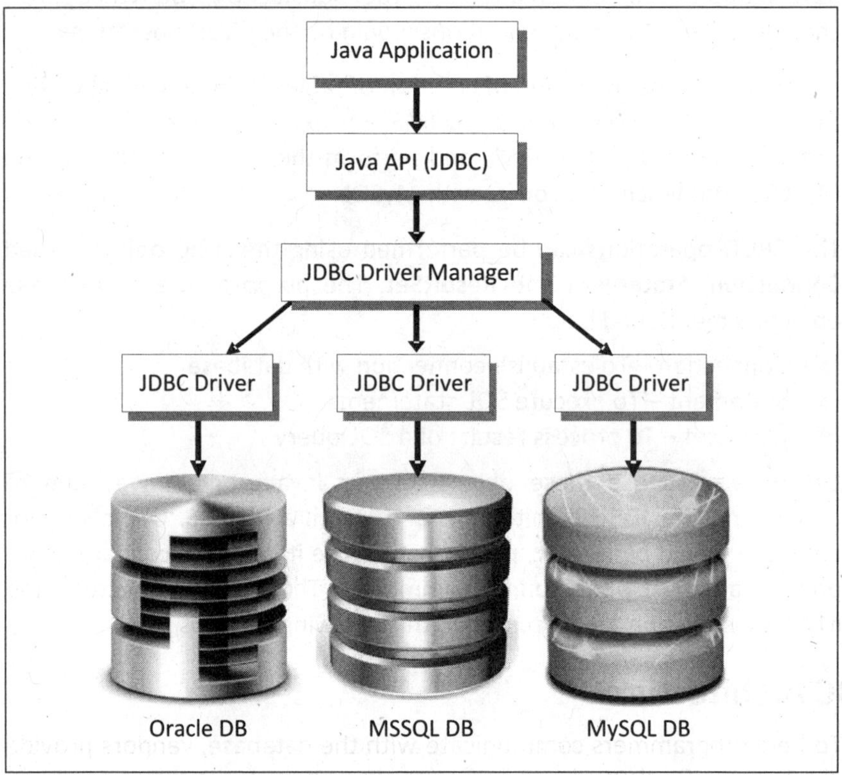

Figure 21.1

JDBC Driver Types

Java implementations are available for a wide variety of Operating Systems and hardware. These platforms themselves have evolved over the years. There are different JDBC driver implementations for these different platforms. All these drivers are classified into 4 categories—

Type 1 driver, Type 2 driver, Type 3 driver and Type 4 driver. Most legacy applications would use Type 1, 2, or 3 driver, whereas to connect with modern databases Type 4 driver is used. For programs in this book Type 4 driver would have to be installed.

MySQL Database Installation

We wish to install MySQL on a Windows machine. To do this we need to first download the MySQL Installer. This is available for download at https://dev.mysql.com/downloads/windows. Once downloaded, execute this MySQL Installer. When presented with options to install components, choose MySQL database and JDBC driver. At the time of writing this book the JDBC driver was available in mysql-connector-java-5.1.40-bin.jar.

Once the MySQL database and driver stand installed, download MySQL Workbench for your version of Windows from URL given below and install it.

https://dev.mysql.com/downloads/workbench/

The Workbench provides an integrated tool for carrying out the following operations:

(a) Database Design
(b) Trying SQL queries
(c) Database Administration
(d) Database Migration

In a later part of the chapter we would see how to use the MySQL Workbench to create a database and its tables(s). We would also see how to use the JDBC driver to work with the database programmatically.

Common JDBC API Components

The JDBC API provides different classes and interfaces. In a previous section we had seen the purpose three classes—**Connection, Statement** and **ResultSet**. Apart from them, JDBC API also provides several other classes and interfaces. The important amongst them are as follows:

(a) **DriverManager**: This class provides services for loading and managing JDBC drivers.

(b) **Driver**: This is an interface. Each JDBC driver implements this interface. It handles the communications with the database server.

In a Java program we rarely interact with **Driver** directly. Instead, we use **DriverManager** objects, which in turn manages the **Driver** objects.

(c) **SQLException**: This class handles any errors that occur in a database application.

Putting it to Work

We have now understood the data organization, SQL statements for database operations, JDBC architecture and JDBC API components. We have also seen how to install MySQL and MySQL Workbench. So it is now time to write a Java program that accomplishes the following:

(a) Create a Schema called "study". Insert a table in it called "Accounts" and add three fields to it—ID, Name and Balance.

(b) Add 4 records to the table using MySQL Workbench containing following data:

ID	Name	Balance
1011	Neha	4000.50
1023	Sunil	5000.00
1021	Rohit	6000.75
1044	Rahul	5600.55

(c) Create a record with field values 1001, Joe, 5000.00.

(d) Retrieve and print all existing records.

(e) Update record – Change Sunil to Sanjay.

(f) Delete record whose ID is 1044.

Out of these, steps (a) and (b) are to be performed using MySQL workbench, whereas the rest are to be performed through the Java program.

So let us now create a schema, add table to it and then add 4 records to it. Carry out the following steps to achieve this:

(a) Start MySQL workbench by double-clicking its icon. Create a new schema (database) by selecting from the menu File | New Model. By default a schema by the name **mydb** would get created. It would be shown under the "Physical Schemas" tab.

(b) Double click on **mydb** schema. A dialog would popup. Through this dialog change the **Name** of this schema to "study".

(c) From the "study" tab double click the "Add Table" icon. Given the table name as "Accounts".

(d) Click on the Columns tab at the bottom of the page and create three columns with following properties.

Column Name	Datatype	Primary Key
ID	INT	Yes
Name	VARCHAR(255)	No
Balance	FLOAT	No

(e) Click on "Inserts" tab at the bottom of the screen. The columns ID, Name and Balance would be shown. Add 4 records with values mentioned in the problem statement above.

Now finally we have reached a stage where we can write a Java program to carry out steps (c), (d), (e) and (f) given in the problem statement. Here is the program...

```
package myjdbccrud ;
import java.sql.* ;

public class MyJdbcCRUD
{
    static final String  jdbcDriver = "com.mysql.jdbc.Driver" ;
    static final String  dbURL = "jdbc:mysql://localhost/study" ;

    public static void main ( String[ ] args ) throws Exception
    {
        Connection  conn = null ;
        Statement  stmt = null ;
        ResultSet  rs = null ;

        try
        {
            Class.forName ( jdbcDriver ) ;
            conn = DriverManager.getConnection( dbURL,
                                                "root", "admin" ) ;

            stmt = conn.createStatement( ) ;
```

```
            String sql ;
            sql = "INSERT INTO Accounts VALUES ( 1001, 'Joe',
                  5000.0 )" ;
            stmt.executeUpdate ( sql ) ;

            sql = "UPDATE Accounts SET NAME = 'Sanjay'
                        WHERE ID = 1023" ;
            stmt.executeUpdate ( sql ) ;

            sql = "DELETE FROM Accounts WHERE ID = 1044" ;
            stmt.executeUpdate ( sql ) ;

            sql = "SELECT * FROM  Accounts" ;
            rs = stmt.executeQuery ( sql ) ;

            int id ;
            String name ;
            float balance ;

            while ( rs.next( ) )
            {
                  id = rs.getInt ( "ID" ) ;
                  name = rs.getString ( "Name" ) ;
                  balance = rs.getFloat ( "Balance" ) ;

                  System.out.println ( id + " " + name + " " + balance ) ;
            }

            rs.close( ) ;
            stmt.close( ) ;
        }
        finally
        {
            if ( conn != null )
                  conn.close( ) ;
        }
    }
}
```

Let us now to try to understand the program. The project name given was **MyJdbcCrud**, hence the classes in this program would belong to the package **myjdbccrud**, as indicated in the package statement at the beginning of the program.

The **import** statement ensures that the classes declared in **java.sql** package for database access are available to the program.

Now we need to open a communication channel with the database. For this we need to load and register the JDBC driver. This registration needs to be done only once in the program. We have done this registration through the call

Class.forName (jdbcDriver) ;

where **jdbcDriver** is a string that has been initialized to "com.mysql.jdbc.Driver". This call dynamically loads the driver's class file into memory, which automatically registers it. Naturally if we use a different RDBMS than MySQL then the driver name and hence the string would change as given below.

ORACLE RDBMS - oracle.jdbc.driver.OracleDriver
DB2 RDBMS - COM.ibm.db2.jdbc.net.DB2Driver

Now we need to open a connection with the database. This is done using the statement

conn = DriverManager.getConnection (dbURL, "root", "admin") ;

The **getConnection( )** method needs three parameters—the database URL which indicates the name and location of the database, login name and password to access the database. We have initialized the **dbURL** to "jdbc:mysql://localhost/study".

Here **localhost** refers to the local machine and **study** refers to the database name. If the database is present on a different machine, then **localhost** should be replaced by IP address or name of the machine where the database is hosted.

Once again for Oracle and DB2 the **dbURL** string would be different. For these databases the following strings should be used:

Oracle RDBMS - jdbc:oracle:thin:@hostname:port Number:databaseName
DB2 RDBMS - jdbc:db2:hostname:port Number/databaseName

While creating the database we have given the login name as "root" and password as "admin". Hence same have been used in the call to **getConnection( )**. This call creates a **Connection** object and returns it, which we promptly collect in **conn**.

Once the connection with the database is established, we have performed the CRUD operations. For this we have to create a **Statement** object by calling **createStatement( )** on the connection object. Next, we have to create the query string and pass it to **executeUpdate( )** method of **Statement** object to execute the query. This sequence of operations is shown below.

```
stmt = conn.createStatement( ) ;
String  sql ;
sql = "INSERT INTO Accounts VALUES ( 1001, 'Joe', 5000.0 )";
stmt.executeUpdate ( sql ) ;
```

Create, update and delete operations are similar in the sense that to perform all of them the **executeUpdate( )** method has to be called. The Read operation is a bit different. For it we need to call the **executeQuery( )** method on the **Statement** object. When we do this, the query is fired on the database and all the records that qualify the query are returned in the form of a **ResultSet** object. For example, when we fire the query "SELECT * from Accounts" all the records in the **Accounts** table would qualify this query and hence would be returned together in a **ResultSet** object.

We can iterate through all the records in the **ResultSet** object through a **while** loop. Each time through the loop we can extract the individual field values in the record by calling the **ResultSet** methods as shown below.

```
id = getInt ( "ID" ) ;
name = rs.getString ( "Name" ) ;
balance = rs.getFloat ( "Balance" ) ;
```

We have extracted the values and displayed them on the screen. Once all the records have been iterated, **rs.next( )** returns a false, whereupon the loop is terminated.

That brings us to the final stage of the program where we need to do the cleanup operations. We do this by calling the **close( )** methods on **Statement**, **ResultSet** and **Connection** objects.

One small thing needs to be done before you can execute the program. We need to add the JDBC library. Carry out the following steps to do this:

(a) Right click on "Libraries" node of the "MyJDBCCrud" project in the project window.

(b) From the menu that pops up select "Add JAR/Folder".

(c) Navigate to the suitable directory where you have downloaded the "mysql-connector-java-5.1.40-bin" file.

(d) Click Open followed by OK.

Once the library has been added we can now use F6 to build and execute the program.

Exercise

[A] State True or False:

(a) A database can contain multiple tables.

(b) MySQL is an open source RDBMS.

(c) Modern databases use T3 type of JDBC driver.

(d) Advantage of JDBC is that the same driver can be used to connect multiple RDBMSs.

(e) A call to **class.forName( )** loads and registers the JDBC driver.

(f) Records from a table can be deleted using call to **executeQuery( )** method of **Statement** object.

(g) To read a set of records from a table we must use the **executeUpdate( )** method of the **Statement** object.

(h) **Driver** class's method should be called from your program to obtain a **Connection** object to interact with the database.

(i) Different **dbURL** connection strings should be used to connect to different RDBMSs.

(j) A set of records is returned while reading a database table into a **RecordSet** object.

[B] Answer the following:

(a) Write a program which lets you carry out the CRUD operations through a GUI shown in Figure 21.2. Use the same database and table discussed in the section "Putting it to Work".

Note that all the records added to the table should get displayed in the list box. Before carrying out Delete or Update operations the record should be searched using the ID. A new record should be added or the existing record should be modified on clicking the Commit button.

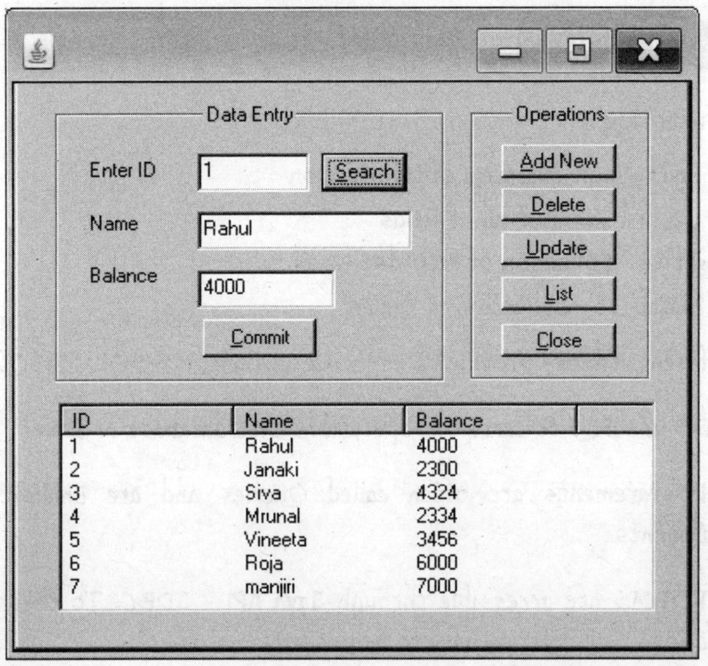
Data Entry
Enter ID
1
Search
Name
Rahul
Balance
4000
Commit
Operations
Add New
Delete
Update
List
Close
ID
Name
Balance
1 Rahul 4000
2 Janaki 2300
3 Siva 4324
4 Mrunal 2334
5 Vineeta 3456
6 Roja 6000
7 manjiri 7000

KanNotes

- Terminology :
  - Field - Individual item of information
  - Record - Collection of fields
  - Table - Collection of records
  - Database - Collection of tables
- Different vendors provide RDBMS. Ex. : Oracle, MS SQL, MySQL
- All DB use SQL to carry out operations on a database or tables
- SQL statements are often called Queries and are English like statements
- All RDBMS are accessible through Java API - JDBC. To these API functions SQL queries have to be passed
- Common database operations - Create / Modify / Drop Table
- Examples of database operations :
  - CREATE TABLE Persons (ID int, Name varchar (255))
  - ALTER TABLE Persons ADD DateOfBirth date
  - ALTER TABLE Persons DROP COLUMN DateOfBirth
  - DROP TABLE Customers
- These database operations are usually done using Tools that come with each DB. Ex. : MySQL WorkBench that comes with MySQL
- Common operations on Table – CRUD (Create, Read, Update, Delete)
- Examples of operations on a table :
  - INSERT INTO Persons (ID, Name) VALUES (1001, 'Sunil')
  - SELECT * FROM Employees
  - UPDATE Persons SET Name = 'Satish' WHERE EmpID = 1001
  - DELETE FROM Persons WHERE EmpID = 1244
- These operations are done programmatically using JDBC objects

- Common JDBC objects used are :
  - Connection object – establishes connection with database
  - Statement object – executes SQL statements
  - Resultset object – processes results of a query
- Add library "mysql-connector-java-5.1.40-bin" before using JDBC objects
- Software Installations required - MySQL Installer and Workbench

Index

Search it, the easy way...

Let Us JAVA

3rd Edition

!

A

B

C

D

E

F

G

H

I

M

N

O

P

R

S

T